Social Studies

myWorld

INTERACTIVE

3

SAVVAS

LEARNING COMPANY

Savvas would like to extend a special thank you to all of the teachers who helped guide the development of this program. We gratefully acknowledge your efforts to realize the possibilities of elementary Social Studies teaching and learning. Together, we will prepare students for college, careers, and civic life.

SAVVAS
LEARNING COMPANY

ISBN-13: 978-0-328-97310-1
ISBN-10:   0-328-97310-6
Printer code TK

Program Authors

Dr. Linda B. Bennett
Faculty, Social Studies Education
College of Education
University of Missouri
Columbia, MO

Dr. James B. Kracht
Professor Emeritus
Departments of Geography and
Teaching, Learning, and Culture
Texas A&M University
College Station, TX

Reviewers and Consultants

Program Consultants

ELL Consultant
Jim Cummins Ph.D.

Professor Emeritus,
Department of
Curriculum, Teaching,
and Learning
University of Toronto
Toronto, Canada

**Differentiated Instruction
Consultant**
Kathy Tuchman Glass

President of Glass
Educational Consulting
Woodside, CA

Reading Consultant
Elfrieda H. Hiebert Ph.D.

Founder, President and
CEO, TextProject, Inc.
University of California
Santa Cruz

Inquiry and C3 Consultant
Dr. Kathy Swan

Professor of Curriculum
and Instruction
University of Kentucky
Lexington, KY

Academic Reviewers

Paul Apodaca, Ph.D.

Associate Professor,
American Studies
Chapman University
Orange, CA

Warren J. Blumenfeld, Ed.D.

Former Associate
Professor, Iowa State
University, School
of Education
South Hadley, MA

Dr. Albert M. Camarillo

Professor of History,
Emeritus
Stanford University
Palo Alto, CA

Dr. Shirley A. James Hanshaw

Professor, Department
of English
Mississippi State
University
Mississippi State, MS

Xiaojian Zhao

Professor, Department
of Asian American
Studies
University of California,
Santa Barbara
Santa Barbara, CA

Teacher Reviewers

Mercedes Kirk
First grade teacher
Folsom Cordova USD
Folsom, CA

Julie Martire
Teacher, Grade 5
Flocktown Elementary School
Long Valley, NJ

Kristy H. Spears
K-5 Reading Specialist
Pleasant Knoll Elementary School
Fort Mill, SC

Kristin Sullens
Teacher, Grade 4
Chula Vista ESD
San Diego, CA

Program Partner

Campaign for the Civic Mission of Schools is a coalition of
over 70 national civic learning, education, civic engagement,
and business groups committed to improving the quality and
quantity of civic learning in American schools.

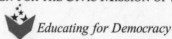

CAMPAIGN FOR THE CIVIC MISSION OF SCHOOLS

Educating for Democracy

🌐 Geography Skills Handbook

✏️ Writing Workshop

🔍 Using Primary and Secondary Sources

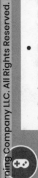
The BIG Question How do we interact with our planet?

Rap About It! How Do We Interact With

Quest Explore a National Park!

Chapter 2 Economics

The BIG Question How do people get what they want and need?

Chapter 3 Communities Build a Nation

The BIG Question How does our past affect our present?

GO ONLINE FOR DIGITAL RESOURCES

 eTEXT

 VIDEO

- **Field Trip Video**
  Independence Hall

 AUDIO

Rap About It! lyrics and music

👆 **INTERACTIVITY**

- **Big Question Activity**
  Why do we have government?
- **Quest Interactivities**
  Quest Kick Off
  Quest Connections
  Quest Findings
- **Lesson Interactivities**
  Lesson Introduction
  Lesson Review
- **Digital Skill Practice**
  Compare and Contrast
  Interpret Graphs

 **GAMES**

Vocabulary Practice

☑ **ASSESSMENT**

Lesson Quizzes and Chapter Tests

The **BIG Question** Why do we have government?

Chapter 5 Citizenship and Civic Engagement

 eTEXT

 VIDEO

- **Field Trip Video**
Volunteering:
Mentor, Tutor,
Friend

 AUDIO

Rap About It! lyrics
and music

 INTERACTIVITY

- **Big Question Activity**
How can I participate?
- **Quest Interactivities**
Quest Kick Off
Quest Connections
Quest Findings
- **Lesson Interactivities**
Lesson Introduction
Lesson Review
- **Digital Skill Practice**
Ask and Answer Questions
Fact and Opinion

 GAMES

Vocabulary Practice

 ASSESSMENT

Lesson Quizzes and Chapter Tests

The BIG Question How can I participate?

Chapter 6 A Growing Nation

GO ONLINE FOR
DIGITAL RESOURCES

 eTEXT

VIDEO

- **Field Trip Video**
  National Inventors
  Hall of Fame

 AUDIO

Rap About It! lyrics
and music

 INTERACTIVITY

- **Big Question Activity**
  How does life change throughout history?
- **Quest Interactivities**
  Quest Kick Off
  Quest Connections
  Quest Findings
- **Lesson Interactivities**
  Lesson Introduction
  Lesson Review
- **Digital Skill Practice**
  Compare Primary and Secondary Sources
  Draw Conclusions

GAMES

Vocabulary Practice

ASSESSMENT

Lesson Quizzes and
Chapter Tests

The BIG Question How does life change throughout history?

Chapter 7 Celebrating Our Communities

GO ONLINE FOR DIGITAL RESOURCES

 eTEXT

 VIDEO

- **Field Trip Video** Different Communities: Exploring Nearby Communities

 AUDIO

Rap About It! lyrics and music

 INTERACTIVITY

- **Big Question Activity** How is culture shared?
- **Quest Interactivities** Quest Kick Off Quest Connections Quest Findings
- **Lesson Interactivities** Lesson Introduction Lesson Review
- **Digital Skill Practice** Generalize Take Informed Action

 **GAMES**

Vocabulary Practice

 ASSESSMENT

Lesson Quizzes and Chapter Tests

The BIG Question How is culture shared?

Quests

Ask questions, explore sources, and cite evidence to support your view!

Maps

Where did this happen? Find out on these maps in your text.

Maps continued

Charts and Graphs

Find these charts, graphs, and tables in your text. They will help you pull it together.

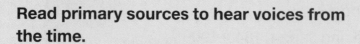

Primary Sources

Read primary sources to hear voices from the time.

People to Know

Read about the people who made history.

Citizenship

Biographies Online

Abigail Adams

John Adams

Samuel Adams

Elsie Allen

James Armistead

Benedict Arnold

Clara Barton

Delilah Beasley

James Beckwourth

Chaz Bono

William Bradford

Sergey Brin

Jerry Brown

Edmund Burke

Juan Rodriguez Cabrillo

Tani Gorre Cantil-Sakauye

Christopher "Kit" Carson

César Chávez

Louise Clappe

Thomas Clifford

Christopher Columbus

Hernán Cortés

Juan Crespi

Charles Crocker

Hallie M. Daggett

Juan Bautista de Anza

Pedro Menéndez de Avilés

Samuel de Champlain

People to Know continued

Gaspar de Portolá

Antonio Lopez de Santa Anna

María Angustias de la Guerra

Bartolomeu Dias

John Dickinson

Walt Disney

Frederick Douglass

Ralph Waldo Emerson

William Fargo

First Lady Pat Nixon

Wong Chin Foo

Benjamin Franklin

John C. Fremont

Eric Garcetti

John Gast

Nathan Hale

Alexander Hamilton

John Hancock

Kamala D. Harris

Mary Ludwig Hays

Patrick Henry

Mark Hopkins

Henry Hudson

Dolores Huerta

Collis P. Huntington

Anne Hutchinson

Daniel Inouye

Joseph James

Thomas Jefferson

Hiram Johnson

Billie Jean King

Martin Luther King, Jr.

King Charles III

King George III

Dorothea Lange

Lewis and Clark

Abraham Lincoln

Henry Wadsworth Longfellow

Lord Dunmore

Ferdinand Magellan

Wilma Mankiller

James Wilson Marshall

John Marshall

Biddy Mason

Louis B. Mayer

Sylvia Mendez

Metacom

Harvey Milk

James Monroe

Samuel Morse

John Muir

Nicolás José

Thomas Paine

Charley Parkhurst

William Penn

William Pitt

James K. Polk

Prince Henry the Navigator

Edmund Randolph

Ronald Reagan

Paul Revere

Sally Ride

People to Know continued

Jackie Robinson	Levi Strauss
Eleanor Roosevelt	John A. Sutter
Sarah Royce	Mary Tape
Bernarda Ruiz	Archie Thompson
Sacagawea	Tisquantum
Haym Salomon	Harriet Tubman
Deborah Sampson	Mariano Guadalupe Vallejo
José Julio Sarria	Earl Warren
Dalip Singh Saund	Mercy Otis Warren
Junípero Serra	George Washington
Roger Sherman	Henry Wells
Sir Francis Drake	Phillis Wheatley
John Drake Sloat	Narcissa Whitman
Jedediah Smith	Roger Williams
John Smith	Sarah Winnemucca
Leland Stanford	John Winthrop
John Steinbeck	Jerry Yang

Skills

Practice key skills in these skills lessons.

Literacy Skills

Skills continued

Critical Thinking Skills

Map and Graph Skills

Gold found at Sutter's Mill.

Cali
bec

848   1849   1850

Skills Online

Analyze Cause and Effect	Deliver an Effective Presentation
Analyze Costs and Benefits	Distinguish Fact and Opinion
Analyze Images	Distinguish Fact From Fiction
Ask and Answer Questions	Draw Conclusions
Classify and Categorize	Draw Inferences
Compare and Contrast	Evaluate Media Content
Compare Viewpoints	Generalize
Conduct Research	Generate New Ideas
Create Charts	Identify Bias

Skills Online continued

Identify Main Idea and Details

Interpret Cultural Data on Maps

Interpret Economic Data on
  Maps

Interpret Graphs

Interpret Physical Maps

Interpret Timelines

Make Decisions

Predict Consequences

Resolve Conflict

Sequence

Solve Problems

Summarize

Use and Interpret Evidence

Use Latitude and Longitude

Use Primary and Secondary
  Sources

Use the Internet Safely

Work in Cooperative Teams

Welcome to Your Book!

**Your Worktext is made up of chapters and lessons.
Each lesson starts with pages like this.**

Look for these words as you read.

Words with yellow highlight are important social studies words. The sentence with the word will help you understand what the word means.

Lesson 1 Land and Water

🕐 INTER ACTIVITY
Participate in a class discussion to preview the content of this lesson.

Unlock The BIG Question

I will know how land and water change from place to place.

Vocabulary

continent
landform
mine
adobe

Academic Vocabulary

area
region

Mountains, valley, and a lake

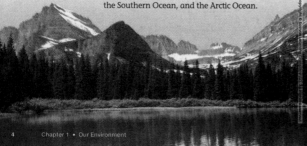

JumPstart Activity

Think about what you already know about mountains, rivers, lakes, and the ocean. Work with a partner. Choose a type of land. Take several turns saying a word to describe it. Then choose a type of water and do the same thing.

Geography is the study of Earth and its people. Earth is made up of both land and water. The largest land areas on Earth are the seven **continents**: North America, South America, Europe, Africa, Asia, Australia, and Antarctica. The five oceans are the Pacific Ocean, the Atlantic Ocean, the Indian Ocean, the Southern Ocean, and the Arctic Ocean.

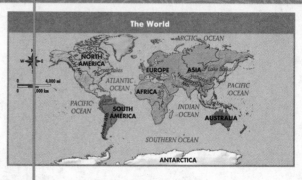

The World

Landforms and Bodies of Water

Each continent has many different landforms. A **landform** is the form or shape of part of Earth's surface. Landforms include glaciers, mountains, hills, islands, and peninsulas. Glaciers are made up of ice and snow. Mountains are landmasses that rise above the surrounding land. Hills are usually lower than mountains and have rounded tops. Islands are **areas** of land surrounded on all sides by water. Peninsulas are connected to a mainland and usually have water on only three sides.

Bodies of water are different shapes and sizes, too. On the map, find the five oceans. Oceans are Earth's largest bodies of salt water. Lakes and rivers provide people with freshwater. The Great Lakes in the United States are the largest freshwater lakes in the world. These lakes include Lake Superior, Lake Michigan, Lake Huron, Lake Erie, and Lake Ontario.

Academic Vocabulary

area • *n.*, a part of a larger place

1. ☑ **Reading Check**
Circle a landform in North America. **Underline** a body of water north of Asia.

Reading Checks will help you make sure you understood what you read.

Your Turn!

Flip through your book with a partner.

1. Find the start of another lesson.
   What do you see on the page?

This book will give you a lot of chances to figure things out. Then you can show what you have figured out and give your reasons.

The Quest Kick Off will tell you the goal of the Quest.

Watch for Quest Connections all through the chapter.

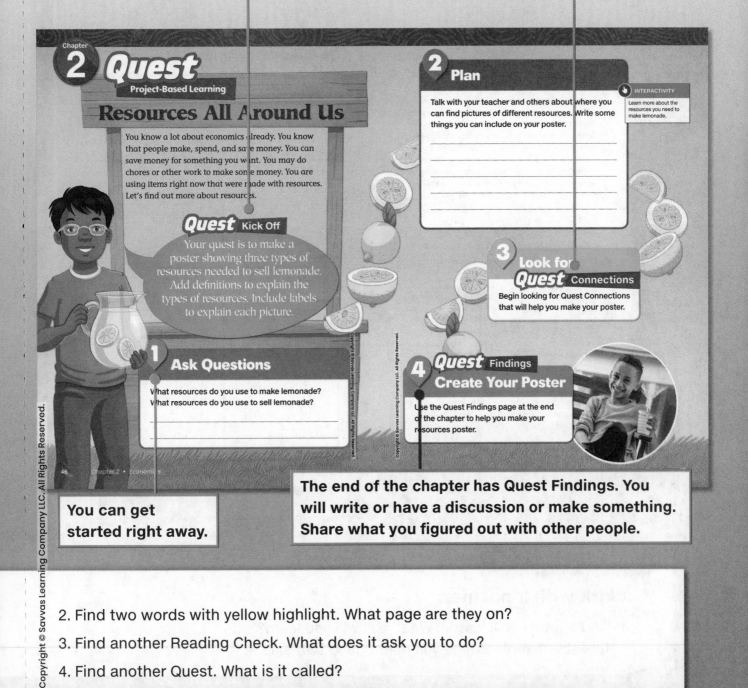

Chapter 2 Quest
Project-Based Learning

Resources All Around Us

You know a lot about economics already. You know that people make, spend, and save money. You can save money for something you want. You may do chores or other work to make some money. You are using items right now that were made with resources. Let's find out more about resources.

Quest Kick Off

Your quest is to make a poster showing three types of resources needed to sell lemonade. Add definitions to explain the types of resources. Include labels to explain each picture.

1 Ask Questions

What resources do you use to make lemonade? What resources do you use to sell lemonade?

2 Plan

Talk with your teacher and others about where you can find pictures of different resources. Write some things you can include on your poster.

INTERACTIVITY
Learn more about the resources you need to make lemonade.

3 Look for Quest Connections

Begin looking for Quest Connections that will help you make your poster.

4 Quest Findings
Create Your Poster

Use the Quest Findings page at the end of the chapter to help you make your resources poster.

You can get started right away.

The end of the chapter has Quest Findings. You will write or have a discussion or make something. Share what you figured out with other people.

2. Find two words with yellow highlight. What page are they on?

3. Find another Reading Check. What does it ask you to do?

4. Find another Quest. What is it called?

Learn to use important skills.

> **Read the explanation. Look at all the text and pictures.**

> **Practice the skill. You'll be ready to use it whenever you need it.**

Literacy Skills

Cause and Effect

Oil gushes from a well at Spindletop.

To understand what you read, look for causes and effects. A *cause* is the reason why something happens. An *effect* is the result. Suppose more people want to buy clothing made of cotton. Because of this need, farmers grow greater amounts of cotton. Needing cotton is the cause. Growing greater amounts of cotton is the effect. You can use the word *because* in a sentence to help you figure out a cause. *Because* people want to buy clothing made of cotton, farmers grow greater amounts.

An effect can have more than one cause. A cause may lead to more than one effect. As you read about events in Texas history, look for how events are connected and how one event might cause another.

Read the following paragraph and answer the questions.

For many years, people drilled for oil at Spindletop in Texas. Then workers got a new part for their drill so they could dig deeper into the ground. On January 10, 1901, mud began to bubble up from the well. Then suddenly a stream of oil shot up more than 100 feet high! The nearby city of Beaumont was changed forever. Since oil had been found near it, people from all over the country rushed to Beaumont in search of oil. The number of people living in Beaumont rose from 10,000 to 50,000 people. Now that there was plenty of oil, automobiles and factories started to use more of this natural resource.

Your Turn!

INTERACTIVITY
Review and practice what you learned about cause and effect.

1. What is one effect from the cause?

Cause		Effect
Workers got a new part for their drill.	→	

2. What is one cause of the effect?

Cause		Effect
	→	People from all over the country rushed to Beaumont.

3. Use the photo and the text about oil at Beaumont to fill in your own cause and effect.

Cause		Effect
	→	

Your Turn!

Work with a partner.

1. Find another skill lesson. What skill will you learn? Talk about another time you might need that skill.

Every chapter has primary source pages. You can read or look at these sources to learn right from people who were there.

Find out what this source is about and who made it.

These questions help you think about the source.

🔍 Primary Source

From an Essay by Rachel Carson

A primary source is a source created at an event or during a certain time period. A primary source may provide the reader with insight into what was happening during a specific time in history. It might also offer a person's views on important events.

An essay is one kind of primary source. You can read an essay to find out ideas or issues that the writer considers important. You can also read it to identify the writer's purpose.

Read the excerpt from an essay by environmentalist Rachel Carson.

Vocabulary Support

Parts where plants and animals live and humans have not changed the land

Area kept as a national or state park, refuge, or other wilderness habitat

emblem • *n.*, a symbol
refuge • *n.*, a place that provides protection
marsh • *n.*, an area of soft, wet land with grasses
retain • *v.*, to keep

If you travel much in the wilder sections of our country, sooner or later you are likely to meet the sign of the flying goose—the emblem of the national wildlife refuges. You may meet it by the side of a road crossing miles of flat prairie in the Middle West, or in the hot deserts of the Southwest. You may meet it by some mountain lake, or as you push your boat through the winding salty creeks of a coastal marsh. Wherever you meet this sign, respect it. It means that the land behind the sign has been dedicated by the American people to preserving for themselves and their children, as much of our native wildlife as can be retained along with our modern civilization.

—Rachel Carson,
Introduction to *Conservation in Action*

36 Chapter 1 • Our Environment

This is the source.

Close Reading

1. **Circle** the sentence that tells about the two regions of the United States where you might meet the flying goose.

2. What does it mean to respect the emblem?

_____

_____

_____

Wrap It Up

Why do you think Rachel Carson made these statements? What did she hope to encourage people to do?

_____

_____

Primary Source • From an Essay by Rachel Carson 37

Pull it all together.

2. Find another primary source lesson in your book. What is the source about?

Geography Skills Handbook

Using Maps

Vocabulary

political map
title
map legend
map key
symbol
scale
compass rose

The map titled "Southeast United States" is a political map. A **political map** shows information such as state or national borders. Political maps often show the capital cities and major cities of states or countries.

Knowing how to read a map is an important skill. There are tools on the map to help you. Look at the Southeast United States political map and find each of these map tools.

Title: The title tells you what the map shows.

Map legend or **map key**: The legend or key explains the meaning of the symbols on the map.

Symbol: A symbol is a marking or color that stands for something else.

Scale: The scale on the map shows distance. It helps you see how far apart locations are.

Compass rose: A compass rose shows you the cardinal directions of north, south, east, and west.

1. ☑ Reading Check **Describe** what a political map shows.

_____

_____

_____

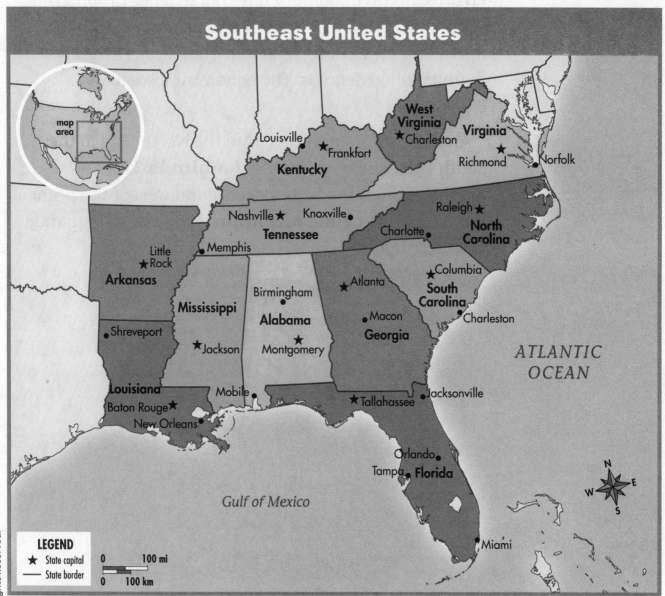

Southeast United States

Louisville

West Virginia
★Charleston

Virginia
Richmond ★   ● Norfolk

★Frankfort

Kentucky

Nashville ★   Knoxville ●

Raleigh ★

Tennessee   Charlotte ●   **North Carolina**

● Memphis

Little ★Rock

★Columbia

Arkansas   ★Atlanta   **South Carolina**

Birmingham ●   ● Macon   Charleston ●

Mississippi   **Alabama**   **Georgia**

● Shreveport   ★Jackson   ★Montgomery

ATLANTIC OCEAN

Louisiana   ● Mobile

Baton Rouge ★   ★Tallahassee   Jacksonville ●

New Orleans ●

Orlando ●

Tampa ●   **Florida**

Gulf of Mexico

Miami ●

LEGEND
★ State capital
— State border

| 0 | 100 mi |
| 0 | 100 km |

N
W E
S

2. ☑ **Reading Check** **Analyze** the map and answer these questions.

Locate and circle the title on the map. Circle the symbol that is used for the state capital. Find the scale on the map. About how far is Atlanta, Georgia, from the Atlantic Ocean?

_____

Copyright © Savvas Learning Company LLC. All Rights Reserved.

Geography Skills Handbook   **SSH1**

Using Globes

A **globe** is a model of Earth, so it is in the shape of a sphere. You can find the equator on the globe. The **equator** is an imaginary line that extends around the center of Earth. Lines of **latitude** measure distances north and south of the equator. The lines are numbered in units called degrees. The equator is located at 0 degrees (0°).

Another set of lines runs from the North Pole to the South Pole. These are lines of **longitude**. Lines of longitude measure distances east and west of the prime meridian. The **prime meridian** is the line of longitude marked as 0°.

North Pole

Equator

South Pole

3. ☑ **Reading Check** **Identify** and trace the equator on the globe.

4. ☑ **Reading Check** **Locate** and circle the North Pole on the globe.

The equator and the prime meridian divide Earth into hemispheres, or parts. Each **hemisphere** is half of Earth. The equator divides Earth into the Northern Hemisphere and the Southern Hemisphere. The prime meridian and the line opposite it on the other side of Earth form the Western Hemisphere and the Eastern Hemisphere. The United States is in the Northern Hemisphere and the Western Hemisphere.

Vocabulary

globe
equator
latitude
longitude
prime meridian
hemisphere

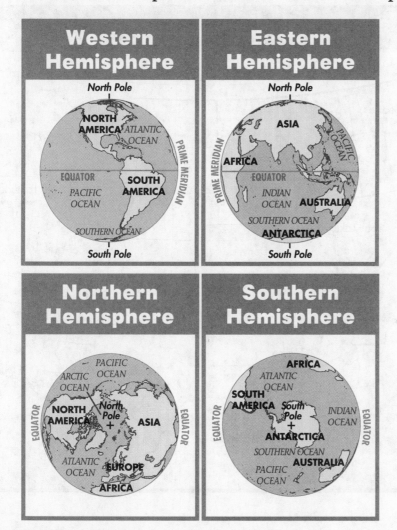

5. ☑ Reading Check **Identify** the hemisphere that all of South America is located in.

_____

6. ☑ Reading Check **Identify** the line that separates the Northern Hemisphere from the Southern Hemisphere.

_____

Absolute Location

Absolute location tells the exact location of a place on Earth. A place's absolute location does not change. You can find the absolute location of a place on a map or globe by finding its latitude and longitude. For example, the absolute location of San Francisco is 38° N, 122° W.

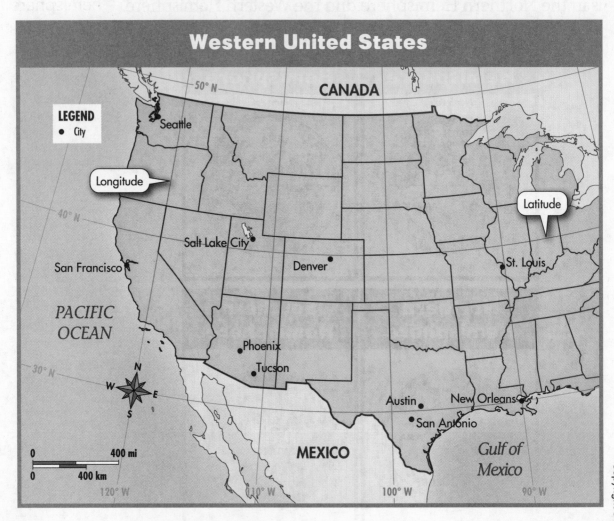

Western United States

7. ☑ **Reading Check** **Determine** the absolute location of New Orleans.

_____

Relative Location

Relative location describes where a place is in relation to another place. You might say that your school is across the street from the park. You can also use the directions in the compass rose to explain the relative location of a place. Look at the map titled "Western United States." San Francisco is south of Seattle. St. Louis is east of Denver. San Antonio is southwest of Austin. Tucson is southeast of Phoenix.

Vocabulary

absolute location
relative location

8. ☑ **Reading Check** Use the map titled "Southeast United States" to **describe** the relative location of Alabama.

_____

_____

_____

_____

_____

9. ☑ **Reading Check** How is relative location useful?

_____

_____

_____

_____

_____

Physical Geography

The natural features of a place are its **physical geography**. Natural features include landforms, such as mountains, deserts, valleys, and plains. They also include bodies of water, such as rivers, lakes, and oceans. A **physical map** shows the landforms and bodies of water found in a place.

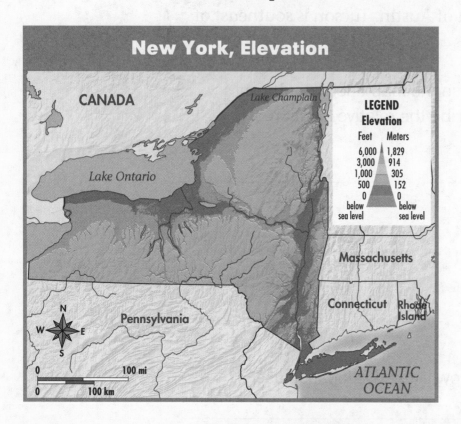

A physical map may also show elevation. **Elevation** is the height of land above sea level. For example, valleys have lower elevations than mountains. The legend helps you understand what the colors on the map mean. Different colors show lower and higher elevations.

10. ☑ **Reading Check** Choose one physical feature shown on the map. **Describe** how people might use it.

_____

_____

_____

11. ☑ **Reading Check** What does an elevation map show?

_____

This table also gives information about elevation, as well as other facts about features in the Northeastern United States.

Vocabulary

physical geography
physical map
elevation

The Northeast's Amazing Features	
Highest elevation	Mt. Washington (New Hampshire): 6,288 feet
Longest river	Saint Lawrence River: 744 miles long
Largest lake	Lake Ontario: 7,340 square miles
Coastline	about 700 miles long (Maine, New Hampshire, Massachusetts, Rhode Island, Connecticut, New York)

Source (for length of shoreline): *Department of Commerce, National Oceanic and Atmospheric Administration, National Ocean Service*

Graphs can also help you learn about physical geography. This graph shows how much land is covered by water in the Northeastern United States.

12. ☑ **Reading Check** About how many more square miles are covered by water in Maine than in Massachusetts?

_____

_____

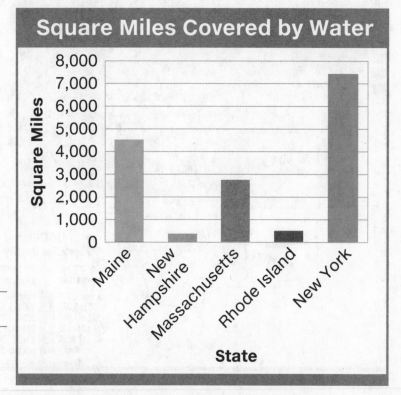

Source: *https://water.usgs.gov/edu/wetstates.html*

Human Geography

Human geography explains how people affect Earth's surface. For example, people may build a tunnel through a mountain or build a dam on a river. These actions change the land. When people build roads or towns, they also change the land. Often when people change the land, those changes can make a place unique. For example, the Golden Gate Bridge is a unique human characteristic of San Francisco.

Some maps show the human geography of a place. A **population map** shows where people live. Cities are centers of business and government. Many people live and work near them. Other parts of a region have fewer cities and jobs. Fewer people live there.

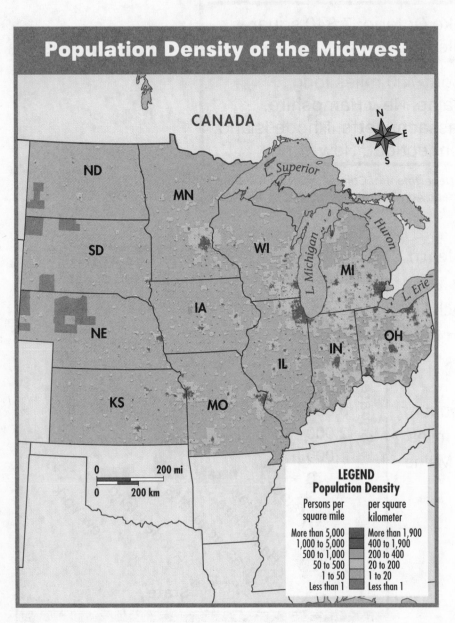

Population Density of the Midwest

LEGEND
Population Density

Persons per square mile	per square kilometer
More than 5,000	More than 1,900
1,000 to 5,000	400 to 1,900
500 to 1,000	200 to 400
50 to 500	20 to 200
1 to 50	1 to 20
Less than 1	Less than 1

13. ☑ **Reading Check** Look at the population map. **Identify** which state looks to have a higher population, Iowa or Ohio.

_____

Charts can also show the human geography of a place. The chart shows the ten cities in the Midwest where the most people live.

Vocabulary

human geography
population map

Largest Cities in the Midwest, 2016	
Name	**Population**
Chicago, Illinois	2,704,958
Columbus, Ohio	860,090
Indianapolis, Indiana	855,164
Detroit, Michigan	672,795
Milwaukee, Wisconsin	595,047
Kansas City, Missouri	481,420
Omaha, Nebraska	446,970
Minneapolis, Minnesota	413,651
Wichita, Kansas	389,902
Cleveland, Ohio	385,809

Source: *U.S. Census Bureau*

14. ☑ **Reading Check** Use the chart and population map to **determine** which area of the Midwest has the most populous cities. Why do you think this is so?

_____

_____

_____

_____

_____

Writing Workshop

Keys to Good Writing

Good writers follow five steps when they write.

Plan	• Brainstorm to choose a topic. • Find details about the topic. • Take notes from sources. • Write down your sources. • Plan how to use the details.
Draft	• Write down all of your ideas. • Think about which ideas go together. • Put ideas that go together in groups. • Write a sentence for the introduction and write a sentence for the conclusion.
Revise	• Review what you wrote. • Check that your ideas and organization make sense. • Add time-order words and transitions (words and phrases such as *because* or *for example*). • List any more sources that you used.
Edit	• Check for correct grammar, spelling, and punctuation. If using a word processor, use spell-check. • Make a final copy.
Share	• Use technology to print or publish your work. • Make sure that you list all of your sources.

1. ☑ **Reading Check** **Explain** Why is it important to edit?

_____

_____

_____

The three main writing genres are opinion, informative, and narrative. They all have a different purpose.

Opinion Writing

When you write an opinion piece, you share your point of view on a topic. Your goal should be to make your viewpoint clear. You also need to support your point of view with evidence. Read the steps and sample sentences to see how to write effective opinion pieces.

Homesteaders sometimes used a spinning wheel, like the one shown, to make yarn from wool.

1	**Introduce the topic.** *The number of settlers moving west grew after 1862. Many moved west to set up a homestead.*
2	**State your opinion.** *People who moved west after 1862 were smart because they could buy 160 acres of land for little money.*
3	**Support your opinion with reasons and evidence.** *To be a homesteader, a person had to build a house and live there for five years. Then, the person owned the land.*
4	**Make sure that your ideas are clear and organized to support your purpose.**
5	**Support your opinion statement with a conclusion.** *I think that the settlers who moved west to start homesteads were smart because they had an opportunity to own land and support their families for little money.*

2. ☑ **Reading Check Analyze** How might using technology make your writing more effective?

_____

_____

American Indians relied on the natural resources available to them.

Informative Writing

Informative writing is also called explanatory writing. When writing an informative piece, your purpose is to inform, or tell. Credible, or reliable, sources are very important to use in this kind of writing. Make sure to avoid plagiarism. This means using someone else's words without giving that person credit. Take notes on your sources, including what they say and where you found them. Read the steps and sample sentences.

1
Introduce the topic.
Many different groups of American Indians lived off the land before settlers came.

2
Develop the topic with facts, definitions, and concrete details.
The Indians of North America used the natural resources in their environment to live. Natural resources are things in nature that people use, such as water, soil, plants, and trees. Some groups that lived on the coast used shells for jewelry and for money to trade. Another natural resource that they used for money was beads.

3
Use precise language and content words.
The Chumash made bead money from Olivella shells, which came from sea snails. Some shells were rare, so they were very valuable.

4
Write a conclusion that supports your introduction.
American Indians lived off the land by using the natural resources available to them.

3. ☑ **Reading Check** **Infer** Discuss with a partner the following question: What could be added to the conclusion?

Narrative Writing

Writing a narrative is telling a story. The story can be about a real or made-up event or experience. Use sensory words to show, rather than tell, the reader what happened. Sensory words describe what a person sees, hears, touches, tastes, or smells. The events in your narrative should be clear, in order, and connect to each other. Read the steps and sample sentences.

4. ☑ **Reading Check** Based on the description in the story, **underline** the setting, or place where an event takes place.

1	**Introduce the story and characters.** *Lin was getting ready for the Chinese New Year.*
2	**Use dialogue and sensory words.** *"Mrs. Chen, would you like some oranges? We just unloaded them from the farmer's truck. They're sweet and juicy." Mrs. Chen bit into an orange slice and it squirted Lin in the face. Lin wiped the sticky juice away from her cheek.*
3	**Use details to develop your writing.** *Lin dashed to the front of the store to help her mother at the cash register. A long line twisted around the shelves of fresh fruit she had stocked early that morning.*
4	**To connect the events in your writing, use words that express sequence.** *Finally, it was 1:00 and time to close the store to get ready for the parade.*
5	**Make sure that the order of events in your story is organized.**
6	**Write a strong conclusion to close the narrative.** *As Lin grabbed her sweater, someone in a colorful dragon costume passed by the shop. Lin called out to her parents, "Let's follow that dragon!"*

Researching on the Internet

Look at sites before you use information from them. Web sites with .org, .edu, or .gov are good choices. You cannot always rely on facts and details from sites that end in .com. If you do use them, check one or two other sources from a .org, .edu, or .gov site.

5. ☑ **Reading Check**

   Infer Discuss the following question with a partner. How might you use your Library Media Center to find information on American Indian groups who lived where you live today?

Using a Library Media Center to Write a Research Paper

When you are writing a research paper, it is helpful to use the resources available in your Library Media Center. To use them effectively, make sure that you:

- use both print and electronic sources and also make sure the sources are reliable to use.
- use more than one source and check the information in the sources to see if it matches.
- take short notes from your sources.
- ask a librarian for help if you are unsure which sources to use for your topic.

Follow these steps to write a research paper:

1. Write down two or three questions to help you with your research.
2. Use reliable sources to answer the questions you wrote. Change your questions if needed.
3. Based on the answers to your questions, organize your topic so that details for each part of your topic are together.
4. Write a sentence about your topic based on your research. This will become your introduction.
5. Use details, examples, and quotes to support your statement.
6. Use transitions and clauses to connect ideas and events.
7. Write a strong conclusion that goes back to what you stated in the introduction.
8. Make a list of your sources.

Using Primary and Secondary Sources

Primary and Secondary Sources

A **primary source** is a source made or written by a person at an event. A primary source can be a historical document, such as the U.S. Constitution. Other examples of primary sources are letters, diaries or journals, and photographs. Maps and artwork are also primary sources. Even **architecture**, which is how buildings are designed, can be a primary source. It helps us understand the people who designed the buildings.

A **secondary source** is material that was written or made by someone who did not witness an event. This textbook is a secondary source. Encyclopedias, online or in print, are also secondary sources. Secondary sources may include primary sources. For example, textbooks include photographs and often journal entries that are primary sources. Encyclopedias include information about people, places, and events from other sources.

Artifacts like this basket made by the Pomo Indians are considered to be primary sources. An **artifact** is an object that was made and used by people.

A **biography** is a story about a person's life that was written by someone else. Because the author did not see or live through the events he or she describes, a biography is a secondary source.

Vocabulary

primary source
architecture
secondary source
artifact
biography
oral
eyewitness

Pomo Indian basket

1. ☑ **Reading Check** **Underline** in the text one example of a primary source and **circle** one of a secondary source. **Explain** your answers to a friend.

Miners panning
for gold

Primary sources can also be oral or spoken. Family stories that are told to children and grandchildren are **oral**, or spoken, histories. Oral histories can tell us how individual people contributed to the history of a place. Songs can also be oral histories. Read the words from a song written by a miner who did not have the money to go home after he came to California to find gold. Note that *lousy* means "of poor quality." As you read, think about who wrote the song and why. Also think about what it tells you about the past.

Primary Source

It's four long years since I reached this land,
In search of gold among the rocks and sand;
And yet I'm poor when the truth is told,
I'm a lousy miner,
I'm a lousy miner in search of shining gold. . . .
Oh, land of gold, you did me deceive [trick],
And I intend in thee my bones to leave;
So farewell, home, now my friends grow cold,
I'm a lousy miner,
I'm a lousy miner in search of shining gold.

– "The Lousy Miner," from *Put's Original California Songster,*
edited by John A. Stone, 1854

2. ☑ **Reading Check** **Draw Conclusions** What does the song tell you about why the writer came to California? How do you know that it is a primary source?

_____

_____

_____

Distinguishing Between Primary and Secondary Sources

To distinguish between primary and secondary sources, think about who created the source and when. If a person at an event creates the source, it is a primary source.

An **eyewitness** is a person who sees or experiences an event. Eyewitness accounts are primary sources. A journal entry about witnessing the horse and buggy being replaced by the first car would be a primary source. If you wrote a report about the different kinds of transportation people have used over the past 100 years, the report is a secondary source. Your report is a secondhand account because you were not there 100 years ago.

A film can be a primary or secondary source. If you make a video of your family or friends at the beach, that video is a primary source. You are creating a film or video while you are experiencing the event. A film is a secondary source if it is made about a time in the past, such as a movie about people who settled in the west in the 1800s. The film might include primary sources like historical documents or photographs, but the film itself is a secondary source. The people who made the film were not alive when the events in the film took place.

Making videos of the sunset

3. ☑ **Reading Check** **Analyze** and **describe** how a film can be either a primary source or a secondary source.

_____

_____

How to Interpret a Primary Source

We can learn who, what, where, and when from primary sources. Read part of a speech by Chief Sitting Bull. Under his leadership, the Sioux worked together to preserve their way of life. After gold was discovered in the Black Hills of South Dakota, which was sacred land to the Sioux, conflicts with U.S. authorities grew. Sitting Bull is most famous for defeating U.S. General George Armstrong Custer and his troops at the Battle of Little Bighorn in 1876.

Primary Source

They claim this mother of ours, the earth, for their own, and fence their neighbors away; they deface her with their buildings and their refuse. They threaten to take [the land] away from us.

—Sitting Bull's Speech at the Powder River Council, 1877

Asking questions about sources helps us identify what type of source we are using. Questions also help us understand what the source can teach us.

4. ☑ Reading Check Answer these questions based on the primary source.

Who delivered this speech? _____

What does the speech tell you about how Sitting Bull felt about settlers from the east? _____

_____

_____

When was the speech delivered? _____

How to Interpret a Secondary Source

Your textbook has information about American Indians, but the information was not written by someone who was there, like Sitting Bull. The authors did not see or live through the events that are described. They got their information by reading other people's writing or looking at other primary sources, like photographs, diaries, and artifacts. We can ask the same questions to interpret secondary sources that we used to interpret primary sources. Read this passage from your textbook that talks about American Indians.

> The Cherokee first settled in North America more than 1,000 years ago. They were hunters and farmers. They ate meat, fruit, and vegetables.

The textbook is different from Sitting Bull's speech because the writers of the textbook were not there 1,000 years ago. They did not meet the Cherokee in person. Notice that the writers do not use *I* or *we*. They did not interact face to face with the Cherokee.

5. ☑ **Reading Check** **Compare** the speech and the textbook excerpt. **Write** how they are different.

_____

_____

_____

_____

_____

_____

1 Our Environment

▶ VIDEO

👆 INTERACTIVITY

🔊 AUDIO

🎮 GAMES

☑ ASSESSMENT

📖 eTEXT

The BIG Question How do we interact with our planet?

▶ VIDEO

Lesson 1
Land and Water

Lesson 2
Weather, Climate, and Forces of Nature

Lesson 3
Using Earth's Resources

Lesson 4
Interacting With the Environment

JumPstart Activity

👆 INTERACTIVITY

People interact with their environment in many different ways. Think about all the different things you like to do outside. Stand up and pretend you are doing your favorite outdoor activity.

How Do We Interact with Our Planet?

Preview the chapter **vocabulary** as you sing the rap.

Let's talk about geography—
   the Earth and its people,
Seven **continents**, five oceans to see too.
Five different **regions** in the U.S.A.,
With **landforms** like mountains, hills, valleys
   and plains.

A region's **climate** depends on its location
And **affects** animals and plant life, **vegetation**.

Natural resources like soil, trees,
Minerals, and water help meet people's needs.
Some are **essential** for us to survive,
And so we need to **conserve**,
   or protect them to thrive.

Most communities **develop**
   near water and land,
People **adapt** to environments
   the best they can.

Quest
Document-Based Writing

Explore a National Park!

The United States has many wonderful and exciting places to visit. Some of those places are the country's national parks. Each one has its own unique features and landscape. These natural wonders have one thing in common—they have been preserved for everyone to enjoy.

Quest Kick Off

Your quest is to discover our national parks and choose one to investigate. Write and then present a sightseeing guide about your national park including its features and how people use its land and water.

1 Ask Questions

What national park will you describe? Where is it located? How do people use its land and water features?

....

....

....

....

INTERACTIVITY

Complete the activities to get started on your sightseeing guide.

3 Look for Quest Connections

Begin looking for Quest Connections that will help you plan and write your sightseeing guide.

2 Research

Visit Web sites about national parks. Use "national parks" as your search words. Select one and click on its name to find out more about it. What are three things that make this an exciting and interesting place to visit?

....

....

....

....

4 Quest Findings
Create a Sightseeing Guide

Use the Quest Findings page at the end of the chapter to help you write and present your sightseeing guide to the class.

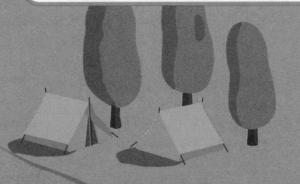

INTERACTIVITY

Participate in a class discussion to preview the content of this lesson.

Unlock The BIG Question

I will know how land and water change from place to place.

Vocabulary

continent
landform
mine
adobe

JumpStart Activity

Think about what you already know about mountains, rivers, lakes, and the ocean. Work with a partner. Choose a type of land. Take several turns saying a word to describe it. Then choose a type of water and do the same thing.

Academic Vocabulary

area
region

Mountains, valley, and a lake

Geography is the study of Earth and its people. Earth is made up of both land and water. The largest land areas on Earth are the seven **continents**: North America, South America, Europe, Africa, Asia, Australia, and Antarctica. The five oceans are the Pacific Ocean, the Atlantic Ocean, the Indian Ocean, the Southern Ocean, and the Arctic Ocean.

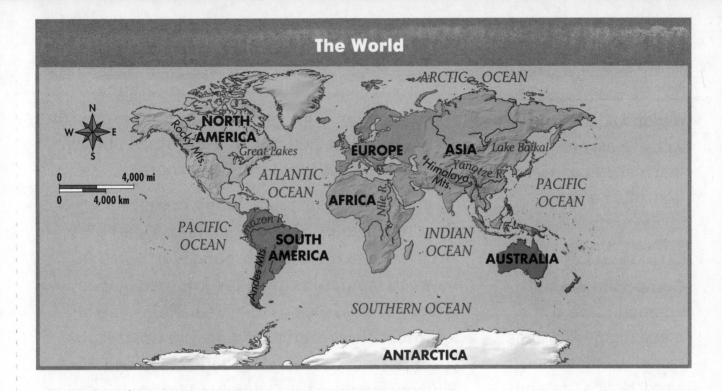

The World

Landforms and Bodies of Water

Each continent has many different landforms. A **landform** is the form or shape of part of Earth's surface. Landforms include glaciers, mountains, hills, islands, and peninsulas. Glaciers are made up of ice and snow. Mountains are landmasses that rise above the surrounding land. Hills are usually lower than mountains and have rounded tops. Islands are **areas** of land surrounded on all sides by water. Peninsulas are connected to a mainland and usually have water on only three sides.

Bodies of water are different shapes and sizes, too. On the map, find the five oceans. Oceans are Earth's largest bodies of salt water. Lakes and rivers provide people with freshwater. The Great Lakes in the United States are the largest freshwater lakes in the world. These lakes include Lake Superior, Lake Michigan, Lake Huron, Lake Erie, and Lake Ontario.

Academic Vocabulary

area • *n.*, a part of a larger place

1. ☑ **Reading Check**
Circle a landform in North America.
Underline a body of water north of Asia.

Land and Water in the United States

Academic Vocabulary

region • *n.*, a large area with at least one feature that makes it different from other areas

Word Wise

Compound Word A compound word is made up of two words joined to create a new word. Notice the word *Northeast*. How do the smaller words *north* and *east* help you know what *Northeast* means? Find other compound words. Use the smaller words to determine their meaning.

Geographers often organize the United States into five regions: the West, the Midwest, the Northeast, the Southeast, and the Southwest. The states in each region are grouped based on their location and the landforms they share.

Different landforms are found in the regions of the United States. The Appalachian Mountains stretch across the Southeast and Northeast. In between mountains there are low areas called valleys. Plains, such as the Great Plains, are also low areas. They tend to be flat. The Great Plains cover parts of the Midwest, Southwest, and West. Plateaus, such as the Columbia Plateau located in the West, are high areas that have steep sides and flat tops. Mountains are also found in the West.

The largest bodies of water in the United States are rivers and lakes. Locate the Mississippi River on the map. More than 2,000 miles long, it is the second longest river in the country. It runs through the Midwest and Southeast. The Great Lakes, in the Midwest and Northeast, form part of the border between Canada and the United States.

The West

The Midwest

The Northeast

United States Regions

Columbia Plateau

Rocky Mountains

Great Plains

Great Lakes

Mississippi R.

Ohio R.

Appalachian Mts.

PACIFIC OCEAN

ATLANTIC OCEAN

Rio Grande

LEGEND
- Northeast region
- Midwest region
- Southeast region
- Southwest region
- West region

2. ☑ **Reading Check** **Review** the map. Label the states in each of the five United States regions. **Identify** the region you live in.

_____

_____

The Southeast

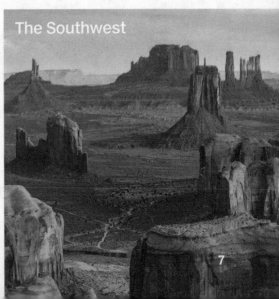

The Southwest

Quest Connection

In which region is your national park located? What different landforms and bodies of water are features in your park?

👆 INTERACTIVITY

Talk with a partner about some ways people interact with each park's different features.

Homes made of adobe are found in the Southwest region.

Five Regions of the United States

The Northeast region has some of the largest cities in the United States, such as New York City in New York, and Philadelphia, Pennsylvania. This region has areas of hills, rocky coastlines, and farmland. Many people also fish along the coast. Coasts are areas of flat land that are located near water.

Early settlers in the Southeast region built large farms called plantations. However, the region is best known for its long coastlines today. Along the coasts, people fish, enjoy the warm weather, and visit the beaches. Farther inland, many people farm the rich soil.

The Midwest region is one of the flattest areas in the United States. In this region, many people work on farms. Other people **mine**, or dig for materials, such as coal and iron.

Many states in the Southwest region were once a part of Mexico. The deserts of this region are home to many American Indians. Long ago, early settlers and American Indians used sun-dried bricks called **adobe** [uh DOH bee] to build shelters and other buildings. In the Southwest today, people still build with adobe.

The West is a region of mountains. The Rocky Mountains are in this region. They are some of the tallest mountains in the United States. Other mountain ranges include the Coast Ranges and the Alaska Range. The West region also has a long coast. Many people visit the West to hike, fish, and camp. People also come to visit the beaches.

3. **☑ Reading Check** Of the regions you just read about, **discuss** with a partner which region you would like to visit and why.

_____

_____

_____

☑ Lesson 1 Check

INTERACTIVITY

Check your understanding of the key ideas of this lesson.

4. **Cause and Effect** Choose one region of the United States. **Explain** how the landforms may affect some of the activities people do. **Identify** clues in the maps and photographs.

_____

_____

_____

5. **Describe** the landforms and bodies of water that you live near. **Identify** how they affect the activities you do.

_____

_____

_____

6. **Understand the _Quest_ Connections** **Explain** why people might want to spend time in a region that has mountains and lakes.

_____

_____

_____

Weather, Climate, and Forces of Nature

INTERACTIVITY

Participate in a class discussion to preview the content of this lesson.

Vocabulary

weather
climate
elevation
vegetation
ecosystem

Academic Vocabulary

affect
structure

Unlock The BIG Question

I will know how climate affects the land, plants, and animals.

JumpStart Activity

Think about the different kinds of weather that happen where you live. Write five words to describe your favorite weather. Swap lists with a partner and guess each other's favorite weather. Then show each other what you like to do during that kind of weather.

This rain forest is in a warm and wet climate. Many unique plants and animals live here.

Weather relates to the daily conditions outside such as hot or rainy. **Climate** is the weather a place has over a long period. A region's climate consists of temperature (how hot or cold it is), precipitation (the amount of rain or snow that falls), and wind.

Climate Regions

A region's climate depends on its location on Earth. Places located close to the equator get more direct sunlight. Places far from the equator get less direct sunlight.

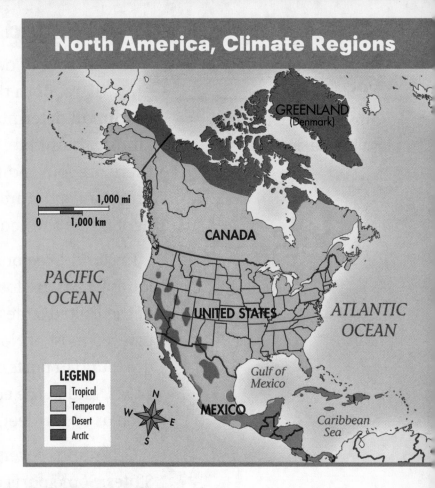

North America, Climate Regions

GREENLAND (Denmark)

CANADA

PACIFIC OCEAN

UNITED STATES

ATLANTIC OCEAN

Gulf of Mexico

MEXICO

Caribbean Sea

0   1,000 mi
0   1,000 km

LEGEND
Tropical
Temperate
Desert
Arctic

N W E S

Bodies of water shape the climate of places near them and affect the amount of rain that falls. They also change the temperature since they warm and cool more slowly than land. Winds that blow from the water cool the land in summer. Winds that blow from the water warm the land in winter. The **elevation**, or the height of land above sea level, affects climate, too. High places and mountains are cool most of the year.

The map shows North America's climate regions. Arctic climates are mostly cold. Tropical climates are mostly wet and hot. Temperate climates are not as cold as arctic climates or as hot as tropical climates. Most of the United States is in a temperate climate region. However, parts of the West have dry desert climates where there is little rainfall. Temperatures may be hot during the day and cold at night.

Climate and Plants

Academic Vocabulary

affect • *v.*, to have an influence on

The climate of a place **affects** the plants that grow there. Both the temperature and the amount of rainfall determine the types of **vegetation**, or kinds of plant life, that grow. In the United States, there are four main types of vegetation: forests, grasslands, tundra, and deserts. Different animals depend on the vegetation that grows in an area.

In climate regions that have plenty of rainfall, large forests are found. Forests grow in many parts of the United States. In fact, not long ago, forests covered most of North America! Many forests today are found in parts of the West region, near the Great Lakes, and in the eastern United States. Animals such as bears, deer, and raccoons live in forests.

Grasslands cover much of the plains in the United States. Some parts of the Great Plains get enough rain for tall grasses, berry bushes, and even small trees to grow. However, in the western Great Plains, there is less rain. Short grasses are found here. The prairie dogs that live in this region dig underground and eat the grasses.

Caribou in Alaska search for food in the tundra.

Both tundra and desert vegetation are found in places that have dry climates. In Alaska's arctic climate, the land is called tundra. The ground is frozen nearly all year long. It is too cold for trees to grow. However, moss, lichens, and some shrubs grow. Deer called caribou use their hooves to scrape away snow and eat the moss and lichens off the frozen land.

In desert climates, the only plants that can survive are those that can live with little water. In some deserts, grasses and shrubs are found. In the deserts of the West region, there are large cactuses called saguaros [suh GWAR ohs]. Saguaros grow in Mexico, too. Saguaros have long roots that allow them to get water from a wide area. A saguaro can grow to be 50 feet high. That is nearly as tall as a five-story building!

Animals that live in deserts can survive the hot temperatures during the day. Some animals, such as desert tortoises, keep cool by spending much of their time underground. Other animals only come out at night when it is cooler.

 **Quest Connection**

What kinds of plants and animals live in your national park? What does that tell you about its climate?

INTERACTIVITY

Talk with a partner about the different kinds of plant and animal life throughout the United States.

1. ☑ **Reading Check** **Main Idea and Details Identify** two details about each type of vegetation, then fill in each box.

Forests
_____
_____
_____
_____

Grasslands
_____
_____
_____
_____

Tundra
_____
_____
_____
_____

Desert
_____
_____
_____
_____

Plants and Animals Work Together

Forests, deserts, and grasslands each have different ecosystems. In an **ecosystem**, all living things, such as the plants and animals, interact with each other.

In both forest and rain forest ecosystems, birds, squirrels, and other animals depend on trees. Some of the seeds the animals eat drop into the soil and grow into new trees. The vegetation in these ecosystems needs animals to help spread the seeds.

In the desert, cactuses are important to many animals. Bats, such as the lesser long-nosed bats, drink nectar from the cactus flowers. By doing this, the bats spread pollen from cactus to cactus. This helps the cactus fruit grow. Other animals, including jack rabbits, eat parts of the cactus.

Places with similar vegetation can have different ecosystems. The grasslands in the middle of the United States do not have the same ecosystem as the grasslands on the continent of Africa. Some of the grasslands in Africa get more rainfall.

In the lake and swamp ecosystems in the southeastern United States, alligators dig large pond-like holes. Alligators use the holes as a place to rest. The holes also provide shallow water for birds and fish.

Lesser long-nosed bat

2. ☑ **Reading Check** **Cause and Effect Explain** the effect the animals have on the vegetation in an ecosystem.

_____

_____

_____

Natural Hazards

Have you ever watched a weather forecast? Perhaps you have heard about events in nature, called natural hazards. Some examples of natural hazards are volcanoes, hurricanes, and earthquakes. These physical processes can cause changes to the land. Some physical processes such as these are dramatic and happen quickly. Other physical processes, like erosion, happen slowly.

A volcano is a mountain that erupts in an explosion of molten rock (lava), gases, and ash. The lava, gases, and ash are forced out of the volcano. Hot lava flows down the side of the volcano. When it cools, it changes the land. The ash that falls down can make the soil rich, which helps plants grow. Volcanic eruptions have helped form some of the greatest mountain chains around the world.

A hurricane is a big storm with strong winds and a lot of rainfall. Heavy rains and wind from hurricanes can cause flooding. These factors shape and change the land.

An earthquake is a violent shaking of the earth. Many earthquakes strike along faults, or cracks in Earth's crust. The crust is the outer layer of Earth. Earthquakes can cause landslides and mudslides, which can change the landscape.

Hot lava flows from Kilauea Volcano in Hawaii.

Natural Disasters

Natural hazards can change the land in the environment. When they cause damage, they are natural disasters. A disaster is something that can cause damage to human-made structures such as buildings and bridges. It can wipe out land or form new land.

In 2005, the most destructive hurricane to hit the United States moved ashore along the Gulf Coast. In New Orleans after the **structures** built to prevent flooding failed, about 80 percent of the city was underwater. Millions of people became homeless, and it has taken years to recover from the disaster.

Earthquakes have caused major damage around the world. More earthquakes strike California than any other state in our country.

Academic Vocabulary

**structure • ** *n.*, something that is constructed

New Orleans faces extreme flooding during Hurricane Katrina in 2005.

16

3. **☑ Reading Check** **Main Idea** How do natural disasters impact the land?

_____

_____

_____

_____

INTERACTIVITY

Check your understanding of the key ideas of this lesson.

☑ Lesson 2 Check

4. **Cause and Effect Identify** one natural hazard. **Explain** its effect on the land.

_____

_____

_____

5. **Describe** how the weather or climate affects how you live.

_____

_____

_____

6. **Understand the** _Quest_ **Connections** **Explain** how climate impacts living things.

_____

_____

_____

Use Digital Tools to Understand Geography

Digital geography tools are electronic helpers for finding out more about Earth and its people, plants, and animals. One digital geography tool is the *Global Positioning System*, or *GPS*, which makes use of satellites to identify the locations of places on Earth. Today, many people use GPS devices to help them find directions as they drive.

Another digital geography tool is Global Information System, or GIS. GIS lets people find, store, and view information about Earth. GIS creates maps, but it does so in layers. For example, one layer might show the kind of landforms in a place. Another might show roads there. Still another might show natural resources. In that way, people can easily compare different kinds of geographic information.

GIS has allowed people to create huge geographic databases. A *geographic database* is a collection of information about a geographic topic, such as natural resources, lakes, or weather. GIS also helps people make better maps. It even allows people to make their own maps. In addition, GIS lets people view images of places they might not otherwise ever see.

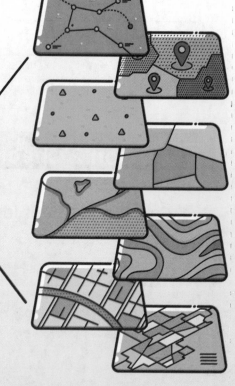

GIS uses layers of different maps.

1. Suppose you want to start a farm. What map layers might help you decide the best place for your farm?

INTERACTIVITY

Review and practice what you learned about using digital tools to understand geography.

_____

_____

_____

2. How has your family used GPS?

_____

_____

_____

_____

3. **Analyze** this image of a moving hurricane. Why do you think a weather database would be useful?

_____

_____

_____

_____

Weather forecast database

3 Using Earth's Resources

INTERACTIVITY

Participate in a class discussion to preview the content of this lesson.

Unlock The BIG Question

I will know how natural resources are used.

Vocabulary

agricultural region
industrial region
renewable resource
nonrenewable resource
conserve
erosion
recycle

Academic Vocabulary

consume
essential

People enjoy using natural resources.

JumpStart Activity

Work with a partner. Together, draw a picture of a tree with at least four branches. On each branch, write one way people use trees. Then add a body of water to your drawing. By the water, write ways people use water.

Earth has many different natural resources. Some natural resources, such as soil and trees, are found on the land. Other natural resources are minerals like gold and iron. Water is another important natural resource. People use water to meet many of their needs.

United States Resources

LEGEND
- Agricultural area
- Industrial area
- Other uses
- Region border
- Oil
- Coal
- Iron
- Gold
- Timber

Natural Resources

North America has many natural resources. Canada has minerals, forests, and rich soil. Mexico has iron and gold. Oil is found in Trinidad and Tobago, and the Caribbean islands have forests and rich soil.

Parts of the West region have forests, rich soil, and minerals. In the Southwest region, the land is used for mining and to raise animals such as cows. Oil, a natural resource used for fuel, is also found in parts of Oklahoma and Texas. Parts of the Midwest, Northeast, and Southeast have rich soil so many crops are grown there. Notice on the map that coal is found in these regions, too. Iron is found in the northern part of the Midwest region.

1. ☑ **Reading Check**
Circle three resources in the Southwest. **Underline** the most common resource found in the West region.

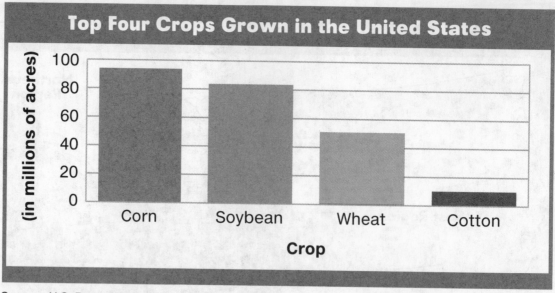

Top Four Crops Grown in the United States

Source: U.S. Department of Agriculture, National Agricultural Statistics Service, 2016

Agriculture and Products

People use natural resources to make products they need. In an **agricultural region**, or a place where there is much flat land and rich soil, people use the land and soil to farm.

Farmers grow many different crops. The top four crops grown in the United States are corn, soybeans, wheat, and cotton. Some crops are grown for people to **consume**, and some are made into products. Cotton is made into fabric for clothing. People buy plastic containers and car seats made from soybeans.

In other agricultural regions, vegetable and fruit crops are grown for people to eat. People also use grasses to feed animals such as cows and sheep.

People make other products from the natural resources that grow on the land. In some forest regions, people cut down trees. The trees are then sent to mills and made into timber, or lumber, for building. Wood from trees is also turned into pulp to make paper products.

Academic Vocabulary

consume • *v.*, to eat or drink something

Industry and Products

People make products from the resources found underground, too. Many of these products are made in industrial regions.

An **industrial region** is a place where many kinds of factories are located. In the United States, many industrial regions are located near large cities such as Chicago, Illinois, and Detroit, Michigan.

In many places with oil and natural gas, people pump them from underground. The oil is then made into fuel such as gasoline. Oil can also be heated to make plastic. Then the plastic is used to make many different products such as telephones, plastic bags, and even toys! Most people use gasoline to power automobiles. They also use gas or oil to heat their water and their homes. People mine coal, copper, zinc, and iron. Coal is used to help make electricity. Coins, including pennies, are made from copper and zinc. Iron is used to make steel. Steel is used in making automobiles and building materials.

Word Wise

Homonym A homonym is a word that sounds the same as another word but has a different meaning. Find the word *mine* in the text. What does the word mean as it is used in the sentence? Explain another meaning for the word *mine*.

2. ☑ **Reading Check**
Write the natural resource used to produce the products.

Products Produced From Natural Resources

Products	vegetables wheat	lumber paper	telephones toys
Natural Resource	_____ _____ _____	_____ _____ _____	_____ _____ _____

Protecting Resources

Some resources people use, such as trees and soil, are renewable resources. A **renewable resource** is one that can be replaced in a short time. Many of the resources found underground are nonrenewable resources. **Nonrenewable resources** are those that take a long time to replace or cannot be replaced after they are used. Coal, oil, and natural gas are all nonrenewable resources. In order to make sure that everyone has enough **essential** natural resources to live, people find ways to **conserve**, or to save and protect, them.

One way people conserve resources is by using less of them. Many people try to use less natural gas or water. People also conserve resources when they use them more carefully. Some farmers plant trees near their crops or strips of grass in between rows of crops. These plants help prevent **erosion**, or the washing away of soil by rain, wind, and nearby rivers. The plants help to hold the soil down.

Another way to protect natural resources is by recycling them. To **recycle** means to use an item again. Plastic bottles, newspapers, aluminum cans, and glass bottles are all items that people recycle every day. In many neighborhoods, trucks pick up these items from bins that line the streets. Many factories use recycled materials instead of natural resources to make new products.

Academic Vocabulary

essential • *adj.*, absolutely necessary

Recycled materials can be used again.

While many people work hard to protect natural resources, sometimes people's actions can harm them. Chemicals used in factories and on farms can pollute the air and nearby waterways. Smoke from burning fires can also pollute the air.

3. ☑ **Reading Check** **Cause and Effect** **Write** an effect of recycling items you use every day.

_____

_____

_____

☑ Lesson 3 Check

Check your understanding of the key ideas of this lesson.

4. **Cause and Effect** **Describe** a cause of pollution.

_____

_____

5. **Identify** the natural resources you use most during the week. What could you do to conserve these resources?

_____

_____

_____

_____

6. How are renewable resources different from nonrenewable resources? Give an example of each.

_____

_____

Cause and Effect

Oil gushes from a well at Spindletop.

To understand what you read, look for causes and effects. A *cause* is the reason why something happens. An *effect* is the result. Suppose more people want to buy clothing made of cotton. Because of this need, farmers grow greater amounts of cotton. Needing cotton is the cause. Growing greater amounts of cotton is the effect. You can use the word *because* in a sentence to help you figure out a cause. *Because* people want to buy clothing made of cotton, farmers grow greater amounts.

An effect can have more than one cause. A cause may lead to more than one effect. As you read about events in Texas history, look for how events are connected and how one event might cause another.

Read the following paragraph and answer the questions.

For many years, people drilled for oil at Spindletop in Texas. Then workers got a new part for their drill so they could dig deeper into the ground. On January 10, 1901, mud began to bubble up from the well. Then suddenly a stream of oil shot up more than 100 feet high! The nearby city of Beaumont was changed forever. Since oil had been found near it, people from all over the country rushed to Beaumont in search of oil. The number of people living in Beaumont rose from 10,000 to 50,000 people. Now that there was plenty of oil, automobiles and factories started to use more of this natural resource.

Your Turn!

INTERACTIVITY

Review and practice
what you learned about
cause and effect.

1. What is one effect from the cause?

Cause	Effect
Workers got a new part for their drill.	_____

2. What is one cause of the effect?

Cause	Effect
_____	People from all over the country rushed to Beaumont.

3. Use the photo and the text about oil at Beaumont to fill in your own cause and effect.

Cause	Effect
_____	_____

INTERACTIVITY

Participate in a class discussion to preview the content of this lesson.

Vocabulary

adapt

modify

irrigate

Academic Vocabulary

method

enable

Unlock The BIG Question

I will know how people affect the environment.

JumpStart Activity

What do you think the environment looked like before people lived in it? Why do you think the environment has been changed over time? Stand with a partner and share your ideas about changes to the environment. Then tell about something that has changed recently in the environment in which you live.

Think about what makes up your environment. Landforms, bodies of water, vegetation, natural resources, and climate are all things that make up the environment of a place.

The Environment Affects People

The environment affects where people live, work, and play. Most communities develop in regions where there is plenty of land and freshwater. People also settle in communities near natural resources. People live near forests to cut and plant trees. Other people live near the coast to fish. In the mountains and in desert areas, there are fewer settlements. These places do not always have flat land or enough water to grow crops.

People adapt to the environment to fit their needs. To **adapt** is to change the way you do something. People may change the way they dress or how they travel. In arctic climates, people dress in warm clothes to protect themselves from the cold. They ski or sled to travel down snow-covered hills. People drive snowmobiles in areas where it is difficult or unsafe to drive automobiles.

People in states such as Texas and Florida, and in the countries of Central America, have changed how they make buildings. In these areas, heavy rains and hurricanes can bring strong winds and a quick rise in the water level. Many people in these places use building materials that can stay up in strong winds. Other people in these areas settle farther inland to avoid rising waters.

The Havasupais live in the Grand Canyon.

In Arizona, Native Americans called Havasupais [hah vah SOO pyez] live in a village in the Grand Canyon. This environment affects how they travel in and out of their village. People cannot drive automobiles down the canyon. Mail and other supplies are carried into the village by the country's last mule train or are flown in by helicopter.

Climate Affects People

As you have learned, the environment affects people and how they live. So people adapt to their environment to best meet their needs.

Flooding in Georgia after a storm

In desert climates, conditions are often dry and hot, but they can be cool at night. Water can be limited. People build homes that will stay cool in the day and warm at night. They may practice conservation to make sure that there is always a water supply.

People who live in wetland climates may have to live with a lot of rainfall, humidity, and little farmland. Unlike in desert climates, wetlands often have a lot of water. Sometimes the land is waterlogged from having too much water. This can make it difficult to grow crops. People can change the direction of the flow of water by building dams. People who live in wetlands have to consider the kind of homes they build. They must make sure that the land is solid.

1. ☑ **Reading Check** **Cause and Effect** Look at the photo of flooded areas in Georgia. What might cause these floods? **Explain** one effect.

_____

_____

_____

_____

Mountain climates are different from desert climates because they are cool and wet. Farming can be difficult because of the elevation. Since there is less oxygen at high elevations, living things cannot grow. The climate in a mountain community may be harsh in winter. People may need to collect enough food, water, and firewood to prepare for a winter storm.

Living on the plains has its own set of challenges. The climate is often cold in winter and warm in the summer. The plains may have low rainfall, but they do have sources of water such as rivers. The land can be good for growing crops. However, because it is usually flat it can be very windy. Wind can wear away the soil. Poor soil or no soil makes it hard to grow crops. These areas, however, can work well for herding cattle and ranching.

2. ☑ **Reading Check** **Compare** how people adapt to different environments to meet their needs.

Desert	Mountains
_____	_____
_____	_____
_____	_____

Wetlands	Plains
_____	_____
_____	_____
_____	_____

The Hoover Dam, a national historic landmark, is considered one of the greatest designs and construction of a dam in modern times.

People Modify Environments

People interact with, or act on, their environment in many ways. One way is to **modify**, or change something. In areas with dry land, farmers **irrigate**, or bring water in through pipes. Other farmers break up the soil to kill weeds and to keep the soil rich. They may add chemicals to grow more crops or others to kill insects.

People modify the land when they use large machines to pump oil from the earth. In Pennsylvania and West Virginia, miners dig tunnels deep underground to reach minerals. Miners also carry away soil and rock to uncover coal. Land in some forests is cleared as workers cut down trees to sell as lumber. In some countries, people also burn forest areas so the land can be used for farms or homes.

The areas near these resources have also been modified. People move to the area to work. They build homes, buildings, roads, bridges, and railroads.

People modify rivers when they build dams across rivers to block the flow of the water. Dam gates **enable** some water to flow through, which forms lakes behind the dams. People use the lakes for water activities and to irrigate nearby farms. The rushing water that passes through the Hoover Dam and some other dams is used to make electricity.

Academic Vocabulary

enable • *v.*, to make possible

The beaver told the rabbit as they stared at the Hoover Dam: "No, I didn't build it myself, but it's based on an idea of mine!"

—Charles Hard Townes

Effects of Population

The number of people who live in an area can also affect the physical environment. In the late 1800s and early 1900s, new tools and equipment made farming easier. Fewer farmworkers were needed. Many people moved to cities in the East to work in factories. So more space was needed for people to live.

People began to build out from the center of the city. People built homes and other buildings. They laid railroad tracks and built roads so people could travel in and out of the city. People also built upwards. They built tall buildings called skyscrapers. Over time, people used improved materials to build skyscrapers that were much taller.

Today, in areas with large populations, people modify the land to meet the changing needs in a community. More means of transportation are added and roads may be widened so they can fit more cars, trucks, and buses. Additional rail lines may be built, too, so people can more easily travel into and out of the city.

3. ☑ **Reading Check** **Explain** why people modify the land.

_____

_____

_____

People and the Land

Some of the activities that people do can help or harm the environment. Scientists and others look for **methods** to improve the environment and how resources are used. Over the years, farmers learned that planting the same crops every year can harm the soil. As a result, many farmers today rotate, or take turns, growing different crops. Farmers also plan for a period of rest when they do not plant any crops. By doing so, the soil is moist and better able to grow crops.

Miners also work to help the environment. After they carve out soil in search of minerals, the land has little or no vegetation left. Miners then work to plant trees and other vegetation on the land.

Community leaders help the environment with some of the decisions they make. Leaders pass laws to prevent people from throwing garbage on the ground. They also pass laws to keep the drinking water clean. Some laws protect the oceans. These laws do not allow companies to dump materials that can harm the ocean or sea life.

Other people help the environment by their actions every day. Some people buy automobiles that do not pollute the air. People also use the heat from the sun or the wind to power things. Others organize groups to help clean up beaches, parks, and lakes. When people clean up the land, they make it safe for people and animals.

Academic Vocabulary

method • *n.*, a particular way of doing something

Quest Connection

Yellowstone National Park, home to Old Faithful, was the first national park. What facts about your national park make it special?

Old Faithful erupts several times a day in Yellowstone National Park.

Another way people help the environment is by conserving land. People conserve land when they set aside some of it in state parks or national parks. The first national park was created in 1872. Today, there are more than 400 national parks in the United States. This land is protected. People may not build or settle on this land.

INTERACTIVITY

Talk with a partner about why our country has national parks.

4. ☑ **Reading Check** **List** three ways people help the environment.

_____

_____

INTERACTIVITY

Check your understanding of the key ideas of this lesson.

☑ Lesson 4 Check

5. **Cause and Effect Explain** the effect of a law that helps the environment.

_____

_____

6. **Describe** ways the land has been modified in your community.

_____

_____

_____

7. **Understand the** *Quest* Connections Do you think it is a good idea to have land that is protected? Why?

_____

_____

From an Essay by Rachel Carson

A primary source is a source created at an event or during a certain time period. A primary source may provide the reader with insight into what was happening during a specific time in history. It might also offer a person's views on important events.

An essay is one kind of primary source. You can read an essay to find out ideas or issues that the writer considers important. You can also read it to identify the writer's purpose.

Read the excerpt from an essay by environmentalist Rachel Carson.

Vocabulary Support

Parts where plants and animals live and humans have not changed the land

Area kept as a national or state park, refuge, or other wilderness habitat

emblem • *n.*, a symbol
refuge • *n.*, a place that provides protection
marsh • *n.*, an area of soft, wet land with grasses
retain • *v.*, to keep

If you travel much in the wilder sections of our country, sooner or later you are likely to meet the sign of the flying goose–the emblem of the national wildlife refuges. You may meet it by the side of a road crossing miles of flat prairie in the Middle West, or in the hot deserts of the Southwest. You may meet it by some mountain lake, or as you push your boat through the winding salty creeks of a coastal marsh. Wherever you meet this sign, respect it. It means that the land behind the sign has been dedicated by the American people to preserving for themselves and their children, as much of our native wildlife as can be retained along with our modern civilization.

–Rachel Carson,
Introduction to *Conservation in Action*

Close Reading

1. **Circle** the sentence that tells about the two regions of the United States where you might meet the flying goose.

2. What does it mean to respect the emblem?

_____

_____

_____

_____

Wrap It Up

Why do you think Rachel Carson made these statements? What did she hope to encourage people to do?

_____

_____

_____

_____

_____

Quality:

Individual Responsibility

Hallie M. Daggett
First Female Fire Lookout

Hallie M. Daggett was a woman who took on a big responsibility. She was the first female fire lookout hired by the United States Forest Service. Beginning in the summer of 1913, she worked in the Klamath National Forest in northern California, atop a high mountain peak. Her job was important. She had to look out over the entire area and watch for forest fires. She had to deal with terrible weather, too. She also had to be careful of grizzly bears and other wild animals.

Perhaps most difficult of all, Daggett's job required her to spend many hours all alone atop Klamath Peak. It was 9 miles away from her home. The other lookouts—all men—never thought she would continue working. They were wrong. She loved her job and worked hard at it for 14 years.

Find Out More

1. In what way did Hallie M. Daggett have a lot of responsibility?

_____

_____

_____

2. There are a lot of people in your community who have jobs with a lot of responsibility, such as police officers, doctors, and firefighters. Ask an adult who works in one of those jobs to talk about his or her responsibilities. Report back to the class what you learn. Would you like to have a job with a lot of responsibility?

Visual Review

Use these graphics to review some of the key terms, people, and ideas from this chapter.

Land and Water

- Landforms: glaciers, mountains, hills, islands, peninsulas
- Bodies of water: oceans, lakes, and rivers
- United States regions: West, Midwest, Northeast, Southeast, and Southwest

Our Environment

Weather, Climate, and Forces of Nature

- Climate includes temperature, precipitation, and wind
- Climate regions: arctic, tropical, and temperate
- Natural hazards include volcanoes, hurricanes, and earthquakes

Using Earth's Resources

- Natural resources include forests, soil, minerals, and oil
- Natural resources can be renewable or nonrenewable
- Ways to conserve include using less and recycling

Interacting With the Environment

- People modify their environment based on their needs
- Ways to protect the environment include using nonpolluting cars, using the sun or wind for power
- Some lands are protected as national parks

☑ Assessment

Vocabulary and Key Ideas

1. Draw a line from the term to its definition.

conserve   the form or shape of part of Earth's surface

landform   all the living and nonliving things that interact in a certain place

adapt   to save and protect resources

ecosystem   to change the way you do something

2. **Compare and Contrast** What is the difference between a renewable resource and a nonrenewable resource?

_____

_____

3. **Identify** Look at the image. Which region of the United States is it most likely showing?

_____

4. **Describe** Fill in the circle next to the best answer. What happens when there is a volcanic eruption, hurricane, or earthquake?

Ⓐ People move from the farm to the city.

Ⓑ People tear down bridges.

Ⓒ The landscape may change.

Ⓓ The landscape remains the same.

Critical Thinking and Writing

5. **Identify** Which region in the United States is home to many mountains? Give examples.

_____

_____

6. **Contrast** ways people can adapt to desert climate and wetland climate.

_____

_____

_____

_____

_____

_____

7. **Cause and Effect** Factories use natural resources to make products. What is one effect of factories on the environment?

_____

_____

8. What are some ways in which you interact with our planet?

_____

_____

_____

_____

9. **Writing Workshop: Write Informative Text** On a separate sheet of paper, identify the region of the United States in which you live. Describe its physical geography, including its natural features, landforms, resources, and ecosystems.

Analyze Primary Sources

Any fool can destroy trees . . . God has cared for these trees . . . but he cannot save them from fools—only Uncle Sam can do that.

—John Muir, "The American Forests," 1897

10. John Muir was an environmentalist, or a person who works to protect the environment. What does he think the United States government should do to care for the environment? (Hint: "Uncle Sam" means the same thing as the United States government.)

_____

_____

_____

Cause and Effect

11. How does building a dam contribute to where people settle?

_____

_____

_____

_____

_____

_____

_____

Quest Findings

INTERACTIVITY

Complete the activities to get started on your sightseeing guide.

Create Your Sightseeing Guide

You have read the lessons in this chapter, and now you are ready to write and present your sightseeing guide. Remember that your goal is to tell others about one national park and explain what it has to offer visitors.

1 Prepare to Write

Decide on three features in your national park that you think people should be sure to visit. Write them down on a piece of paper and explain how people use these features. Then find pictures of these features on the Internet, in magazines, or draw ones.

2 Write Your Sightseeing Guide

Use your notes and write a sightseeing guide in which you tell others about each of the features. For each feature include

- the name of the feature,
- a catchy phrase about the feature,
- how people interact with the feature, and
- an image of the feature.

3 Share With a Partner

Trade sightseeing guides with a partner. Check that your partner has included all the items needed. Share ideas to make each part better.

4 Revise and Share

After you have thought about your partner's suggestions, make changes to your sightseeing guide. Then present it to your classmates.

2 Economics

The BIG Question

▶ VIDEO

How do people get what they want and need?

Lesson 1
Goods and Services

Lesson 2
Types of Resources

Lesson 3
Economic Choices

Lesson 4
Human Capital and Your Future

JumpStart Activity

👆 INTERACTIVITY

Write five things that are valuable. Include two that do not cost money. Share your list with a partner. On the board, put your two lists in order from least to most important. Talk about your reasons.

_____

_____

_____

_____

♪ ♪ **Rap** About It! ♪

🔊 AUDIO

What You Need, What You Want

Preview the chapter **vocabulary** as you sing the rap:

We all have some **needs**,

We can't live without these items.

We all have some **wants**,

Like them but can live without them.

Needs and wants can be **goods**,

Like a home, some food, or a purse.

Services help others,

Like teaching or being a nurse.

What are goods made of?

Mostly **natural resources**.

How are the goods made?

By people, **human resources**.

Plus machines and tools,

Those are **capital resources**.

2 **Quest**

Project-Based Learning

Resources All Around Us

You know a lot about economics already. You know that people make, spend, and save money. You can save money for something you want. You may do chores or other work to make some money. You are using items right now that were made with resources. Let's find out more about resources.

Quest Kick Off

Your quest is to make a poster showing three types of resources needed to sell lemonade. Add definitions to explain the types of resources. Include labels to explain each picture.

1 Ask Questions

What resources do you use to make lemonade?
What resources do you use to sell lemonade?

....

....

2 Plan

Talk with your teacher and others about where you can find pictures of different resources. Write some things you can include on your poster.

INTERACTIVITY

Learn more about the resources you need to make lemonade.

....

....

....

....

....

3 Look for Quest Connections

Begin looking for Quest Connections that will help you make your poster.

4 Quest Findings
Create Your Poster

Use the Quest Findings page at the end of the chapter to help you make your resources poster.

INTERACTIVITY

Participate in a class discussion to preview the content of this lesson.

Unlock The BIG Question

I will know how goods and services have changed over time and where goods are produced.

Vocabulary

goods
services
consumer
local
producer
import
export

Academic Vocabulary

rely
purchase

Academic Vocabulary

rely • *v.*, to depend on, to trust

JumpStart Activity

You are going on a label hunt. Look for labels that tell where a product is made. List the places you find.

_____

_____

You see people spend and earn money every day. You can spend money to buy goods. Your teacher earns money by providing a service. **Goods** are items you can see, like pencils or cars. Businesses sell goods for people to use. **Services** are work that people do, such as fixing a car or cutting your hair. You are a **consumer**, or user, of goods and services.

Early Economies

Early American settlers had to **rely** on themselves to provide everything they needed. They had to grow their own food, build their own homes, and mend their own clothes. They had to use what they found nearby.

As settlements grew, people traded or earned money to get what they needed. They bought **local** goods, or things made near where they were sold. For example, suppose a family grew extra beans. They might trade or sell the beans to someone who had fruit or knew how to repair a wagon wheel. As time went on, entrepreneurs built businesses to provide goods or services for growing towns. Many businesses that started long ago are still in business today. They helped shaped other businesses.

1. ☑ **Reading Check** **Use Evidence From Text**
   Underline ways the economies of later settlements and towns changed from the economies of the early settlers.

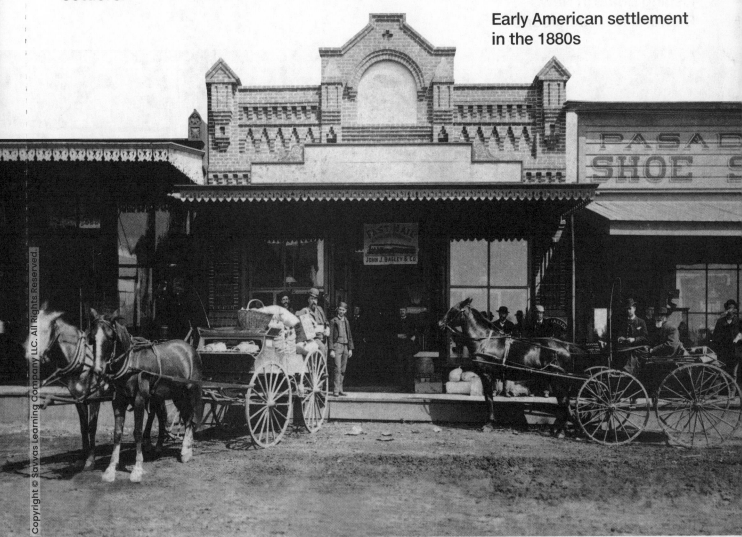

Early American settlement in the 1880s

Quest Connection

Think about some products that are produced near where you live. What resources are used to make them?

INTERACTIVITY

Take a closer look at resources.

Fishing boats in New Bedford, Massachusetts

Producing and Buying Local Goods

In the 1800s, immigrants from Cape Verde (islands off the coast of West Africa) settled in the port of New Bedford, Massachusetts. They were known for their hard work on whaling and fishing boats. Cape Verdeans bought boats, called packet boats, to carry passengers and goods between Cape Verde and New Bedford. Today millions of pounds of cod, haddock, and scallops are processed in New Bedford every year.

Producers, the makers of goods, often build their businesses near the things they need to make the goods. Why? Being close to the resources saves money shipping the resources to other places. If they save money, the goods cost less to sell.

As you have read, settlers had only local products to choose from. Today, we have choices from near and far. Even so, many people still try to buy products that are produced nearby. They might do this for several reasons. Perhaps they like to support small businesses that people in their community own. They might like to save the cost of shipping goods from far away. They may feel that food produced closer is fresher. In some ways, buying locally produced goods is like returning to an earlier time.

Strawberries ripen in a field.

2. ☑ **Reading Check** **Identify** and add details to the diagram to support the main idea.

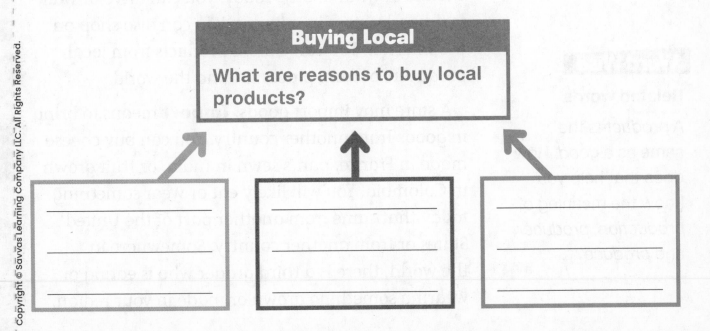

Buying Local

What are reasons to buy local products?

Freight containers on a ship in a U.S. port

Goods From Far Away

Long ago, traveling in a horse-pulled wagon to get supplies could take a day or longer. When settlers got to the store, they would have only a few choices of what to buy. Today, you can drive or walk to a nearby store in minutes. You can also shop on the Internet. You can choose products from local producers or from places around the world.

A store may import goods. **Import** means to bring in goods from another country. You can buy cheese made in France, pants sewn in India, or fruit grown in Colombia. You will likely eat or wear something today that came from another part of the United States or from another country. Somewhere in the world, there is a third grader who is eating or wearing something grown or made in your region.

Word Wise

Related words

A *product* is the same as a *good*. How does that help you know the meaning of *production*, *producer*, and *produce*?

Producers may get, or secure, new customers if they export their products to faraway places. **Export** means to send goods out to another country. Having new consumers increases the amount of money a business makes. Consumers often like to try new products or **purchase** products that are not made near them. Even though oranges do not grow in Alaska, a child in Alaska can drink orange juice for breakfast. That orange juice may have been made in Florida. The next time you are in a store, look to see where products are grown or made.

Academic Vocabulary

purchase • *v.*, to buy with money

3. ☑ **Reading Check** **Talk with a partner** about why you would buy or sell products from far away.

INTERACTIVITY

Check your understanding of the key ideas of this lesson.

☑ **Lesson 1 Check**

4. **Explain** how shopping would be different if you were an early American settler.

_____

_____

_____

5. **Identify** and circle the word to complete each sentence.

An (import export) is a product brought into a country for sale.

An (import export) is a product sent out of a country for sale.

6. **Quest** Connections In this lesson, you thought about products made near you and the resources used. Write other things that might be needed to make those products. (Hint: Think about workers or machines.)

_____

_____

Advertisement From Early America

A primary source may be just text, like a letter or diary. A primary source might also be just a picture, like a painting or photograph. The advertisement on this page contains both text and a picture. It is important to look at both to understand the information.

Think about what you already know about advertisements you see every day. Ads are designed to sell you something and make you feel good about it. The ad on this page is from a fruit box label in the 1930s. It tries to make you think good things about the apples.

This label makes people think that Rainbow Apples get lots of sun and rain.

Fun Fact
Many family farmers showed images of their farms on their fruit labels.

Close Reading

1. **Identify** and circle parts of the advertisement that tell about or show what is being sold.

2. **Identify** and write words from the advertisement that **describe** the product.

_____

_____

Wrap It Up

Look at the advertisement from today. **Compare** it with the early advertisement. How are the two ads alike? How are they different?

_____

_____

_____

INTERACTIVITY

Participate in a class discussion to preview the content of this lesson.

I will know the three types of resources used to create a product.

Vocabulary

human resource
capital resource

Academic Vocabulary

sufficient
technology

JumpStart Activity

In small groups, select one of these products: a car, desk, book, carton of milk, tube of toothpaste, or loaf of bread. Your group will then list resources needed to make that product. The resources should include materials, people, and tools needed.

A logging truck carries timber to a mill.

What is needed to make a product? Many of the objects we use each day take many steps to create. In this lesson, you will learn about resources that producers need.

Natural Resources

Native Americans, and the white settlers who came after them, used the natural resources they found in America. These resources helped them meet their needs for food, shelter, and clothing. Natural resources are items found in nature that people use. They include trees, water, minerals, and soil. We still use natural resources to meet our needs. Farmers use water and soil to raise crops. A factory uses wood from trees to make furniture. To get to school, a school bus needs gasoline from oil found underground.

1. ☑ **Reading Check** **Explain** what a natural resource is.

_____

_____

Human Resources

How did early American Indians know how to make pots or use the skins of deer? How did settlers know how to herd cattle, plant crops, or heal a cough? They learned from their parents or other members of a group. Knowing how to make or do something is an important resource. **Human resources** are people's talents and skills.

Academic Vocabulary

sufficient • *adj.*, enough

Just having trees is not **sufficient** if you want to make a table. You also need the skill to cut the tree into lumber. You need to make the pieces of wood fit together to make a table.

Without the human resources of cooks, you would not get a hot bowl of vegetable soup. A skilled scientist helps make certain medicine is safe and can help heal a cut.

Milk: From Farm to Store

1 Farmers raise dairy cows.

2 Farmers milk the cows.

3 A truck driver takes the milk to a factory.

Look at the diagram showing how milk is made. It shows that many people work together to get milk to stores. For any product, there might be people who designed it, worked in a factory, tested the product for safety, wrote ads for the product, and brought the product to a store. There were likely many more people (human resources) involved in making the product and getting it to the consumer.

We can plant trees to grow more. What can we do to increase our human resources? You are doing something right now that increases your value as a human resource. You are learning. Learning, trying new things, and observing others are ways we each can become more valuable human resources.

2. ☑ **Reading Check** **Use Evidence From Text** Underline details in the text that show how human resources are needed to get goods to a consumer.

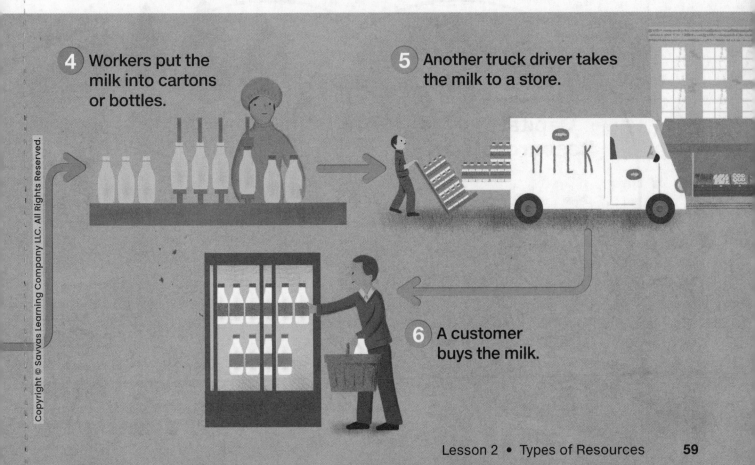

4 Workers put the milk into cartons or bottles.

5 Another truck driver takes the milk to a store.

MILK

6 A customer buys the milk.

Capital Resources

There is another resource that people need to create products. **Capital resources** are human-made items used to make other goods or provide services. Some American Indians made fish weirs to catch fish. Settlers used plows to help with planting. A barber uses scissors to cut hair. Tools and buildings are capital resources.

Think about milk again. What capital resources are used to get the milk from the cow to the store? There are barns, milking machines, tanks, bottles, trucks, and the refrigerator at the grocery store. You can probably think of others. The early settlers may have used only their hands and a bucket to get milk. Times have changed!

3. ☑ **Reading Check Compare and Contrast** Fill in the diagram to **compare and contrast** capital resources and natural resources. In the center, **describe** how they are alike.

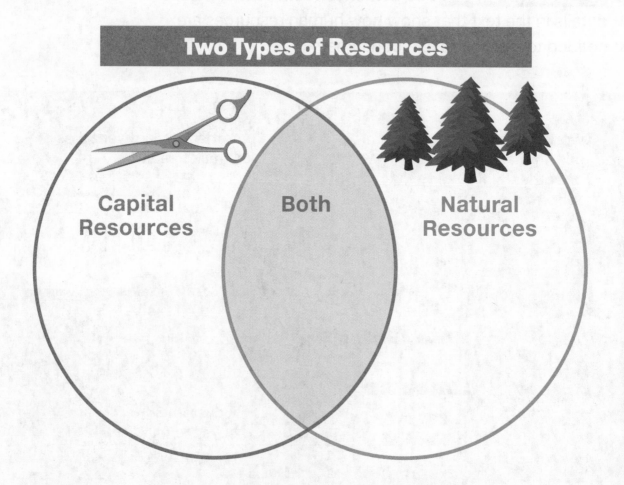

Two Types of Resources

Capital Resources

Both

Natural Resources

This hand-powered dental drill was used long ago. Today, dental drills are powered by electricity.

Some of our tools and capital resources have changed over time. None of us would want to go to a dentist who uses tools from a hundred years ago! As time passes, **technology** advances. For example, it used to take a long time to place metal letters to print one page of a newspaper. Now a news story can be delivered to someone's phone or tablet very fast. Computers are an important capital resource. They are used in most businesses today.

Academic Vocabulary

technology • *n.*, the use of science to solve problems and make things work better

 INTERACTIVITY

Check your understanding of the key ideas of this lesson.

 **Lesson 2 Check**

4. **Identify** Soil, water, forests, and minerals are examples of what type of resource?

_____

5. **Explain** two ways people can become more valuable human resources.

_____

_____

6. **Identify** and list one natural resource, one human resource, and one capital resource used to make a salad.

_____

_____

INTERACTIVITY

Review and practice what you learned about summarizing.

Summarize

When you summarize you tell the most important parts. Have you explained a book or movie to a friend? There is no time and no need to tell every detail. You have to summarize and just tell the main idea and most important points.

Read about the restaurant. If the chef told a friend about a day at the restaurant, how would the chef summarize the day?

People in the restaurant work very hard. Everyone has a job to do. Chef Angela arrives at the restaurant at 6 A.M. She turns on the ovens and heats up the grill. She mixes pancake batter for breakfast, and chops fruit. She checks that all of her cooking supplies and tools are nearby. The first customer arrives. Chef Angela is ready to cook!

By 7 A.M. the restaurant is very busy. The seats are filling up, and the servers have all arrived. They make hot drinks, and fill people's cups. They take breakfast orders from customers, and give the orders to the cooks. They carry plates of hot and cold food to people. Later, they take away the empty plates from tables and bring customers the bill. Servers have no time to rest because breakfast is a busy time.

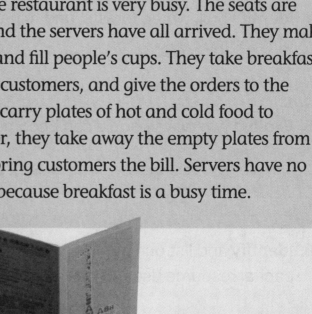

Your Turn!

1. What are the main ideas and details of the paragraphs describing the restaurant? **Fill in** the organizer showing the main idea and details from the first paragraph. Use the box labeled "Summary" to **write** a short statement that summarizes the paragraph. Use your own words to sum up what you have read.

MAIN IDEA

_____
_____
_____
_____
_____

DETAILS

_____
_____
_____
_____
_____

SUMMARY

_____
_____
_____
_____

2. Read the second paragraph. **Underline** the main idea and important details. Then **write** a sentence or two that summarizes that paragraph.

_____
_____

3 Economic Choices

INTERACTIVITY

Participate in a class discussion to preview the content of this lesson.

Unlock
The **BIG**
Question

I will know how economic choices are made.

Vocabulary

trade-off
cost
opportunity cost
benefit
need
want

Academic Vocabulary

adjust
responsible
option

JumpStart Activity

Stand with a partner. Play a game of "You Choose." Think of two things your partner may want, such as a video game or a fun toy. Have your partner say which of the two he or she would rather have. Then switch. Think of at least five pairs of things.

We may wish to have unlimited resources, but none of us do. People, families, communities, and even states and countries have to work with the resources they have. Limited resources cause us to make careful choices about goods and services we use. Sometimes we have to **adjust** what we expect to get.

Academic Vocabulary

adjust • *v.*, to change or shift

Why We Have to Choose

When settlers were deciding if and where to move, they had to weigh the good and bad things. For example, they might find good soil for growing crops, or they might lose everything in a drought. Today, communities might have to choose to use money to build a new school or repair pipes. There might not be enough money to do both. People have to make economic choices, too. For example, suppose you must decide whether to buy soccer shoes or a soccer ball. You cannot do both. Whatever you choose, that choice is a **trade-off**. In a trade-off, you give up one thing for another.

1. ☑ **Reading Check** **Summarize** Why does everyone have to make economic choices?

_____

_____

_____

A family compares bicycles to decide which one to buy.

Possible Costs

How much does it cost? You have probably asked that question. **Cost** is the price needed to get something else. The cost of something is more than just the price on the tag. There may be other costs. For example, a new kitten may cost $40. There are other costs to think about, however. There is the cost to feed it. There might also be costs if the kitten scratches a chair or sofa. It will also cost time to take care of the kitten. The kitten costs more than the $40 to buy it.

An **opportunity cost** is what you have to give up to have something else. Suppose you have $10. You can spend that money on a movie ticket or on a collar for your dog. You do not have enough money for both. If you do one, you cannot do the other. The one you cannot do is called the opportunity cost.

2. ☑ **Reading Check**
Main Idea and Details Add details to the graphic organizer that support the main idea.

Cost of a Pet

Main Idea
The cost of a pet is more than just the price to buy it.

Detail	Detail	Detail
_____	_____	_____
_____	_____	_____

Possible Benefits

If there is a cost to something, why would you buy it? There needs to be a benefit of a good or service. A **benefit** is a useful result. A benefit can mean you get something you need or want. The benefit of having a kitten is that it is fun to play with, it helps you learn to be **responsible**, and you feel good about giving it a home. One benefit of paying a person to fix your broken bicycle is that you can ride it again. The benefit of buying a sandwich is that it removes your hunger. A benefit may be something that is helpful. It may be something that makes you feel good.

This produce costs money. But it has other costs, too. It costs the time it takes to go to the store. It may also cost gasoline and wear and tear on a car.

Academic Vocabulary

responsible • *adj.*, able to be trusted to do what is right

3. ☑ **Reading Check** **Define** What is a benefit?

_____

_____

Making Choices

When making a good choice, you need to see if the benefits are greater than the costs. Here are some steps to help when trying to make a good choice.

Academic Vocabulary

option • *n.*, a choice that can be made

1. List your **options**, or choices that can be made.

2. Identify the costs to each option.

3. Identify the possible benefits to each option.

Here is how a town might study the decision between updating a library or updating a school.

Options	Update the Library	Update the School
Costs	• $8 million dollars • Takes one year	• $16 million dollars • Takes two years
Benefits	• Makes people want to move to the community • A place to go that is free • Fixes an old library that has many problems • Provides resources and enjoyment for everyone	• Helps with crowding • Provides space if more students move to town • Is modern; uses new technology • Provides resources and enjoyment for students

You make economic choices each day. To make a good choice, ask questions. Is it something you need? A **need** is something you must have to live. Is it something you want? A **want** is something you would like to have but do not need. Do you give up something to save money for something else? Do you do extra chores to earn money for something you want? At the store, do you ask a parent for a new eraser or your favorite snack? Your choices tell a lot about what is important to you.

4. ☑ **Reading Check** **Opinion** Look at the chart. **Turn and talk** with a partner. What decision do you think the town should make based on the costs and benefits? Circle the benefits that you think are most important. Underline the most important cost.

Quest Connections

With a partner, think of some of the natural, human, and capital resources needed to build a new school.

👆 **INTERACTIVITY**

Take a closer look at natural, human, and capital resources.

👆 **INTERACTIVITY**

Check your understanding of the key ideas of this lesson.

☑ **Lesson 3 Check**

5. **Summarize** why people and communities have to make economic choices.

_____

_____

6. **Identify** and circle the correct word to complete the sentence.

The (cost benefit) of a good or service is the price you have to pay.

7.  **Quest** Connections What capital resources do you use in your classroom each day to get your education?

_____

_____

_____

Analyze Costs and Benefits

When making an important decision, first weigh the costs and the benefits. For example, think about the costs and benefits to a family during the 1860s. They want to decide if they should move to lands in the West or stay in Missouri. In Missouri, they live on their parents' land. Read to learn about the costs and benefits of each option.

Options	Move West	Stay in Missouri
Costs	• Buy a wagon and supplies • Trip takes four months • No income during trip • Dangerous journey • Moving far from family • Future unknown	• Land belongs to parents • Share all farm money with parents • Difficult winters • Little money from farm • Hard to earn a living • Small plot of land
Benefits	• Better farmland • Own the land • Adventure • More future possibilities	• Support of family • Easy to stay • Known future • Nearby school • Already have farm and house

1. **Identify** and circle the one cost of moving to lands in the West that you think would be the biggest problem.

2. **Explain** why the benefits are different for each option.

INTERACTIVITY

Review and practice what you learned about analyzing costs and benefits.

_____

_____

_____

3. Create your own cost-benefit chart about an economic choice you can make. **Compare** two choices for how to spend, save, or donate some money.

Options		
	_____	_____
Costs		
Benefits		

Human Capital and Your Future

Copyright © Savvas Learning Company LLC. All Rights Reserved.

INTERACTIVITY

Participate in a class discussion to preview the content of this lesson.

Vocabulary

invest
human capital
occupation

Academic Vocabulary

prepare
fund

Jobs such as a veterinarian, electrician, and farmer use different skills.

Unlock The BIG Question

I will know how I can prepare for my future with my work today.

JumpStart Activity

Think of a job you might like to do when you grow up. Work with a partner. Take turns acting out skills needed for that job.

Do you enjoy working with numbers and shapes? Studying math and science may lead to becoming an architect or a game creator. Do you enjoy learning about people? Studying history, the arts, and reading may lead to becoming a historian or an entertainer. What do you enjoy?

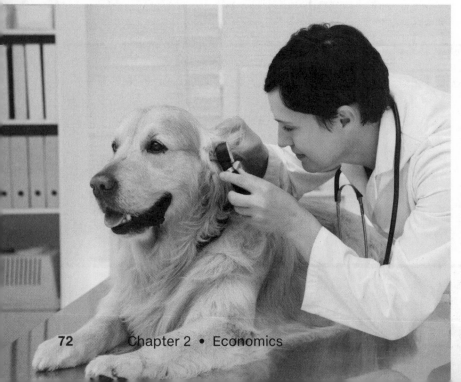
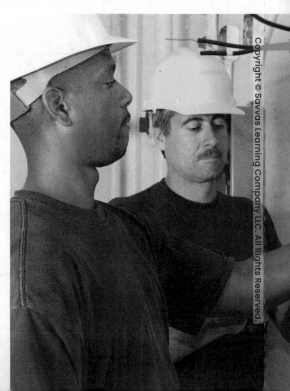

Planning Ahead

Each day you learn is a day you invest in your future. **Invest** means to spend now in the hope of future reward. The time and effort you put into learning now will reward you as you get older. Every doctor, teacher, electrician, singer, or other adult learned while in school. Even if you do not know what adult job you might like, you can begin to **prepare** now. You can grow your human capital. Your **human capital** is your skills, knowledge, and experiences. You can develop good habits now. These habits will help you be a learner your whole life.

Academic Vocabulary

prepare • *v.*, to get ready

1. ☑ **Reading Check** **Explain** how working and studying today is an investment in your future.

_____

_____

_____

Taxpayers may pay for school buses to take students to school.

Education Matters

Education helps prepare you for the future. You work in school. This work helps you learn skills and habits that help you as an adult. Educated people make good citizens. They have the knowledge for a good work and family life.

Americans believe in the importance of education. They pay for every child in the United States to go to school. Taxpayers **fund** your education. They pay for the school building, your teacher, the playground, and your books. They believe in you, and they believe in the value of a good education.

Academic Vocabulary

fund • *v.*, to pay for

2. ☑ **Reading Check** **Cause and Effect** What is the effect of citizens believing in the value of a good education?

_____

_____

What Does It Take to Succeed on the Job?

Success means many different things to people. For some, success is doing what you enjoy and making a difference. Others like earning enough money to own a home or raise a family. Most would agree that doing well on the job makes people successful. You can learn how to do well on the job by talking to people about how they prepared for work. Shop owners might tell you how they use art to present their goods. Nurses might tell you how they use science to help those who are sick. Truck drivers might tell you how they use geography to deliver goods.

A student talks to a peace officer to find out more about his job.

3. ☑ **Reading Check** **Ask Questions** What questions would you ask an adult to learn about how to do well on the job?

_____

_____

_____

_____

_____

_____

Big Dreams Plus Hard Work

A big dream can lead to a future occupation. An **occupation** is a job or work. A big dream might also lead to rewarding volunteer work. Helping others can be a way to make a difference. Whether the work is paid work or volunteer work, we all want to do work that is worth doing.

Word Wise

Parts of Speech
Volunteer can be used as a noun, a verb, or an adjective. How is it used in this sentence? We would like to *volunteer* to help with the clean up.

Primary Source

Far and away the best prize that life offers is the chance to work hard at work worth doing.

—President Theodore Roosevelt, Address to the New York State Agricultural Association, 1903

How is this boy working hard at something worth doing?

4. ☑ **Reading Check** **Opinion** Who do you think Roosevelt was talking to? What kind of hard, rewarding work might they do?

_____

_____

_____

_____

INTERACTIVITY

Check your understanding of the key ideas of this lesson.

☑ Lesson 4 Check

5. Identify and circle the correct word.
His (occupation volunteer) is a chef, but he also helps as a (occupation volunteer) at the food bank.

6. Explain how your education is an investment in your future.

_____

_____

_____

7. How does the work you do in school improve your human capital? **Describe** ways your skills, knowledge, and experiences have grown in school this year.

_____

_____

_____

_____

_____

**Quality:
Determination**

Jerry Yang
A Leader in Technology

Jerry Yang moved from Taiwan to the United States when he was about ten. Mr. Yang says that the only word he understood when he got to the United States was *shoe*. He studied hard and became a very good student. He graduated with the highest grades in his high school. He was also voted class president.

Mr. Yang was interested in computers and the Internet. He and a college friend, David Filo, started a Web site called *Jerry and David's Guide to the World Wide Web*. They started a company based on a search engine, which helps users search the Internet for information.

Mr. Yang is often called one of the top innovators in the world. He continues to work with technology companies by providing funding through his latest company.

Find Out More

1. How did Jerry Yang show determination?

_____

_____

_____

2. Research Go online to find out the names of three search engines.

_____

_____

_____

Visual Review

Use these graphics to review some of the key terms and ideas from this chapter.

EXPORTS
Goods that are sent out of a country to be sold in a different country.

IMPORTS
Goods that come into a country from a different country.

Three Types of Resources

	Natural Resources	Human Resources	Capital Resources
Definitions	items found in nature that people use	talents and skills that people have and use	human-made items used to make goods or provide services
Examples	forests, water, minerals, soil, gasoline, oil	skills to do a job, such as repairing a car or treating an illness	computers, buildings, tools, machines

☑ Assessment

 GAMES

Play the vocabulary game.

Vocabulary and Key Ideas

Identify and circle the correct word to complete each sentence.

1. A person who creates products is called a _____. producer consumer

2. Trees and water are _____. natural resources capital resources

3. Equipment and buildings are _____. human resources capital resources

Critical Thinking and Writing

4. **Summarize** How has the way people use resources changed over time?

_____

_____

_____

_____

5. **Explain** why people need to make trade-offs when making economic decisions.

_____

_____

_____

_____

6. **Cost-Benefit Analysis** Ella's family made a cost-benefit chart to help them decide between adopting a puppy or an adult dog.

Options	Adopt a Puppy	Adopt an Adult Dog
Costs	• $200 fee • Training tools • Time spent training • Food and supplies	• $100 fee • Unknown past • Food and supplies
Benefits	• Very cute • Known past	• Very cute • Already trained

Explain why Ella's family decided to adopt an adult dog.

_____

_____

_____

_____

7. **Revisit the Big Question** How do people get what they want and need?

_____

_____

_____

_____

8. **Writing Workshop: Write a Narrative Text** On separate paper, write a short story about a person who has to decide between buying something now or saving for something to buy in the future. Include the costs and benefits involved with the decision.

9. **Describe** the photograph using the words *import* and *export*. What questions do you have about this photo?

_____

_____

_____

_____

_____

Analyze Costs and Benefits

10. **Analyze** the difference between a cost and a benefit.

_____

_____

_____

_____

Quest Findings

Resources All Around

INTERACTIVITY
Use this activity to help you make your poster.

You have read about many resources people use. Now it's time to show what you have learned. Make a poster showing the resources needed to make and sell lemonade.

1 Prepare Your Poster

Make headings for each of the three types of resources. Next to each heading give a short definition of that type of resource.

2 Gather the Pictures

Look for pictures of natural resources, human resources, and capital resources that could be used to make lemonade. Look in old magazines, newspapers, and on the Internet. Figure out the group where each picture should be placed. Leave space for the labels. Do not paste on your pictures yet.

3 Share With the Class

With your poster flat on your desk and the pictures where you want them, show your poster to the class. Everyone will look at each poster to help make sure the pictures are in the correct groups. If any are not in the right place, move them.

4 Add Details

Complete your poster by pasting on the pictures. Add labels telling why each picture is an example of that resource. Hang up your poster for everyone to see!

Chapter 3

Communities Build a Nation

GO ONLINE FOR
DIGITAL RESOURCES

- ▶ VIDEO
- 👆 INTERACTIVITY
- 🔊 AUDIO
- 🎮 GAMES
- ☑ ASSESSMENT
- 📖 eTEXT

The BIG Question

▶ VIDEO

How does our past affect our present?

JumpStart Activity

👆 INTERACTIVITY

Think about something you learned how to do in the past or an action you took in the past. Act it out for a partner. Then talk about what it has to do with you now.

Lesson 1
America's First Peoples

Lesson 2
Early Explorers

Lesson 3
Early Spanish Communities

Lesson 4
Early French Communities

Lesson 5
Early English Communities

Lesson 6
Creating a New Nation

Communities Built a Nation: The U.S.A.

Preview the chapter **vocabulary** as you sing the rap.

North America was first settled by different
   American Indian groups.
They had their own cultures, and their own
   customs too.

Some also worked with European settlers
   who came.
Explorers traveled from Portugal, France,
   England, and Spain.
Some came for gold, spices, riches, or fame
And built **forts** to help **defend** land they'd claim.

The British built colonies and many people
   came for
Religious freedom, like the **pilgrims** and **Quakers**.

The British **imposed** taxes, but colonists
   weren't represented
And this led to **protests**, and a fight for
   independence.

The Past and You!

When you think of our country's past, does a person or event come to mind? Identifying people or events from the past is one way to learn about history and what it has to do with your life today.

Quest Kick Off

What is something from the past that has made a difference in your life? Write about the event or person from history so others can see how something like this might affect them.

1 Ask Questions

What questions can you ask to find out about people or events that are important to our country's past? How does it relate to your life?

....

....

....

2 Plan

What evidence will help tell why a person or event was important? What evidence will explain how this person or event impacted your life? Write down some ideas.

....

....

....

INTERACTIVITY

Complete the activities to get started on your persuasive text.

3 Look for *Quest* Connections

Begin looking for Quest Connections that will help you write your persuasive text.

4 *Quest* Findings
Write Your Persuasive Text

Use the Quest Findings page at the end of the chapter to help you write your persuasive text.

Lesson 1 America's First Peoples

INTERACTIVITY

Participate in a class discussion to preview the content of this lesson.

Vocabulary

custom
longhouse
confederacy
cooperate
reservation
government
tradition

Academic Vocabulary

purpose
generation

Unlock The BIG Question

I will know how geography influences communities and how the past connects to the present.

JumpStart Activity

Stand in one of the five areas of your classroom that represent the five regions of the United States. Think about that region's land, water, climate, and resources. Make a drawing that shows what life may have been like for Native Americans living there long ago.

Native Americans settled throughout North America. This settlement was in the Northeast.

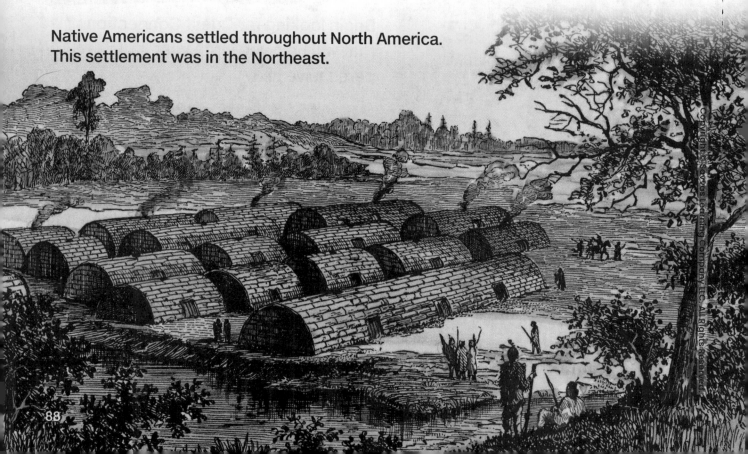

Every community has a history shaped by the people who first lived there. Your community is special because of its past as well as its present.

Cultural Groups

Native Americans were the first people to settle in North America. There were many Native American groups. Each had its own cultures and **customs**, or special ways of doing things.

Native Americans lived in all regions throughout North America. Each group used the natural resources in its region to meet their needs. Native Americans who lived in the Pacific Northwest caught fish from the Pacific Ocean. Those living on the Plains used the rich soil there for farming.

Cherokee of the Southeast

More than 1,000 years ago, the Native American group called the Cherokee settled in the forests of the southeastern United States. The Cherokee settled in this area because of geography: rich soil, rivers, and trees. They were hunters and farmers. They ate meat, fruit, and vegetables available to the area. They used trees to build houses. They covered the wooden frames with mud from the nearby riverbanks. Later, the Cherokee built log homes that kept out the cold and snow in winter.

A famous Cherokee named Sequoyah (sih KWOI uh) invented a system for writing the Cherokee language. Once people learned the 86 symbols, they could read and write the language.

Word Wise

Word Endings You know that the word *settle* means "to live in a new place or to build a new community." What do you think *settler* and *settlement* mean?

1. ☑ **Reading Check**
Underline why the Cherokee settled in the southeastern United States.

Iroquois of the Northeast

The Iroquois settled in the forests of what is now central and northern New York and southern Canada. Like the Cherokee, the Iroquois chose this area to settle because of geography. The forests had plenty of animals and plants. The Iroquois used rivers for fishing and traveling.

Like the Cherokee, the Iroquois used trees to build their houses. However, Iroquois houses had a different shape than Cherokee houses. They were up to 200 feet long! Since these homes were longer than they were wide, they were called **longhouses**. Longhouses could be home to as many as ten families. Each family had its own living space. Fires were built down the middle of the longhouse, and families on each side shared a fire.

Hiawatha was an Onondaga chief and a member of the Iroquois Confederacy.

More than 500 years ago, the Iroquois formed a confederacy. A **confederacy** is a formal agreement, or treaty, between groups to work together. The Iroquois Confederacy had five groups: the Mohawk, Oneida, Onondaga, Cayuga, and Seneca peoples all shared a similar culture. The Confederacy was also called the Five Nations. It had rules to protect the rights of each of the five groups. Each group voted on important Iroquois decisions.

2. ☑ **Reading Check** **Describe** how the idea to form a confederacy changed communities.

_____

_____

Group Cooperation

As the Iroquois Confederacy shows, some Native American groups **cooperated**, or worked together. Even though the Confederacy allowed each group to rule itself, the Five Nations felt it was best to come together so they could be stronger and more powerful. The main **purpose** of the Iroquois Confederacy was the *Great Law of Peace*. This law said that all decision making had to be done peacefully. No one was allowed to hurt anyone if groups disagreed.

Some Native American groups worked with one another. They also sometimes cooperated with the first settlers from England. When these settlers came about 300 years ago, some Native Americans taught them how to plant crops such as pumpkin, squash, beans, and corn. They also taught settlers different ways to fish in the shallow water.

At times, however, Native American groups went to war against each other. About 400 years ago, the Iroquois fought wars against the Huron, Erie, and Algonquin groups. The Iroquois had traded beaver furs with European settlers for guns and other supplies. When the beaver population began to die out, the Iroquois traveled west into other Native American lands to look for beaver. Because the Iroquois had better weapons than the groups they were fighting against, they won what were called the Beaver Wars.

3. ☑ **Reading Check** **Cause and Effect Identify** and **underline** the effects of the Iroquois groups working together.

Academic Vocabulary

purpose • *n.*, goal or reason

Quest Connection

What might the Iroquois Confederacy have to do with how you act in school and at home?

👆 INTERACTIVITY

Explore why the Iroquois Confederacy was formed and its benefits.

Native Americans Today

Leaders of the Cherokee nation get ready for a Native Nations procession to mark the opening of the National Museum of the American Indian.

Today, there are about 2 million Native Americans living in the United States. About 1 million Native Americans live in Canada.

Some Native Americans in the United States live on **reservations**, or lands that the United States government set aside for them many years ago. Each reservation has its own **government**, or system of ruling people. Native Americans who live on reservations have to obey the laws created by this government. They not only have to follow the laws set up by their reservation's government, but they also have to follow the laws made by the United States government.

Ben Nighthorse Campbell is part of the Northern Cheyenne group and serves as a member of the group's Council of Chiefs. He also served as a member of the United States government for 18 years.

Native Americans have traditions. A **tradition** is a special way that a group does something that is passed down from one **generation** to the next. Some Cherokee traditions include games, dances, songs, and written language. Some Native Americans wear traditional clothing at special events.

Academic Vocabulary

generation • *n.*, people born and living about the same time

4. ☑ **Reading Check** **Identify** who creates the laws on Native American reservations.

_____

_____

INTERACTIVITY

Check your understanding
of the key ideas of this
lesson.

☑ Lesson 1 Check

5. **Main Idea and Details Compare** American Indian settlements.
Then fill in the chart with details that support the main idea.

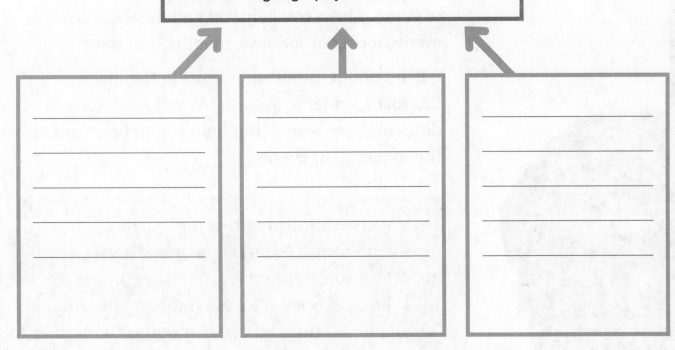

American Indians chose where to settle because of geography.

6. **Describe** traditions in your family or community that came from the past.

_____

_____

7. **Understand the** *Quest* **Connections Identify** evidence from the lesson that explains why cooperation was important to American Indian groups.

_____

_____

_____

Sequence

When you learn about past events, it is important to understand when they happened. The order in which events took place is their sequence. Words such as *first, second, third, then, after, next, finally, past, future, now,* and *later* can help you find the sequence of events. Dates can help you find the sequence of events, too. Look for days, months, and years.

Read about important events in the life of Cherokee leader Sequoyah. As you read, look for dates and key words that help you understand the sequence of events.

Sequoyah certainly deserves a place in American history. After all, he made a very important contribution to Cherokee culture. In 1821, he developed a set of symbols to go with all 86 syllables of the Cherokee language. Born in the 1770s, Sequoyah learned the language of his people. As an adult, he wondered why there was no way to put the language into writing. So he created and introduced his famed writing system. Then the language was taught in all Cherokee schools. Finally, the Cherokee began to print books and newspapers in the Cherokee language.

Your Turn!

1. You read about events in Sequoyah's life. Now put the events in sequence in a chart. Begin with what happened first and write the events in the order they took place.

INTERACTIVITY

Review and practice what you learned about sequence.

2. What clues in the text helped you understand the sequence?

2 Early Explorers

 **INTERACTIVITY**

Participate in a class discussion to preview the content of this lesson.

Vocabulary

explorer
route

Academic Vocabulary

motive
claim

Unlock The BIG Question

I will know the causes and effects of European exploration.

JumpStart Activity

Work with a partner. You are both explorers. Prepare and act out a short skit that tells why you decided to explore other lands. Include what you like about exploring, what you find hard about it, and how you treat the new people you meet.

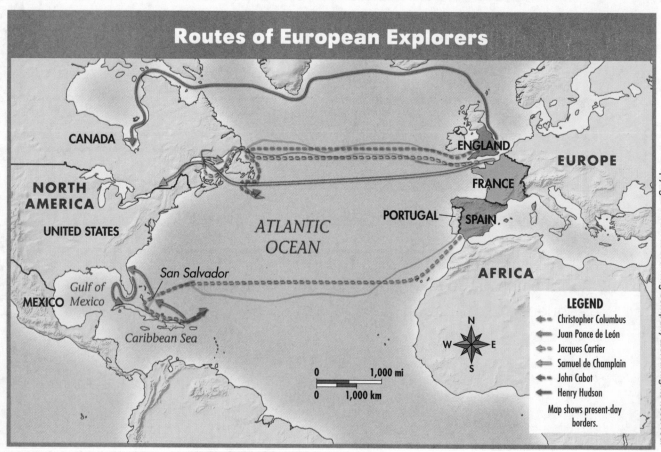

Routes of European Explorers

CANADA

ENGLAND

EUROPE

NORTH AMERICA

FRANCE

UNITED STATES

PORTUGAL

SPAIN

ATLANTIC OCEAN

AFRICA

San Salvador

Gulf of Mexico

MEXICO

Caribbean Sea

0   1,000 mi
0   1,000 km

LEGEND

N
W   E
S

Christopher Columbus
Juan Ponce de León
Jacques Cartier
Samuel de Champlain
John Cabot
Henry Hudson
Map shows present-day borders.

Do you like going to new places and meeting new people? An explorer does! An **explorer** is a person who travels looking for new lands and discoveries.

Explorers Sail From Europe

Explorers from Europe thought traveling to Asia by water might take less time than traveling by land. They all wanted to be the first to find a water route to Asia. A **route** is the course you take to get somewhere.

More than 500 years ago, in the 1480s, explorers from Portugal began to search for a water route to Asia by sailing east around Africa. In the early 1490s, Spain sent explorers west across the Atlantic Ocean looking not only for a way to travel to Asia by water, but also for spices and herbs needed for cooking and medicine. Another **motive** was to find gold, silk, and other riches.

Late in the fifteenth century, England was also trying to find a water route to Asia. In addition, the country wanted to own land in the Americas, so they sent explorers there, too.

By the early 1500s, France was searching for a water route to Asia, too. During the search, French explorers built settlements and traded with Native Americans in what is now Canada.

Academic Vocabulary

motive • *n.*, a reason

1. ☑ **Reading Check** **Sequence** Write the countries in Europe in the order that they began searching for a water route to Asia.

_____

_____

Spanish Explorers

Long ago, spices kept food from spoiling, so people thought they were valuable. In 1492, Spain wanted Christopher Columbus, an explorer born in Italy, to sail to China in search of them. Columbus thought he could reach China by sailing west from Spain. However, he did not find China. Instead he landed on an island off the coast of present-day Florida. On seeing the people living there, he called them "Indians." He thought he had reached the East Indies, near southern China. Then Columbus sailed to other islands. He set up a settlement on an island called Hispaniola (hihs pun YOH luh).

A group called the Taino (TYE noh) already lived on Hispaniola. Their lives changed after the Spaniards, or people from Spain, arrived. Many Taino people died of diseases brought by the Spaniards.

Another explorer who sailed for Spain was Amerigo Vespucci. He explored many places on the present-day continents of North and South America, which are named for him.

Columbus builds a settlement on Hispaniola.

Routes of Vespucci and LaSalle

NORTH AMERICA

Fort Frontenac

NORTH ATLANTIC OCEAN

EUROPE

FRANCE

SPAIN

PORTUGAL

Mississippi River

Fort St. Louis

Gulf of Mexico

Hispaniola

AFRICA

PACIFIC OCEAN

SOUTH AMERICA

SOUTH ATLANTIC OCEAN

LEGEND
- Vespucci, 1499
- Vespucci, 1500
- LaSalle, 1678
- LaSalle, 1684
- Fort

0   1,200 mi

0   1,200 km

French Explorers

The French arrived in North America in the 1520s. They traveled north by river through the center of North America. Jacques Cartier sailed the St. Lawrence River in 1535. Samuel de Champlain explored the St. Lawrence region and the Great Lakes. He founded Quebec City in 1608.

In 1634, Jean Nicolet tried to find the Northwest Passage to India, a water route to link the Atlantic and Pacific oceans. He did not find it, but he explored Lake Michigan. Louis Joliet explored the Mississippi River in 1673. Later, Robert de La Salle explored the Great Lakes and the Mississippi River as well.

2. ☑ **Reading Check** Look at the map. **Identify** which country Vespucci sailed for in 1500 and where he sailed. When did LaSalle reach the Great Lakes?

English Explorers

English explorers wanted to explore the Americas, too. In June 1497, John Cabot arrived on the coast of North America and explored it. Later, England **claimed** all of North America. The English believed that Cabot had been the first person to discover this land.

In 1580, Sir Francis Drake became the first English explorer to sail around the world. He claimed land near present-day San Francisco for England. When Drake finished his trip, he was honored by the queen.

Beginning in 1607, Henry Hudson sailed for England to search for the Northwest Passage to India. After many failed attempts to do so, he moved to Holland. In 1609, he sailed from Holland, again trying to find the Northwest Passage. He could not find it, but he did explore a huge river in North America. The river is called the Hudson River and it is in New York state.

Academic Vocabulary

claim • *v.*, to say that the land belongs to a certain country

3. ☑ **Reading Check**
Identify and **underline** the sentences that tell what each explorer claimed.

Henry Hudson sails into the Hudson River.

☑ Lesson 2 Check

4. Sequence Analyze the list of events. Then fill in the chart by sequencing the events.

- Samuel de Champlain founds Quebec City.
- Jean Nicolet explores Lake Michigan.
- Henry Hudson discovers the Hudson River.

Date	Event
____	____
____	____
____	____

5. Explain how European exploration affected the Americas.

_____

_____

_____

6. Understand the *Quest* **Connections** How did Columbus contribute to the creation of new communities?

_____

_____

Timelines

A timeline shows when events took place. Each event is placed on a timeline in the order in which it happened. The event that happened first, or earliest, is placed on the left part of the timeline. As you read the timeline from left to right, you learn which events happened first, second, third, and then last.

On the timeline each mark stands for 50 years. Notice that some events happen close together in time.

Circle the event on the timeline that happened first.

Underline two events that happened very close together.

1497
Cabot lands on the continent's eastern coast

1535
Cartier sails the St. Lawrence River

1450   **1500**   **1550**

1492
Columbus reaches North America

1524
Vespucci explores South America's coast

Your Turn!

1. What do the numbers on the timeline show?

_____

 INTERACTIVITY

Review and practice what you learned about interpreting timelines.

2. Why are spaces between events different?

_____

_____

_____

3. Did Cartier sail the St. Lawrence before or after Drake's trip around the world?

_____

1580
Drake
sails
around
the world

1607
Hudson explores an
important waterway

1600

1650

1608
Champlain founds
Quebec City

1634
Nicolet searches for
the Northwest Passage

Map and Graph Skills • Timelines   **103**

Lesson 3 — Early Spanish Communities

 INTERACTIVITY

Participate in a class discussion to preview the content of this lesson.

Vocabulary

legend

fort

colony

colonize

mission

citizen

Academic Vocabulary

defend

significant

Ponce de León landed near what is today St. Augustine, Florida.

Unlock The BIG Question

I will know about early Spanish explorers and settlers in North America.

Jumpstart Activity

Imagine you are a Spaniard and have the chance to go to the Americas. Would you go there to live? Stand up and share whether you would make the move and why.

Explorers from Portugal, Spain, France, and England came to the Americas. These explorers and the Native Americans living in the Americas had different cultures. Today, America is a rich mix of all these cultures.

Let's look more closely at the Spanish explorers who brought their culture to America.

Spanish Exploration in Florida

Some explorers who sailed to the Americas wanted gold, gems, and riches. Other explorers wanted to be famous.

Native Americans told a special **legend**, or a story from the past whose facts cannot be checked. The legend was about a magical spring whose water made people young again. Spanish explorer Juan Ponce de León wanted to find the spring. He wanted to find the Fountain of Youth.

In 1513, Ponce de León landed near present-day St. Augustine, Florida, during his search. He took control of the land for Spain. He named the land *La Florida*, which means "land of flowers."

Ponce de León and his men did not find the Fountain of Youth. Ponce de León was very disappointed and left Florida. He sailed to what is known today as Puerto Rico and then back to Spain.

Ponce de León sailed to the west coast of Florida in 1521. He brought with him about 200 settlers, 50 horses and other animals, as well as farm tools. When Ponce de León and his party landed, they went to battle with a group of American Indians. Ponce de León was wounded, and he died soon after.

Ponce de León was the first European to explore the area of Florida that is near St. Augustine. This led to others exploring the area after him.

Ponce de León

Word Wise

Parts of Speech The word *land* is usually used as a noun. Find the word *landed*. What part of speech is *landed*?

Don Pedro Menéndez de Avilés, shown in the statue, had the Castillo de San Marcos built in 1565. The fort still stands today and is a national historic monument.

Spain and France Fight to Settle Florida

Spain and France both wanted to build a settlement in Florida. In 1564, the French set up a fort and a colony on the St. John's River. A **fort** is a strong building or area that can be **defended** against enemy attacks. A **colony** is a place ruled by another country. The French fort was named Fort Caroline.

Fort Caroline was close to where the Spaniards had first landed. The Spanish treasure ships sailed along the Florida coast past Fort Caroline to Spain. The French fort threatened the Spanish ships. King Philip II of Spain wanted to keep his ships safe from enemy attacks. So he sent Don Pedro Menéndez de Avilés [ah vee LAYS], a Spanish explorer, to set up and lead a Spanish colony in Florida. The king knew Menéndez would protect Spanish interests.

Academic Vocabulary

defend • *v.*, to protect or guard from harm

King Philip also told Menéndez to drive out any settlers and pirates from other countries. A pirate is a person who robs ships or boats at sea.

Menéndez arrived in Florida in 1565. Menéndez, his soldiers, and the settlers built a fort for safety. It was named Castillo de San Marcos. Then Menéndez started a settlement, which he called St. Augustine.

About a month later, Menéndez defeated the French at Fort Caroline. As a result, Spain now controlled the coast of Florida. St. Augustine grew since more Spaniards came to settle there. Today, St. Augustine is remembered as the first permanent European settlement in North America. It is also the oldest city in the United States.

Other Spanish Explorers

Around the same time Ponce de León was exploring *La Florida*, Vasco Núñez de Balboa also was exploring for Spain. In 1513, he led an expedition in search of gold, and was the first European to reach the Pacific Ocean. He claimed it and its shores. This helped Spain in later years as the country explored and conquered South America's western coast.

Another Spanish explorer, Hernando de Soto, took part in conquests in Central America and Peru. He also explored the present-day southeastern United States. He was the first European recorded to have seen the Mississippi River in 1541.

1. ☑ **Reading Check** **Sequence** **Underline** the first event that led to Spain's control of Florida. **Circle** what happened as a result of Spain's actions.

The Spanish Explore the Southwest

In the 1500s, many Spaniards lived in New Spain, present-day Mexico. Native Americans told them a legend about the Seven Cities of Gold.

Spanish explorer Francisco Vazques de Coronado went in search of this gold. He found that the city of Cibola was a Native American village. The Zunis told Coronado he might find gold in Quivira. He did not find any gold, and he returned to New Spain in 1540.

In 1598, Juan de Oñate and others returned to again search for Quivira gold. His group crossed the Chihuahuan Desert. On the forty-fifth day, the group ran out of food and water. People searched for plants to eat, but found little. Many people nearly died until they came to the Rio Grande. Their lives were saved.

After resting, hunting, and fishing for ten days, Oñate ordered a day of Thanksgiving. Here is what one member of the group said:

Primary Source

> We built a great bonfire and roasted the meat and fish, and then all sat down to a repast the like of which we had never enjoyed before. We were happy that our trials were over.
>
> —A member of Oñate's group, 1598

Academic Vocabulary

significant • *adj.*, important

Some historians say that this feast was truly the first Thanksgiving. Every year in El Paso, Texas, people reenact this **significant** event.

Spanish Settlements in the Southwest

After the day of Thanksgiving, Oñate colonized New Mexico for Spain. To **colonize** means to settle lands for another country. This was the first Spanish settlement in the Southwest. However, Oñate was a cruel leader. While he was away searching for gold, most of the people left. He was not the only Spaniard to settle the Southwest, though.

In present-day Texas, Spaniards started settlements called missions. A **mission** is a settlement with a church. Its goal is to spread religion to the people who live in the area. In 1691, present-day San Antonio was land where Papaya Indians lived. By 1718, the Mission San Antonio de Valero stood there. That mission later became known as the Alamo.

The Spanish built missions throughout the Southwest including the Mission San Antonio de Valero.

2. ☑ **Reading Check Describe** how Juan de Oñate contributed to the expansion of existing communities or the creation of new communities.

_____

_____

Spanish Settlements in California

The Spaniards also colonized parts of California. Here they began settlements called pueblos. They also built presidios, or forts, and set up missions.

The first missions in California were built in the 1760s. The American Indians who lived there had to learn about Spanish culture and religion. Spain's king sent Father Junípero Serra to set up more missions. He and other leaders forced the American Indians to work hard and to eat Spanish food and to use Spanish.

Spain Loses Power

Spain sent money to support the missions. Then, in the early 1800s, Spain told the religious leaders to stop building missions in California. The last mission was built in 1823.

People moving to California at that time wanted the Mexican government to make the American Indians leave the missions. Mexico had control of California. So, in 1826, the head of government in California allowed many of these American Indians to leave and become Mexican citizens. A **citizen** is an official member of a community. When they left the missions, the American Indians needed new places to live and new jobs. Leaving the missions sometimes made their lives more difficult. However, many California Indians did not like how the missions affected their cultures.

3. ☑ **Reading Check** **Sequence Identify** and **underline** when the first and last missions were built.

One of the last missions built in California

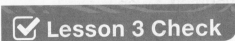 **Lesson 3 Check**

 **INTERACTIVITY**

Check your understanding of the key ideas of this lesson.

4. **Summarize** Write one or two sentences **summarizing** what you learned about Spanish settlements in the Americas.

_____

_____

_____

5. **Identify** reasons the Spanish formed communities in the present-day United States.

_____

_____

6. Spanish explorers were the first Europeans to reach the Pacific Ocean and the Mississippi River. **Explain** why this was important to Spain.

_____

_____

Lesson 4 Early French Communities

INTERACTIVITY

Participate in a class discussion to preview the content of this lesson.

Unlock The BIG Question

I will know about early French explorers and settlers in North America.

Vocabulary

expedition
territory

Academic Vocabulary

undertake
influence

JumpStart Activity

The French and the Native Americans often traded goods. Write five things you use every day but cannot make yourself. Swap lists with a partner. Then act out trading to get the things on the list that you wrote.

Pierre Laclede established a trading post in what is present-day St. Louis, Missouri, around 1760. Today, the riverfront area is named in his honor.

THE HISTORIC RIVERFRONT
LACLEDE'S LANDING
IN OLD SAINT LOUIS

French explorers traveled to many different parts of North America. The explorers brought French culture with them to the places they traveled. Many cities in North America founded by the French have kept parts of French culture.

The French Come to North America

In 1498, Vasco da Gama, an explorer from Portugal, established an all-water route to India. The French thought it might be faster to travel by inland waterways, so they explored rivers and streams.

In 1534, Jacques Cartier landed in Newfoundland. Then he explored the Gulf of St. Lawrence in present-day Canada. Cartier later sailed up the St. Lawrence River. He realized that it was not the direct route to Asia that he was looking for. Rough waters made traveling west too dangerous to **undertake**, so he returned home.

St. Louis, Missouri, is a city that was first settled by the French. In 1700, priests built a mission there. Native Americans joined the priests, but the settlement did not last. Then around 1760, a Frenchman named Pierre Laclede traveled to where the mission had been. Here he set up a trading post. Laclede wanted to buy fur from the Native Americans. He named the area St. Louis for King Louis of France. Laclede said he wanted to set up "one of the finest cities in America." He did!

In time, France lost control of St. Louis. The city opened to new settlers and new businesses. However, French culture is still important in St. Louis today.

Academic Vocabulary

undertake • v., to begin to do

Old Quebec City including
Le Chateau Frontenac

Champlain Builds Quebec City

In 1608, Samuel de Champlain sailed from France to present-day Canada. He built a village near an area where the Huron people already lived. He became friends with the people of this nation.

Champlain called his village Quebec City. England and France fought over this village. They both wanted to take control because of its location. Quebec City was on two waterways, the St. Lawrence and the St. Charles rivers. Settlers could use these rivers for trade and for traveling from one place to another. In 1759, the English won a battle against the French. As a result, French rule in Canada ended.

Today, French culture still **influences** Quebec City. People speak French, and they celebrate French customs and traditions. Old Quebec is a popular place to visit. It is the part of the city on top of a hill. Le Chateau (sha TOH) Frontenac is in the center of Old Quebec. It was built in 1893 on a hilltop overlooking the St. Lawrence River. Standing there, you can see for miles.

1. ☑ **Reading Check** **Explain** why the location of Quebec City was so important.

_____

_____

_____

Academic Vocabulary

influence • *v.*, to have an effect upon

Exploring Waterways

The French explored inland waterways instead of traveling along the coast. In 1634, Jean Nicolet took seven Native Americans with him in a large canoe, and they went on an expedition to Lake Michigan. Nicolet also explored what is now the state of Wisconsin.

In 1672, a Frenchman named Louis Joliet was put in charge of an expedition down the Mississippi River. An **expedition** is a trip made for a special reason. Joliet and a priest named Father Marquette traveled from present-day Canada down the Mississippi River. They traveled to the places that we know today as Green Bay, Wisconsin, and Chicago, Illinois. They learned that the Mississippi River empties into the Gulf of Mexico.

Robert de La Salle

Later in the 1600s, Robert de La Salle explored the Great Lakes, the Mississippi River, and more. He claimed the entire Mississippi region for France.

Because of these explorers and others like them, the French began to gain power and control in North America. They claimed big parts of the continent for France.

2. ☑ **Reading Check** **Sequence** Identify who explored the Mississippi River first: Louis Joliet or Robert de La Salle.

_____

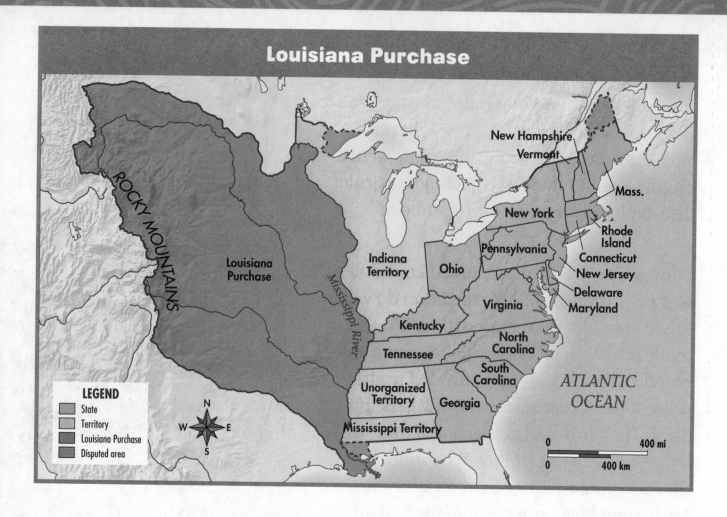

Louisiana Purchase

ROCKY MOUNTAINS

Louisiana Purchase

Mississippi River

Indiana Territory

Ohio

New Hampshire
Vermont
Mass.
New York
Rhode Island
Pennsylvania
Connecticut
New Jersey
Delaware
Maryland
Virginia
Kentucky
North Carolina
Tennessee
South Carolina
Unorganized Territory
Georgia
Mississippi Territory

ATLANTIC OCEAN

LEGEND
State
Territory
Louisiana Purchase
Disputed area

N W E S

0   400 mi
0   400 km

French Lose Power in North America

From 1754 to 1763 Britain and France fought a war for control of northern North America. Some Native Americans helped the French, while others helped the British. When the French lost, both France and their Native American allies had to give much of their land to the British.

France lost more power in 1803, when it sold its Louisiana Territory to the United States. A **territory** is an area of land owned by a country either within or outside the country's borders. This Louisiana Purchase stretched from the Mississippi River to the Rocky Mountains and more than doubled the size of the United States.

3. ☑ **Reading Check**
Trace the outline of the Louisiana Purchase. Then **draw** a dotted line around all of the states.

☑ Lesson 4 Check

4. **Sequence Identify** three main events of the lesson in order from first to last. For each event, **explain** why it was important.

```
┌─────────────────────────────────────┐
│                                     │
│  _____    │
│                                     │
│  _____    │
└─────────────────────────────────────┘
                  │
                  ▼
┌─────────────────────────────────────┐
│                                     │
│  _____    │
│                                     │
│  _____    │
└─────────────────────────────────────┘
                  │
                  ▼
┌─────────────────────────────────────┐
│                                     │
│  _____    │
│                                     │
│  _____    │
└─────────────────────────────────────┘
```

5. **Describe** seventeenth-century exploration of the Mississippi River.

_____

_____

_____

6. Choose one explorer from the lesson. **Describe** how this explorer and his ideas helped shape an area in present-day North America.

_____

_____

_____

_____

Vocabulary

drought
debt
interpreter
Quaker
pilgrim

Academic Vocabulary

require
crucial

Roanoke Colony found abandoned

Unlock The BIG Question

I will know why settlers came from England to North America.

Jumpstart Activity

You live in England long ago. You have been selected to start a new colony in North America. Work with a partner to make an advertisement for others to join you in the adventure. Share it.

North American exploration meant that the Spanish and French had new lands to settle. The English wanted to settle too.

Roanoke Colony

Sir Walter Raleigh sent English settlers to Roanoke Island in present-day North Carolina in 1587. John White was in charge of setting up the colony. When supplies were **required**, White returned to England, but did not come back to Roanoke until 1590.

On his return, White found the word *CROATOAN* carved on a tree, and all of the 113 settlers gone. What happened to the settlers of the Roanoke colony remains a mystery. Some scientists believe that a **drought**, or not enough water, led to the colony's end. Others think that the settlers went to live with American Indians or that they died from disease or hunger.

Academic Vocabulary

require • *v.*, to need

Jamestown

In 1607, 105 English settlers arrived in what is now Virginia. They named their colony Jamestown after King James I.

Long before the English came, American Indians built villages and planted crops in Virginia. Soon after the settlers arrived, they ran out of food. Colony leader Captain John Smith searched for food, but American Indians captured him. Smith was taken to the chief, Powhatan. One legend says Smith's life was saved by Powhatan's daughter, Pocahontas.

When Smith returned to Jamestown, only about 38 settlers were still alive. The rest had died of hunger and disease.

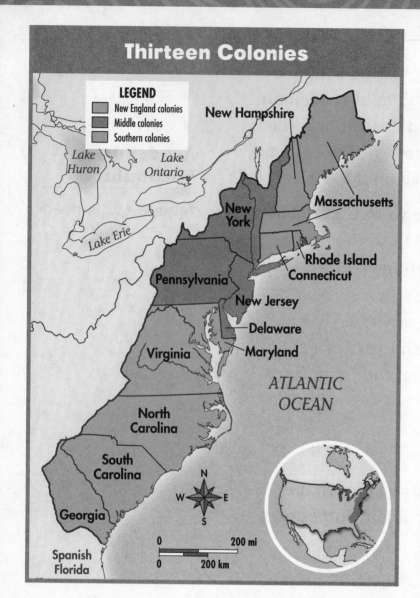

Thirteen Colonies

LEGEND
- New England colonies
- Middle colonies
- Southern colonies

Lake Huron
Lake Ontario
Lake Erie

New Hampshire
New York
Massachusetts
Rhode Island
Connecticut
Pennsylvania
New Jersey
Delaware
Virginia
Maryland

ATLANTIC OCEAN

North Carolina
South Carolina
Georgia
Spanish Florida

N W E S

0   200 mi
0   200 km

England's Colonies

The Roanoke colonists vanished and many of the Jamestown colonists died. Still, the English did not give up. They would go on to settle 13 colonies. By the 1660s, some settlers had moved south and set up Carolina in present-day North and South Carolina.

Settlers to the southern colonies brought enslaved Africans with them. The enslaved people were forced to farm the land.

In 1733, James Oglethorpe founded the Georgia colony. He set up this colony to help people who were in prison for not paying a debt. A **debt** is money that is owed to another person. People owing debts settled in Georgia. Oglethorpe wanted to give them a chance to start a new life in his colony.

Mary Musgrove also played a key role in the founding of Georgia. Musgrove, a member of the Creek Nation, served as an interpreter for Oglethorpe. As an **interpreter**, she helped the English and Native Americans communicate with each other because she was able to speak both languages. She helped the Native Americans and English get along and keep the peace.

1. ☑ **Reading Check**
Identify and **circle** the names of the southern colonies on the map.

Settling the Middle Colonies

New York, New Jersey, Pennsylvania, and Delaware are the middle colonies. Can you guess how they got this name? They are right between the southern colonies and the colonies to the north.

In 1664, Holland lost the land that would later become three of the middle colonies in a war against the English. The Duke of York got one part of the land. He named it New York, after himself. The duke gave the other part of his land to two friends. These other parts eventually became the colonies of New Jersey and Delaware. Pennsylvania, however, was started in a very different way.

William Penn started the colony of Pennsylvania as a "holy experiment." Penn was a Quaker. A **Quaker** is a follower of a religion that believes in peace and equal treatment for all people. Many people came to Penn's colony. People from Germany and Ireland were among the first settlers to come there for religious freedom.

A Philadelphia community honors Ben Franklin's contribution of the city's first fire department.

Benjamin Franklin is one of the most famous people who lived in Philadelphia, Pennsylvania. He moved there because there were many more opportunities than in his home city of Boston, Massachusetts. Wherever Franklin went, he tried to make it a better place to live. He began Philadelphia's first fire department. Thanks to Franklin, Philadelphia became a safer city.

2. ☑ **Reading Check** Choose one of the middle colonies, and **explain** how it was started.

_____

_____

The Mayflower Compact was the first plan of government written in the colonies.

Academic Vocabulary

crucial • *adj.*, very important

3. ☑ **Reading Check** **Sequence Identify** and **underline** the first and second things the Pilgrims did when they came to America.

New England Colonies

Massachusetts, Connecticut, Rhode Island, and New Hampshire were called the New England colonies.

In 1620, William Bradford led a group of Pilgrims on board a ship called the *Mayflower*. A **pilgrim** is a person who travels for a religious reason. Sixty-six days later, they landed in present-day Massachusetts. They came to the colonies to be free to follow their religion.

First, the Pilgrims formed a community in Plymouth, Massachusetts. Then, they wrote a plan of government called the Mayflower Compact. It said the colonists would make laws for the good of the community. A **crucial** part of the plan was that everyone agreed to obey the laws. This was the first time European colonists in America had made laws for themselves.

Bradford became the leader. He was a good leader. The Pilgrims and people of the local Wampanoag Nation began trading food and other items. Squanto, a Wampanoag who spoke English, served as an interpreter. In 1621, the Pilgrims and the Wampanoags sat down to share in a harvest feast. Today, we mark this as the first Thanksgiving.

A woman named Anne Hutchinson did not follow the Pilgrims' beliefs. She began spreading her own beliefs. As a result, in 1634, she was forced to leave Massachusetts. She later founded Portsmouth, Rhode Island.

☑ Lesson 5 Check

4. **Main Idea and Details** Complete the chart with details that support the main idea. **Identify** the needs that cause people to form communities.

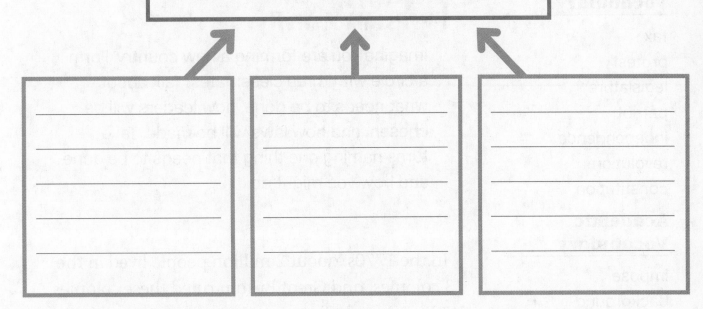

Life was difficult for the early colonists.

5. **Identify** one reason the English settled the Americas. **Explain** why that reason is still important to us today.

_____

_____

_____

6. **Describe** how Benjamin Franklin changed his community by starting Philadelphia's first fire department.

_____

_____

_____

Unlock The BIG Question

I will know the causes and effects of the American Revolution.

Vocabulary

tax
protest
legislature
patriot
independence
revolution
constitution

Academic Vocabulary

impose
background

JumpStart Activity

Imagine you are forming a new country. Form a circle with three classmates. Talk about what needs to be done, how leaders will be chosen, and how laws will be made. Take turns naming one thing that needs to be done and how you might do it.

In the 1770s, about 2 million people lived in the 13 colonies, and Great Britain ruled these colonies. With each year that passed, the colonists wanted more and more to be free to rule themselves.

Angry over British rule, colonists dump tea from British ships into Boston Harbor.

124

Trouble in the Colonies

The British had won the French and Indian War in 1763 and now had a lot of debt. To raise money, Great Britain made the colonists pay taxes. A **tax** is money paid to a government. The colonists became angry and thought this was unfair because they did not have a say in the British government.

In 1764, the British **imposed** the Sugar Act, which taxed most of the sugar brought into the colonies. Then in 1765, Great Britain passed the Stamp Act. The Stamp Act taxed all printed items, such as newspapers and legal papers.

The colonists became more angry, saying, "No taxation without representation!" They would not pay taxes unless they had a say in the government.

The Stamp Act ended, but there were new taxes on paper, glass, and lead. Many colonists refused to buy these things, so the British lost a lot of money.

In 1773, the British passed the Tea Act, which said the colonists could buy tea only from Great Britain. To **protest**, or complain, some colonists went on British ships in Boston Harbor. They dressed themselves as American Indians and dumped all the tea overboard! This was called the Boston Tea Party. The British were angry, so they closed Boston Harbor and also took many powers away from the Massachusetts legislature. A **legislature** is a part of government that makes laws.

The problem was over money, power, and control. Who should rule America: Great Britain or the colonists?

Academic Vocabulary

impose • *v.*, to bring about by force

background • *n.*, a person's culture, knowledge, and experience

Quest Connection

What made Paul Revere take his ride? In which event was he an early participant?

INTERACTIVITY

Explore why the colonists took their actions against the British.

American Patriots

American colonists known as Patriots grew angrier about British rule. A **patriot** is a person who loves and defends the country. The Patriots wanted the American colonies to be free. These Patriots came from different **backgrounds**. For example, Nathan Hale was young and Benjamin Franklin was older. Thomas Jefferson was a leader and Daniel Shays was a farmer. They all worked hard to win **independence**, or freedom, for the colonies.

On April 18, 1775, Patriot Paul Revere rode from Boston to Lexington, Massachusetts, to warn colonial leaders Samuel Adams and John Hancock that British troops were coming to arrest them. Revere also wanted to stop the British from taking the colonists' weapons. He warned everyone on his route about the British.

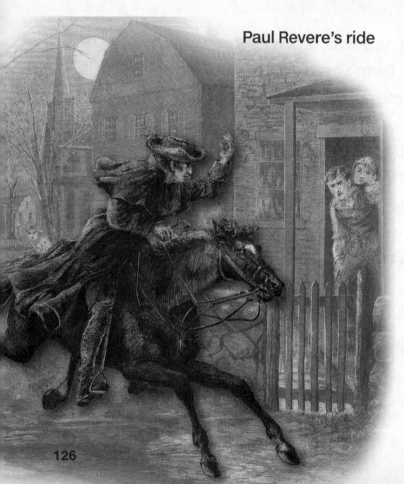

Paul Revere's ride

The War for Independence was beginning. This war between the American colonies and the British is also called the American Revolution. A **revolution** takes place when people want to take over the government that rules them and create a new one. The war started on April 19, 1775, in the towns of Lexington and Concord in Massachusetts.

1. ☑ **Reading Check** **Underline** what the Patriots wanted.

Freedom and Government

Thomas Jefferson wrote the Declaration of Independence in 1776. It told the world why the colonies were breaking away from Great Britain and what the new nation stood for.

The first part said that people have rights that the government must protect. The second part listed the complaints the colonists had against the British king. The third part said the colonies were now free and independent states and not part of Great Britain.

It took eight years for America to win the American Revolution and independence from Great Britain. In 1787, 55 people met in Philadelphia to write a new plan of government, the United States Constitution. A **constitution** is a written plan of government that explains the beliefs and laws of a country. George Washington, Benjamin Franklin, and James Madison were three Founding Fathers. They helped write the Constitution and helped the country grow.

On September 17, 1787, the members completed their work. They had written a new plan of government for the United States. The people, not a king, would rule the new, independent nation.

2. ☑ Reading Check **Summarize** what was included in the three parts of the Declaration of Independence.

_____

_____

Founding Fathers sign our country's plan of government, the U.S. Constitution.

Washington, D.C.

George Washington led the colonial soldiers in the American Revolution. After the war, other leaders wanted Washington to lead the new government.

On February 4, 1789, the people elected Washington our first president. Lawmakers decided to build the new capital at a place they called Federal City. Today, it is known as Washington, D.C. An African American named Benjamin Banneker surveyed, or measured, the land to figure out its border.

In the year 1791, a Frenchman named Pierre L'Enfant designed Washington, D.C. He chose the sites for the two most important buildings there: the Capitol and the White House. He also designed wide streets lined with trees. He set up spaces so that statues could be built to honor important people.

Washington, D.C., is named after George Washington. He is remembered as a great leader who was "first in war, first in peace, and first in the hearts of his countrymen."

3. ☑ Reading Check Identify and **underline** the names of the people who helped create Washington, D.C.

Washington, D.C.

☑ Lesson 6 Check

4. **Sequence Write** the events below in the order of the year they happened.

> - The U.S. Constitution is completed.
> - Great Britain passes the Stamp Act.
> - The French and Indian War ends.
> - Paul Revere rides to Lexington.

1763 _____

1765 _____

1775 _____

1787 _____

5. **Explain** how the Founding Fathers helped build a new nation.

_____

_____

_____

6. **Understand the** Quest Connections **Explain** how the American Revolution impacted the colonies. Then explain its impact on your life.

_____

_____

_____

_____

The Declaration of Independence

The Declaration of Independence is a founding document of the United States. It describes some of the basic ideas and beliefs that shaped the country. It was adopted on July 4, 1776.

Read the excerpt from the Declaration of Independence written by Thomas Jefferson.

Vocabulary Support

We believe that

People give the government the power to act

when the government denies unalienable rights

self-evident • *adj.*, clear, obvious

endow • *v.*, to give

unalienable • *adj.*, not to be given or taken away

derive • *v.*, to get

alter • *v.*, to change

abolish • *v.*, to do away with

We hold these truths to be self-evident, that all men are created equal, that they are endowed by their Creator with certain unalienable Rights, that among these are Life, Liberty and the pursuit of Happiness. – That to secure these rights, Governments are instituted among Men, deriving their just powers from the consent of the governed, – That whenever any Form of Government becomes destructive of these ends, it is the Right of the People to alter or to abolish it, and to institute new Government, laying its foundation on such principles and organizing its powers in such form, as to them shall seem most likely to effect their Safety and Happiness.

–Thomas Jefferson, The Declaration of Independence, 1776

Close Reading

1. Identify and list the rights that all people should have.

_____

_____

2. Identify and **circle** what the Declaration says that people without these rights can do to gain them.

Wrap It Up

Summarize the Declaration of Independence in your own words.

_____

_____

_____

_____

The Declaration of Independence

IN CONGRESS, JULY 4, 1776.

The unanimous Declaration of the thirteen united States of America,

Quality:
Problem Solving

Archie Thompson
Saving the Yurok Language

As one of the last living speakers of the Yurok language, Archie Thompson faced a problem. There was a risk that, in time, no one would know how to speak the Yurok language anymore. The Yuroks were an American Indian nation that settled in Northern California. Thompson wanted to keep the important language alive.

Thompson had grown up with his grandmother, who spoke only Yurok. He understood the importance of Yurok traditions. Thompson helped to save the Yurok language by teaching it at schools in the area. He helped workers at the Yurok Language Project create Yurok dictionaries. Thompson also made recordings of himself speaking Yurok. Because of Thompson and other elders, today the Yurok language is taught in high schools in Del Norte and Humboldt counties in California. In 2013, the year Thompson died, more than 300 people were able to speak Yurok.

Find Out More

1. In what way did Archie Thompson help solve the Yurok language problem?

_____

_____

_____

_____

2. Choose a partner and exchange stories of when you solved a problem. What was the most difficult part of solving it?

3 Visual Review

Use this graphic to review some of the key terms, people, and ideas from this chapter.

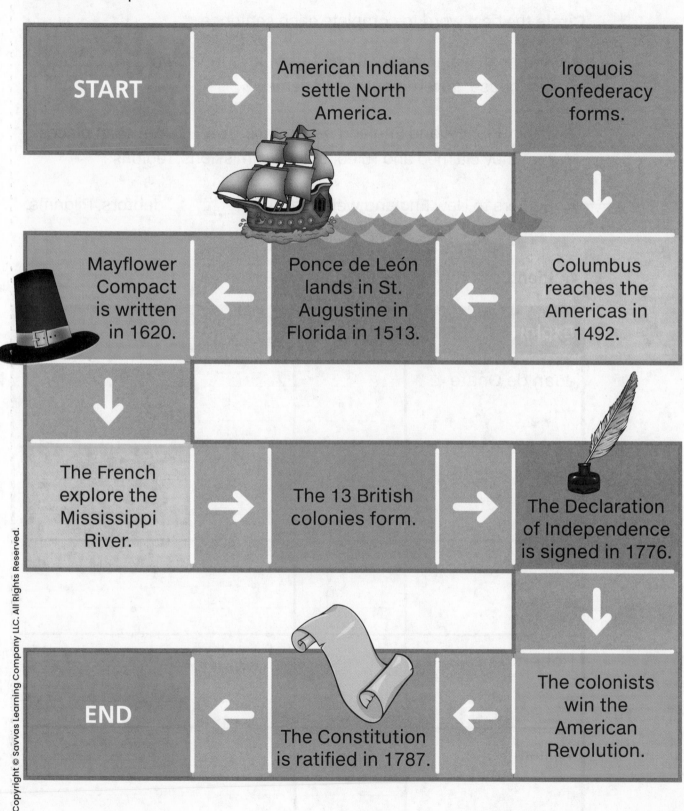

START → American Indians settle North America. → Iroquois Confederacy forms.

Mayflower Compact is written in 1620. ← Ponce de León lands in St. Augustine in Florida in 1513. ← Columbus reaches the Americas in 1492.

The French explore the Mississippi River. → The 13 British colonies form. → The Declaration of Independence is signed in 1776.

END ← The Constitution is ratified in 1787. ← The colonists win the American Revolution.

☑ Assessment

🎮 GAMES

Play the vocabulary game.

Vocabulary and Key Ideas

Circle the best word to complete each sentence.

1. American Indian reservations today have their own _____.
longhouse, government, confederacy

2. Spain, France, and England set up their own _____ in places that they claimed and ruled. colonies, missions, regions

3. Settlers to New England were mainly _____. debtors, Pilgrims, Patriots

4. **Identify** Complete the chart about explorers.

Explorer	Country	Achievement
Juan de Oñate		
Pierre Laclede		
James Oglethorpe		
Robert de La Salle		
William Penn		

Critical Thinking and Writing

5. **Summarize** What were two early forms of government in North America, and why were they created?

_____

_____

_____

6. **Analyze** Why did the Spaniards build pueblos and presidios?

_____

_____

7. **Compare** How did Christopher Columbus, Samuel de Champlain, Don Pedro Menéndez de Avilés, and William Bradford's actions affect North America?

_____

_____

_____

8. **Revisit the Big Question** What is something you learned in second grade that helps you succeed in third grade?

_____

_____

9. **Writing Workshop: Write Journal Entries** On separate paper, write five journal entries from the point of view of one of the explorers in the chapter. Include the country you explored for, when and where you explored, your goals, what you found or claimed, and your overall experiences.

Analyze Primary Sources

"History is who we are and why we are the way we are."

—David McCullough, 1984

10. David McCullough is a writer and historian. A historian is a person who tells about the past. Read McCullough's quote. How does the quote relate to your own life?

_____

_____

Sequence

11. Complete the chart. Place the following events in sequence from what happened first to what happened last.
   • The American Revolution begins.
   • George Washington is elected president.
   • James Madison helps write the Constitution.
   • The Boston Tea Party takes place.

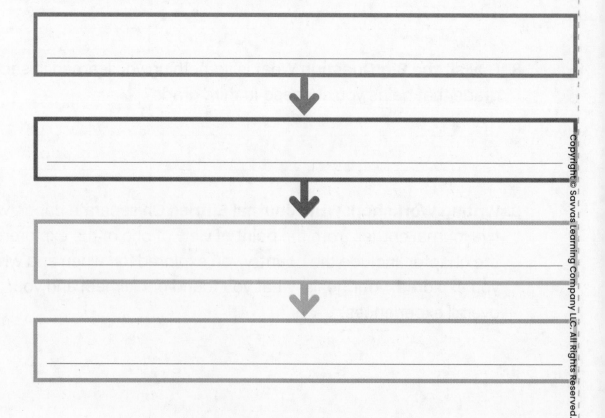

Quest Findings

INTERACTIVITY

Complete the activities to get started on your persuasive text.

Write Your Persuasive Text

You have read the lessons in this chapter, and now you are ready to write your persuasive text. Remember that in a persuasive text you use evidence to support your ideas to help convince others to share your opinion.

1 Prepare to Write

Choose something from the chapter that has made a difference in your life. Write the event or person's name down on a piece of paper and make a few notes.

2 Write a Draft

Use your notes and your answers to the chapter's Quest Connections to write a persuasive text in which you tell how an event or person from the past has made a difference in your life. Provide evidence to support your ideas. You can use specific words and phrases such as *I think this because or In my opinion.*

3 Share With a Partner

Exchange your draft with a partner. Tell your partner what you like about the draft. Ask for some ideas on how to improve your draft and make it more convincing. Listen closely as your partner speaks.

4 Revise

After you have thought about your partner's suggestions, make changes to your draft. Also check for spelling and grammar errors.

137

Government, Landmarks, and Symbols

The **BIG** Question Why do we have government?

▶ VIDEO

JumpStart Activity

👆 INTERACTIVITY

Work in a small group. Suppose there were no rules or laws at all. Write about some things that might happen.

_____

_____

_____

_____

_____

Our Constitution:
The Government Plan

Preview the chapter **vocabulary** as you sing the rap:

Before creating a government, we made the
  Constitution,
An important document that we consider a
  solution,
A plan that explains how our country works
To serve the people and keep our safety first.

Legislative is the branch that makes the laws,
Two houses of **Congress**—each with its own
  cause.

The **executive** branch is headed up by the
  president,
The commander in chief for all our country's
  residents.

The **judicial** branch has a vital contribution:
Making sure laws are fair and sticking to the
  Constitution.

4 Quest

Government at Work

Our government is very big. Many people work for the government. Local government is the government of your community. You have seen local government workers, such as police officers, firefighters, librarians, and others who work for your town or city. You can research to find out more about what they do.

Quest Kick Off

Hello, my first-grade students are having a career day! They will learn about local government jobs. Can you help? Choose a local government job, research it, and tell my students about it at career day.

1 Ask Questions

What local government job did you select? Write two questions you have about that job.

....

....

....

2 Research

Use online or text sources to find out more about the local government job. On the lines, write some sources you can think of.

Complete the interactivity to learn more about local government jobs.

3 Look for *Quest* Connections

Begin looking for Quest Connections that will help you learn about government jobs.

4 *Quest* Findings
Present a Local Government Job

Use the Quest Findings page at the end of the chapter to help you tell about a local job.

Lesson 1

The American Government

INTERACTIVITY

Participate in a class discussion to preview the content of this lesson.

Vocabulary

federal
legislative
Congress
executive
judicial

Academic Vocabulary

consequence
violate

Unlock The BIG Question

I will know how the federal government is organized.

JumpStart Activity

Name three things you and a partner know about the United States government. Then walk around the room with your partner and talk with other pairs. Describe four things you and others know about the nation's government.

On April 30, 1789, George Washington (holding the sword) was sworn in as the first president of the United States. The ceremony took place in New York City.

In the 1700s, Americans wanted to break away from British rule. This led to the American Revolution. The Americans won this struggle. After the revolution, the United States needed a plan for government.

Forming Our Government

During the revolution, American leaders wrote the Declaration of Independence. One idea from it is that government gets its power from "the consent of the governed." This means that the people take part in government. But how? A plan was needed.

In 1787, leaders wrote the United States Constitution. A constitution is a plan for how a country will work. The U.S. Constitution lists goals of the government. It also tells how the government is set up. The states approved the Constitution and must approve any new changes to it today. Also, state laws cannot go against national laws. All Americans depend on the Constitution. It helps to make our country's government work for the people.

1. ☑ **Reading Check** **Summarize** List key information about the United States Constitution.

What Is a Constitution?	Why Is the U.S. Constitution Important?

Donald Trump was elected president of the United States in 2016. He took office in 2017.

Three Branches of the Federal Government

The U.S. Constitution splits the **federal**, or national, government into three parts, or branches. Each branch has some power. No branch has all the power. All three branches meet in the same city. They work in our nation's capital, Washington, D.C.

The **legislative** branch makes the laws. **Congress** is the legislative group. Congress is made up of the Senate and the House of Representatives. People in the states elect legislators—the people who represent them in Congress. Legislators must listen to the people who elect them. They also must do what they believe is best for all the people in the country.

The president of the United States leads the **executive** branch. This branch carries out the laws that the legislative branch makes. The president can sign into law what Congress passes or send it back for changes. The executive branch is also in charge of the departments that make the government work. Some of the departments print money, take care of our national parks, keep our food safe, and protect us.

The **judicial** branch makes certain the laws follow what is in the U.S. Constitution. The judicial branch is made up of federal courts, with the Supreme Court above all other courts. It is important for people to obey the rules and laws. There are **consequences** if people **violate**, or do not follow, laws. It is also important that laws are used in ways that are fair for all.

It takes all three branches to make our national government work. It also takes everyone in the country doing their part by telling legislators what is important, voting, and following the rules and laws.

2. ☑ Reading Check Discuss and **list** some duties of each branch of government.

Academic Vocabulary

consequence • *n*., the result or effect of an action

violate • *v*., to break or fail to follow a rule

What Does Each Branch of Government Do?

Legislative (Congress)	Judicial (Supreme Court)	Executive (President)
_____	_____	_____
_____	_____	_____
_____	_____	_____
_____	_____	_____
_____	_____	_____
_____	_____	_____

National Leaders

Congress, the legislative branch, is made up of senators and representatives from each state. They are elected by the people of each state. Every state elects two senators. The number of representatives differs by state. States with more people elect more representatives. California has the greatest population of any state. It has 53 representatives in the House of Representatives. Seven states (Alaska, Delaware, Montana, North Dakota, South Dakota, Vermont, and Wyoming) have only one representative. How many representatives does your state have?

The president and the vice president of the United States lead the executive branch. They are elected by the whole country, rather than just by one state. They need to represent all of the people. What happens when people do not agree on what the country needs to do? This often happens. It is a hard job to be the president and try to do what is best for the whole country.

The justices of the U.S. Supreme Court decide important legal cases. Their decisions apply to everyone in the nation.

The Supreme Court is the highest court of the judicial branch. Members of the Supreme Court are judges, or justices. They are not elected. The president suggests a justice to be on the Supreme Court. The members of the Senate then vote on the president's choice. The head of the Supreme Court is called the chief justice.

3. ☑ **Reading Check** The three branches of government have different leaders. **Identify** and **list** the leaders of each branch.

Who Leads Each Branch?

Legislative	_____
Executive	_____
Judicial	_____

People vote to elect their leaders in government.

States and the Nation

The federal government makes laws that people in all states must follow. For example, a federal law tells how old you must be to vote anywhere in the country. There are many national laws. Some tell what you can carry on an airplane, what wild animals are protected, how food is kept safe, or that everyone can apply for jobs.

How do people make a difference in the federal government? You know that people vote for the leaders in Congress and vote for president and vice president. People across the country also pay taxes to the national government. These taxes help pay for the military that protects us, highways we travel on, and many other things. Some people may choose to become part of the federal government by becoming a ranger in a national park, joining the military, or even running for Congress. A person can even run for president!

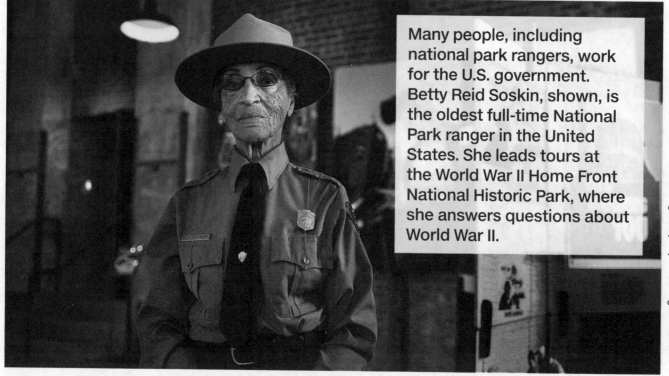

Many people, including national park rangers, work for the U.S. government. Betty Reid Soskin, shown, is the oldest full-time National Park ranger in the United States. She leads tours at the World War II Home Front National Historic Park, where she answers questions about World War II.

People also make a difference by following the rules and laws. One of the most important ways that we all can participate is to let our leaders know what we think. Leaders need to know what issues people think are important and what problems need to be solved. People of all ages have a responsibility to speak up and make suggestions. You can make a difference.

4. ☑ **Reading Check** **Underline** details that show how people take part in the federal government.

INTERACTIVITY

Check your understanding of the key ideas of this lesson.

☑ Lesson 1 Check

5. **Sequence Select** and circle the one that comes first.

A person is elected president of the United States.

Voters in every state vote.

6. **Summarize** why our government needs the U.S. Constitution.

_____

_____

_____

_____

7. **Explain** why it is important to have three branches of government and not just one branch.

_____

_____

_____

_____

Lesson 2

Branches of Government

Unlock The BIG Question

I will know what each branch of government does.

Vocabulary

representative
bill
veto
Cabinet
checks and balances

Academic Vocabulary

role
approve

JumpStart Activity

Move around the room to charts your teacher has put up with the names of government leaders. Write words on each chart to describe what each person should be like. What should we expect these people to do? How should they behave?

United States Capitol

The Legislative Branch

As you learned, Congress has two parts: the Senate and the House of Representatives.

Remember, the Senate is made up of two representatives from each state. A **representative** is a person chosen to speak for others. Citizens vote to choose these representatives. There are 100 senators. Senators are elected every six years, and they can be elected many times.

Congress meets in the U.S. Capitol.

There are 435 representatives in the House of Representatives. Remember, the number of representatives in the House depends on the number of people living in each state. The more people who live in a state, the more representatives the state has. Like senators, representatives speak for the people who vote for them.

The representatives in Congress raise and collect taxes. The money from taxes is used to fund, or pay for, the government. Congress also makes laws for the country. Some laws deal with safety, while other laws make sure that all people are treated fairly. All laws begin as ideas. Once an idea is written down for the government to decide on, it is called a **bill**. Before a bill can become a law, both parts of Congress must vote on it and approve it. The bill is then sent to the president to sign.

The Executive Branch

The president of the United States serves a term of four years and can only be elected for two terms. The president lives and works in the White House in Washington, D.C.

The president has more than one **role** in our government. One responsibility is to sign bills, which are ideas for laws. However, if the president does not agree with a bill, the president may **veto**, or reject, it. If a bill is vetoed, the only way it can become a law is if most of the members of Congress vote again to **approve** it.

The president is in charge of the United States military. This means the president is the commander in chief of members of the Army, the Navy, the Marines, and the Air Force. The president also represents our country to the rest of the world. The president meets with leaders from other countries to solve problems.

The president is commander in chief of all American armed forces personnel.

152

The president also works with the Cabinet. The **Cabinet** is a group of advisors, or people who tell a leader what they think about a subject. Each advisor leads one of the 15 different departments, or groups, in the executive branch. These advisors help provide the president with information about important issues in the country. These issues may be about education, health care, or security. The president selects these advisors. However, the Senate must approve the president's choices.

The president lives and works in the White House.

1. ☑ **Reading Check** **Summarize** Write a summary that **describes** the president's responsibilities.

_____

_____

_____

_____

The Judicial Branch

The judicial branch of the government is made up of the Supreme Court and smaller courts. Judges in the courts make sure that laws are fair. They also decide the consequences for people who break laws.

The Supreme Court has nine judges. Judges in the Supreme Court are called justices. The Supreme Court justices make sure the laws passed by Congress follow the U.S. Constitution. Most cases that the Supreme Court hears are appeals from lower courts. An appeal is a request to review an earlier court decision.

The United States Supreme Court building, completed in 1935, is in Washington, D.C.

The president nominates, or chooses, the justices for the Supreme Court. However, the Senate must approve each choice. Supreme Court justices do not have a term limit. Once a person becomes a justice, he or she can serve for life.

The U.S. Constitution includes ways to make sure that the three branches of government work together. This system is called **checks and balances**. This means that each branch can check the actions of another. This helps make sure that the three branches share the power to rule. One branch does not have more power than the other branches.

2. ☑ **Reading Check** **Describe** the roles of the justices who serve on the U.S. Supreme Court.

_____

_____

_____

_____

INTERACTIVITY

Check your understanding of the key ideas of this lesson.

☑ Lesson 2 Check

3. Main Idea and Details Explain why the total number of senators and representatives for each state is not the same.

_____

_____

_____

4. Describe why we have three branches of government.

_____

_____

_____

_____

5. Use the Internet and other reference materials to **identify** the people who represent you in the national government, and **explain** how they were chosen to represent you.

_____

_____

_____

The Preamble to the United States Constitution

The United States Constitution might be the most important document in our country. The Preamble is the introduction to the Constitution. It tells the goals of the nation and why the Constitution was written. The first words, "We the People of the United States" are perhaps the most meaningful. The power in our government is with the citizens, not a king, queen, president, or any other person.

Vocabulary Support

peace

protection from other nations

encourage the well-being of everyone

our children and their children

make into law

union • *n.*, country
justice • *n.*, fairness
liberty • *n.*, freedom

We the People of the United States, in Order to form a more perfect Union, establish Justice, insure domestic Tranquility, provide for the common defence, promote the general Welfare, and secure the Blessings of Liberty to ourselves and our Posterity, do ordain and establish this Constitution for the United States of America.

—Preamble to the United States Constitution

Fun Fact

The Declaration of Independence and the United States Constitution were both signed in the same building in Philadelphia, Pennsylvania. That building is now called Independence Hall.

Close Reading

1. Who does this primary source say is creating the United States Constitution?

_____

_____

2. Using simpler language than the Preamble, write the six reasons the United States Constitution was written. Number each reason.

_____

_____

_____

_____

_____

Wrap It Up

In what ways do state and local governments have the same goals as the United States Constitution?

_____

_____

_____

_____

_____

_____

Levels of Government

 INTERACTIVITY

Participate in a class discussion to preview the content of this lesson.

Unlock The BIG Question

I will know why the United States has three levels of government and what each level does.

Vocabulary

charter
mayor
council
governor
census

Academic Vocabulary

organize
legal

JumpStart Activity

Think of things the government does, such as fixing roads or making laws. When your teacher calls on you, act out something the government does. Other students can try to guess what you are showing. Then create a list of things the government does.

There are three different levels of government in our country: local, state, and national. Each level provides services to citizens.

Federal and State Constitutions

As you know, the United States has a Constitution. The U.S. Constitution is the highest law in the country, so each state must follow it. Sometimes, people want to change the Constitution. Changes to the Constitution are called amendments. Representatives in both parts of Congress vote on amendments. If Congress approves the amendment, it goes to the states for approval. If 38 of the 50 states approve the amendment, the Constitution is changed.

Each state also has its own constitution. In most states, changes to state constitutions must also be approved by the people before they can be made.

The people expect their elected officials to act on their behalf. If people are unhappy with their officials, they can act. They can share their opinions at town meetings. They can call or write to their officials to discuss issues facing their city, state, or even the country. They can also elect new officials in the next election.

Local Government

Cities and towns have local governments that serve their community. These governments can be **organized** in different ways. The way a city or town government is organized is described in the city or town charter. A **charter** is a **legal** document that describes the powers of the local government.

Word Wise

Multiple-Meaning Words You live in one of the 50 states of the United States. The word *state* can also mean "to say something." You can state that you love living in your state.

Academic Vocabulary

organize • *v.*, to set up

legal • *adj.*, recognized by courts of law

In some cities and towns, people elect a mayor or city manager as the head of the executive branch. A **mayor** is a leader of the community.

The people who make the rules and laws in a community are part of a city or town council. A **council** is a group that makes laws. Council members are often elected. These lawmakers make up the legislative branch. In some cities and towns, the council appoints someone as city manager to carry out the council's laws. Sometimes, the mayor of a city or town is chosen from the council.

The judicial branch is made up of a city's or town's courts. A judge decides what happens to people who do not follow laws. Sometimes a jury, or a group of citizens, decides if a person broke a law. Many local judges are appointed by the mayor or council of the city or town in which they serve. However, some local judges are elected.

Mayor Bill de Blasio of New York talks to students in Brooklyn, New York. With the mayor is U.S. representative Yvette D. Clarke.

The local government provides many services that people in the community use every day. It is in charge of the police department and the fire department. The local government also provides schools, libraries, and parks. It makes sure that trash is collected. It may also cut down trees that have been damaged in storms. The local government takes care of roads. It paves roads so they are smooth, paints lines on roads, and puts up signs so the roads are safe for drivers.

Local governments provide schools for public education.

Where does the local government get the money to pay for all these services? Some money comes from the state government. Other services are paid for by the taxes that the local government collects. Local governments collect taxes on property, such as homes and businesses in the city or town. Some local governments can also charge sales tax on items you buy.

Local government also charges its citizens a fee to use some of its services. These fees help pay for the service. For example, many large cities provide buses for transporting people in the city. However, people must pay to ride the bus.

Quest Connection

Think about your worker. Does the worker do a job for a local government, such as a teacher, librarian, park ranger, or firefighter? If so, which job?

INTERACTIVITY

Take a closer look at the types of jobs people have.

1. ☑ **Reading Check** **Explain** how local governments pay for services they provide.

_____

_____

_____

State Government

Each state has a government that runs it. State constitutions describe the responsibilities of the governor, the legislature, and the courts. The **governor** is the head of a state's executive branch and is elected by the people in the state. The governor can appoint officials to help carry out laws.

The state legislature makes laws for the state. Nearly all 50 states divide the legislative branch into the Senate and the House of Representatives. The people in each state elect the members of their state legislature. These lawmakers meet in the capitol in the state's capital city.

State governments also have courts in their judicial branch. Judges who work in state courts listen to issues that local courts could not solve. In some states, judges are elected by the people. In others, judges are appointed.

The state government provides services, too. It decides the rules for voting, such as if a person must show identification. State governments also work with local governments to keep up state highways. Some of these services are paid for with money from the national government. Others are paid for with taxes the state collects.

2. ☑ **Reading Check** **Identify** and write the name of your governor and your state representatives. **Explain** how they are chosen.

_____

_____

Susana Martinez, the governor of New Mexico, reads with students.

National Government

The three branches of the national, or federal, government serve as a model for local and state governments. The president, members of Congress, and the Supreme Court justices share the responsibilities of running the country. The president and members of Congress are chosen by the people. The president appoints Supreme Court justices. The president also appoints people to the Cabinet to advise on issues.

The national government provides services that cities and states do not. Some of these services are paid for with taxes. Other services are funded by fees paid for by people who use the services. The national government prints paper money and makes coins. It runs the United States Postal Service. It is in charge of trade between states and between countries. The national government also manages the national parks.

People can visit national parks, which are managed and funded by the U.S. government.

The national government serves the whole nation in other ways, too. Every ten years the national government takes a **census**, or a count of the population. This count helps the government decide how much money different communities need. The national government can also organize an army to protect the nation or its people. The government sometimes has soldiers help people and communities after harsh storms.

3. ☑ **Reading Check** **Summarize** Write a summary that **identifies** the services provided by the national government.

_____

_____

Governments Work Together

Even though the local, state, and national governments all have their own responsibilities, they often work together. They work together to complete large projects such as building roads, bridges, and buildings. Local and state leaders may also ask the national government for help if there is a storm or disaster and they need resources to provide help to their citizens.

City and town governments provide many services, including youth sports programs.

The three levels of government do similar kinds of work. They all collect taxes from citizens. This money is used to pay for the services the governments provide. The national government collects taxes on the money people earn from their jobs. Some states also collect this tax. Local governments collect taxes on items people buy and on homes and businesses they own. Local governments also rely on money from the state to fund services. States rely on money from the national government to fund services.

The courts in all three levels also work together. If a local court does not resolve an issue, the case moves to a state court. Cases that are not resolved by state courts may then be decided by the United States Supreme Court justices.

4. ☑ **Reading Check** **Explain** how each level of government pays for the services it provides.

_____

_____

✓ Lesson 3 Check

5. Main Idea and Details Identify three services provided by each of the three levels of government.

Services Provided by Government		
Local Government	State Government	National Government
_____	_____	_____
_____	_____	_____
_____	_____	_____
_____	_____	_____
_____	_____	_____
_____	_____	_____

6. Explain why people elect local, state, and national leaders.

_____

_____

_____

7. Understand the *Quest* **Connections** Think about the local government worker you will represent in your Quest. Which tasks would not get done if a community did not have that worker?

_____

_____

Compare and Contrast

When you compare, you tell how two or more things are alike. When you contrast, you tell how two or more things are different. Writers use words as clues to show what is alike and what is different. Words such as *both*, *alike*, *similar to*, or *in common* show things that are alike. Words such as *yet*, *different*, *but*, and *however* show things that are different.

You can use a diagram to help you compare and contrast information that you read. Read the paragraph below about state and federal governments. Look at the underlined clue words. Then examine the diagram to see what is alike and different about the two governments.

<u>Both</u> state and federal governments make laws. They <u>both</u> also have in common a constitution and a leader who runs the government. <u>However</u>, a governor is the head of a state government. A president is the head of our national government.

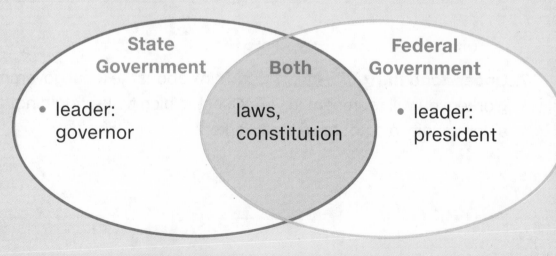

State Government	Both	Federal Government
• leader: governor	laws, constitution	• leader: president

Your Turn!

INTERACTIVITY

Review and practice what you have learned about comparing and contrasting.

1. **Read** more about state and federal governments. **Underline** the clue words. Then **fill in** the chart.

State and federal governments are alike. There are state and federal courts, state and federal laws, state and federal lawmakers, and state and federal taxes. There are both state and national parks, park rangers, and museums. Most states have a state senate and state house of representatives similar to the national Senate and House of Representatives. The people elect both federal and state lawmakers.

However, the federal government provides some things that state governments do not. The federal government prints paper money and mints coins. It runs the U.S. Postal Service. Members of the military are part of the federal government. In addition, the federal government conducts a census every ten years.

Both Governments	Only Federal Government
courts	money
taxes	military
_____	_____
_____	_____
_____	_____

Landmarks, Symbols, and Documents

INTERACTIVITY

Participate in a class discussion to preview the content of this lesson.

Unlock
The **BIG**
Question

I will know some of the documents, symbols, and landmarks that bring us together.

Vocabulary

ideal
document
symbol
landmark

Academic Vocabulary

value
original

JumpStart Activity

You can be a member of many groups, including a classroom, a team, a family, or a country. Describe some of the groups you belong to.

A family views the Constitution of the United States at the National Archives in Washington, D.C.

We belong to many groups. We have things in common with people in those groups. Perhaps we all like the same sport or the same music. What do all Americans have in common? There are many beliefs that Americans share and that make us feel like we belong.

Important Documents

Our American **ideals**, or ideas that we hope will come true, were first stated in 1776 in the Declaration of Independence. It said that the ideal nation would treat people equally. It said that people should have the right to "Life, Liberty, and the pursuit of Happiness." The Declaration of Independence is a **document**, or written record, that makes it clear what Americans **value**. It reminds us that we all believe in the freedom to be the best we can be.

As you know, the U.S. Constitution is another document that we share. Changes have been made to it after it was approved. The Bill of Rights is what we call the first ten changes, or amendments, to the Constitution. Many people value the Bill of Rights for the many rights it protects.

Academic Vocabulary

value • *v.*, to think something is important

1. ☑ Reading Check **Summarize Write** one thing you have learned about the ideals Americans share.

_____

_____

_____

_____

_____

In 1793, George Washington placed the first stone of the United States Capitol building.

CAPITOL CORNERSTONE CEREMONY · 1793

Academic Vocabulary

original • *adj.*, first

The Statue of Liberty was a gift from France.

National Symbols We Honor

If someone from another country visits, what American symbols would you show the person? A **symbol** is something that stands for something else and has meaning for people. The American flag is a symbol for our country. The 50 stars are symbols of the 50 states. The 13 stripes stand for the **original** 13 colonies.

What are some other symbols for our country? The eagle is a symbol of our country's strength. You see the eagle on money and some government buildings. The Statue of Liberty is a landmark that stands for freedom. A **landmark** is an important building, monument, or place that has great meaning to people. When people see the Statue of Liberty in New York Harbor, they may be reminded that the United States has welcomed millions of immigrants to this country. The United States Capitol building in Washington, D.C., is a landmark. It is where Congress meets. It is also a national symbol.

The U.S. Capitol reminds us that we all have a voice and are represented in our country.

We also honor the United States when we stand and say the Pledge of Allegiance. We put our hand over our heart to show that we mean what we are saying with our whole heart:

Primary Source

I pledge allegiance to the flag of the United States of America, and to the Republic for which it stands, one nation under God, indivisible, with liberty and justice for all.

—Pledge of Allegiance to the Flag of the United States, Adopted by U.S. Congress, 1942

Have you heard people singing the national anthem? When we sing "The Star-Spangled Banner," we are letting people know that we are proud of our country. Singing brings us all together. Americans joining together may be the best symbol of all.

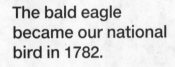

The bald eagle became our national bird in 1782.

2. ☑ **Reading Check** **Ask Questions List** questions about two national symbols.

National Symbol	A Question I Have	Where I Can Find the Answer

Think about how a local government worker can represent the community and its people.

Many people remember the men and women who served our country in the military.

Patriotic Celebrations and Traditions

We all love celebrations. We might celebrate weddings or birthdays with our families. We celebrate as communities and a country as well. Our country celebrates a "birthday" on Independence Day. Each July 4 we remember when our country declared its independence. The U.S. Constitution was signed on September 17, 1787. We celebrate Constitution Day in September to remind ourselves of our country's ideals. The American flag gets remembered on a special day, too. We celebrate the flag and what it stands for on Flag Day on June 14.

Our country honors people who have made and keep our country great. Veterans Day (November 11) and Memorial Day (the last Monday each May) remind us to thank and honor those who have served in our nation's military. Each year on Presidents' Day (the third Monday each February) we remember our founders and those who have come after them to serve as leaders for our country.

3. ☑ **Reading Check** Summarize Why do we have patriotic celebrations?

_____

_____

_____

_____

Celebrating Independence Day is a proud American tradition.

 INTERACTIVITY

Check your understanding of the key ideas of the lesson.

✓ Lesson 4 Check

4. Compare and Contrast How is a landmark different from a celebration?

_____

_____

5. Explain how symbols and celebrations bring people together.

_____

_____

_____

6. Understand the *Quest* **Connections** How can local government workers make us proud of our state?

_____

_____

_____

Interpret Graphs

A graph shows information in a visual way. A graph makes it easier to understand relationships between numbers. Some graphs help us see how things change over time.

When studying a graph, it is important to look at the title. Look also at the labels on the side and bottom of the graph. Notice the source of the data. Then look at how the graph changes.

The federal government employs people to work in our country and the world. These jobs include working for the military, caring for the environment, enforcing laws, or checking that foods and medicines are safe. This graph shows the number of federal government workers in different years. Not every year is shown.

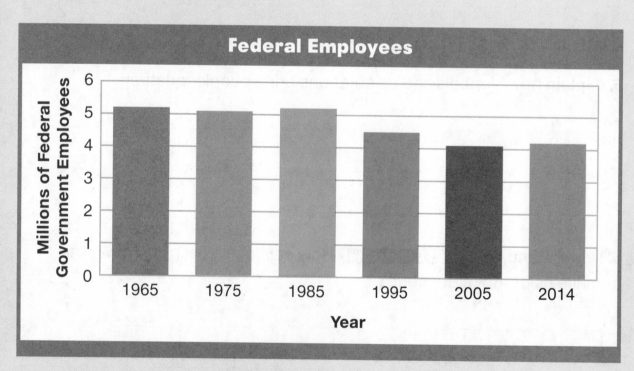

Source: Office of Personnel Management

1. What do the numbers on the side of the graph show?

_____

INTERACTIVITY

Review and practice what you learned about interpreting graphs.

2. What do the numbers at the bottom of the graph show?

_____

3. What generalizations can you make based on the graph? Tell how you know.

_____

_____

_____

_____

_____

Quality:
Leadership

Earl Warren
A Life of Law and Leadership

Even as a young boy Earl Warren knew he wanted to be a lawyer. When older, he went to law school and then began to practice law.

In 1953, the president of the United States appointed Mr. Warren to be the chief justice of the Supreme Court. He was a superb leader, who worked with others to get them to agree.

While he led the Supreme Court, one of its most important rulings made schools open to children of all races. At first, the other justices were divided on this issue. But Warren led them to reach a unanimous decision. Many decisions of the Warren Court increased people's rights.

Primary Source

We conclude that in the field of public education the doctrine of "separate but equal" has no place. Separate educational facilities are inherently unequal.

–Chief Justice Earl Warren, ruling
on *Brown* v. *Board of Education*, 1954

Find Out More

1. What leadership quality did Earl Warren have?

_____

2. When Chief Justice Warren was on the Supreme Court, the court ruled that a child's race should not determine what school the child attends. Talk with a partner about why this is important.

Visual Review

Use these charts to review some key terms, people, and ideas from the chapter.

Governments in the United States

	Federal Government	State Governments	Local Governments
Who Is Governed?	The United States	One state	A city or community
Some of the Leaders	• President • Vice president • Senator • Representative • Supreme Court justice	• Governor • State senator • State representative • Judge	• Mayor • City manager • Council member

Branches of Government

	Legislative	Executive	Judicial
Duties	• Pass laws • Vote on taxes	• Enforce laws • Sign or veto laws	• Decide if laws follow the Constitution • Decide what laws mean
Federal Leaders	Congress	President	Supreme Court Justice
State Leaders	State Legislature	Governor	Judge

😎 **GAMES**

Play the vocabulary game.

Vocabulary and Key Ideas

The United States Constitution is the plan for our national government. **Complete** each sentence with one of these three words: legislative, judicial, executive.

1. The _____ branch decides if laws follow the Constitution.

2. The _____ branch makes the laws.

3. The _____ branch enforces the laws.

4. Use this data to **draw** bars in the bar graph.

   • San Diego has more than 1 million people but less than 2 million people.

   • San Francisco has a little less than 1 million people.

   • Los Angeles has almost 4 million people.

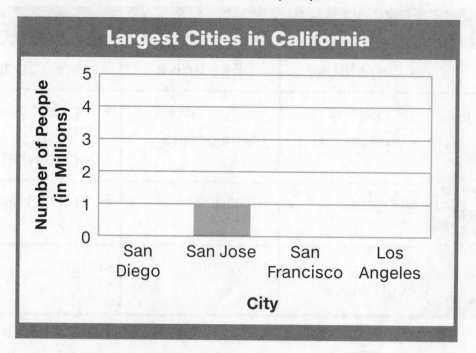

Largest Cities in California

Interpret a Graph Use the information on the graph. What are the two cities with the most people?

Critical Thinking and Writing

5. **Compare and Contrast** Tell how the governor of a state is similar to and different from the president of the United States.

_____

_____

_____

6. **Sequence** Fill in the letter next to the event that happens first when the U.S. Constitution is changed.

Ⓐ The amendment goes to the states for approval.

Ⓑ Thirty-eight or more states approve the amendment.

Ⓒ The Constitution is changed.

Ⓓ Congress votes on and approves an amendment.

7. **Analyze** Why is it important to have national symbols?

_____

_____

_____

8. **Revisit the Big Question** Why do we have government?

_____

_____

_____

9. **Writing Workshop: Write Explanatory Text** On a sheet of paper, **write** a paragraph. Explain how and why we celebrate one of our patriotic holidays.

Analyze Primary Sources

The President shall be Commander in Chief of the Army and Navy of the United States, . . .

–The United States Constitution Article II, Section 2

10. A commander is a leader. What do you think this title means that the president should do?

_____

_____

_____

_____

Compare and Contrast

Both state and federal governments have similarities. But they have differences, too. Both governments have people who make laws. But only the federal government has a military. Both governments collect taxes. But only the national government prints money.

11. How are state and federal governments similar and different?

_____

_____

_____

_____

_____

_____

Quest Findings

Present a Local Government Job

In this chapter, you have read about the levels and branches of government. Now you are ready to prepare and give your presentation about a local government worker. Convince others that you know all about the job!

1 Job Title

What is the title of the job you chose? Write it here.

....

2 Research

Find out more about the job. What tasks does someone who works at this job perform? What training is needed? What qualities should the person have? (For example, does the person need to be fair? Does the person need to be a good leader?)

3 Take Notes

List two duties that are important for this job. Then list two skills needed.

....

....

....

4 Present

On notecards, write what to say about the job. Remember, you will be presenting to first graders, so practice how to be clear. If you like, wear a costume to look like a worker who has the job.

GO ONLINE FOR
DIGITAL RESOURCES

▶ VIDEO

👆 INTERACTIVITY

🔊 AUDIO

🎮 GAMES

☑ ASSESSMENT

📖 eTEXT

The BIG Question How can I participate?

▶ VIDEO

Jumpstart Activity

 INTERACTIVITY

One way to take part in your community is to be nice to others. Work with a partner and act out a time when you were nice to someone. Perhaps you helped someone with a problem or said something nice. Discuss with your partner how being nice to someone makes you feel and how it feels when someone is nice to you.

🔊 AUDIO

Citizenship Is Simple

Preview the chapter **vocabulary** as you sing the rap:

Citizenship is simple.
As **citizens** of the United States
Obey the rules and **laws**.
It is a **responsibility** we take.

You also have **rights**
To cast a vote and even to speak up.
Freedoms of all kinds
All of them granted by the Bill of Rights.

Citizenship is simple.
Sometimes the laws can fall behind the times
And **heroes** have to say,
"Hey! That really ought to be a crime!"

Take part, join a cause.
Being a good citizen's the way to be.

5 Quest

Collaborative Discussion

Vote or Volunteer?

It is important for all of us to take an active part in our community. People can do that in different ways. One way is by voting for our elected officials. Another way is by volunteering. Which way do you think helps a community more?

Quest Kick Off

Hello there! I'm Benjamin Franklin. In this great nation, voting and volunteering are very important. But I can't decide which is more important to a community. Can you? Have a discussion to figure it out.

1 Ask Questions

Why should people vote? How is voting important? Why should people volunteer? Who does that help?

....

....

....

....

2 Plan

What facts do you need to know that will support your opinion?

....

....

....

....

....

INTERACTIVITY

Complete the activities to get started on your discussion.

VOTE FOR ME

COMMUNITY GARDEN

3 Look for Quest Connections

Begin looking for Quest Connections that will help you prepare for your discussion.

BOOK MOBILE

4 Quest Findings
Conduct a Discussion

Use the Quest Findings page at the end of the chapter to help you lead your discussion.

The Reasons for Rules and Laws

👆 **INTERACTIVITY**

Participate in a class discussion to preview the content of this lesson.

Vocabulary

obey
citizenship
responsibility
right
law
fine

Academic Vocabulary

promote
enforce

Unlock The BIG Question

I will know why we have rules and laws and what happens when they are not followed.

JumpStart Activity

Work with a partner. Think of a classroom rule. Talk with your partner about what might happen if that rule is not followed.

People set rules to keep us safe and to help us. Different places have different rules. For example, in school, you should not run in the hallway. At home, you might have a rule to brush your teeth before going to bed. In your community, using a crosswalk during traffic is an important rule. In order for rules to work, people have to **obey**, or follow, them.

When you obey rules at school, you are being a good citizen.

Citizenship

A citizen is a member of a community, state, or nation. Obeying rules is one part of good citizenship. **Citizenship** refers to the character and behavior of a citizen. For example, when you obey the rules of your classroom, you are showing good citizenship. Your school, city or town, state, and nation all value good citizenship. A great way to be a good citizen is to follow the rules of your community.

Good citizenship can change over time, such as when new rules are made. When people obey the new rules, they are **promoting** good citizenship.

Most of the time, citizens follow rules because they feel it is their responsibility to do so. A **responsibility**, or duty, is something that a person should do. For example, many citizens feel it is their responsibility to help other people. They might do that by coaching a youth sports team, or helping people learn how to read.

Academic Vocabulary

promote • *v.*, to encourage or help

1. ☑ **Reading Check** **Identify** and draw a picture of a rule you follow in your daily life.

This person is protesting an environmental issue. The Bill of Rights protects the right to protest.

Academic Vocabulary

enforce • *v.*, to make sure people obey laws and rules

Rights and Laws

Just as citizens have responsibilities, they also have rights. **Rights** are basic ideas or truths that people value. The United States government protects these rights with the Constitution and the Bill of Rights.

You have already read that the Constitution provides a system of government that makes, approves, and **enforces** the nation's laws. A **law** is an official rule. Laws help to keep communities orderly and safe. For example, it is against the law to drive through a red stoplight.

The Bill of Rights, the first ten amendments to the Constitution, protects basic rights for American citizens. Some of the rights include freedom of speech and freedom of religion. Freedom of the press gives citizens the right to hear news that is not controlled by the government. The Bill of Rights also gives people the freedom to gather and peacefully protest a law they disagree with.

The First Amendment of the Bill of Rights explains many of these rights:

Primary Source

Congress shall make no law respecting an establishment of religion, or prohibiting the free exercise thereof; or abridging the freedom of speech, or of the press; or the right of the people peaceably to assemble, and to petition the government for a redress of grievances.

—The Bill of Rights, Amendment I, 1791

Some laws protect the right to vote. For example, people can vote in an election even if they are out of town on the day of an election. Citizens vote to elect leaders who make laws. Voting is both a right and a responsibility.

Quest Connection

Why do we vote for our elected officials?

INTERACTIVITY

Explore some of the reasons for voting.

2. ☑ **Reading Check** **Describe** to a partner how this image shows good citizenship.

People vote to choose their leaders.

Consequences of Breaking Rules and Laws

If people do not obey rules and laws, there can be consequences. The consequences of violating, or breaking, a rule are usually not as bad as the consequences of breaking a law. When you break a classroom rule, for example, you might not be allowed to play outside.

When someone breaks a law, the consequences vary. Violating a traffic law, for example, usually means having to pay money, called a **fine**. Other times, the consequences can be more serious. Some people even go to jail for breaking a law. Lawmakers hope that the consequences of breaking a law will stop people from doing so.

3. ☑ **Reading Check**
Underline some consequences for breaking rules and laws.

There is a law that says cars must stop at stop signs. There are consequences to breaking that law.

☑ Lesson 1 Check

4. Summarize Give three examples of rights that citizens have.

_____

_____

_____

5. Cause and Effect What happens when you do not follow a rule or a law? Fill in the chart to **identify** the consequences of each.

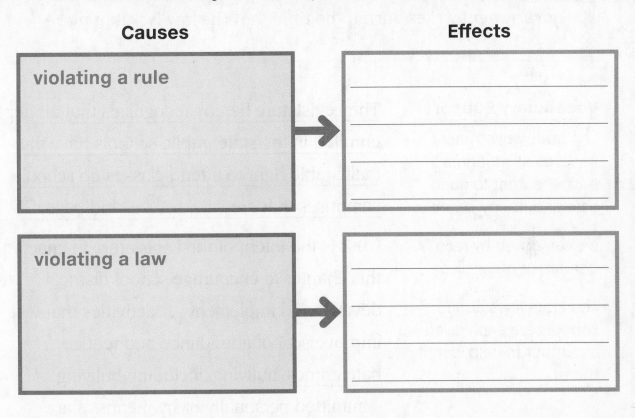

Causes	Effects
violating a rule	
violating a law	

6. Understand the Quest Connections Explain whether this statement is true or false: If we do not like a law, we can vote for different officials who can then change or replace it.

_____

_____

Anti-Bullying Law From California

In 1999, Georgia set up state laws to prevent bullying in schools. Since then, the other 49 states have created some kind of law or policy on bullying. Bullying is when a student teases or hurts another student. Bullying violates good school citizenship. Bullying has consequences. A bully may be suspended from school, or not allowed to attend school for a period of time. A student may be expelled, or kicked out of school, for more serious bullying.

Laws are primary sources because they are documents that a government writes during the time that the law is put in place.

Vocabulary Support

The state government believes all students have the right to go to safe and happy schools.

crimes driven by race, gender, or other bias

The state laws about schools are each given a number to help identify them.

pupil • *n.*, a student
inalienable • *adj.*, not able to be taken away
enact • *v.*, to make happen officially
implement • *v.*, to put into action

The Legislature hereby recognizes that all pupils enrolled in the state public schools have the inalienable right to attend classes on school campuses that are safe, secure, and peaceful . . .

(d) It is the intent of the Legislature in enacting this chapter to encourage school districts . . . to develop and implement . . . activities that will improve school attendance and reduce . . . hate crimes, bullying, including bullying committed personally or by means of an electronic act . . .

—California Education Code §32261

Close Reading

1. What kinds of schools do students have a right to attend? **Identify** and circle those qualities.

2. **Summarize** the intent, or goal, of the law in your own words.

_____

_____

_____

_____

Wrap It Up

How does the law promote both rights and responsibilities?

_____

_____

_____

_____

_____

The opposite of bullying is working together with others, even if they are different from you in some way.

Unlock
The **BIG**
Question

I will know how to be a good citizen.

Vocabulary

public virtue
deed
role model
volunteer
civic
activist
cyberbullying

Academic Vocabulary

issue
aid

JumpStart Activity

As a class, think of ways people can be good citizens. When you have an idea, raise your hand. When your teacher selects you, stand and say your idea. The teacher will then write each idea on the board.

Good citizenship can happen anywhere. You can be a good citizen at home, at school, and in your community. As you have read, part of being a good citizen is obeying laws and rules. Responsibilities, like voting and helping other people, are also part of good citizenship.

When people practice good citizenship, it promotes public virtue. **Public virtue** is the goodness in all citizens and the willingness to work for the good of a community or nation. Public virtue is important. It means that people can get along with one another, so long as they are kind, honest, and respectful.

In the Classroom

One place you can be a good citizen is in your classroom. First, you must follow the rules your teacher has made. That includes raising your hand before you speak, not talking too loudly, and not interrupting your classmates. You should always return things that are loaned to you. It is also a good idea to be a good sport, whether you win or lose a game.

In addition to obeying class rules, you can also do good deeds. A **deed** is an action. Doing good deeds promotes good citizenship and can improve your classroom. For example, you may want to help a classmate with her homework. Or, you could stay after school and help your teacher organize your classroom library.

When you do good deeds, you are acting as a role model. A **role model** is someone whose good behavior sets an example for others. Participating in your classroom in a positive way is a great way to be a good role model.

These students practice good citizenship at school by gathering canned food for those in need.

1. ☑ **Reading Check Identify** and **underline** ways to be a good citizen in the classroom.

In Your Community

Quest Connection

What kind of volunteering do you think you might enjoy doing? Explain.

INTERACTIVITY

Take a closer look at different ways to volunteer.

Good deeds are not limited to your classroom. You can also perform good deeds in your community. The public virtue of a community depends on people helping each other. For example, you and an adult might check in on an elderly neighbor. You could offer to help someone by raking leaves or walking the person's dog. A friend may need plants watered or mail collected while being out of town.

Some people in the community have jobs that require them to perform good deeds. Police officers keep people safe and direct traffic. Firefighters put out fires and respond to accidents. Medical staff help people when they get hurt or very sick.

Some citizens volunteer in their communities. To **volunteer** means to work or give help without being paid. Examples of volunteering include reading to children, working at a food bank, or cleaning up a park.

By helping his grandmother fill out forms, this boy is performing a good deed.

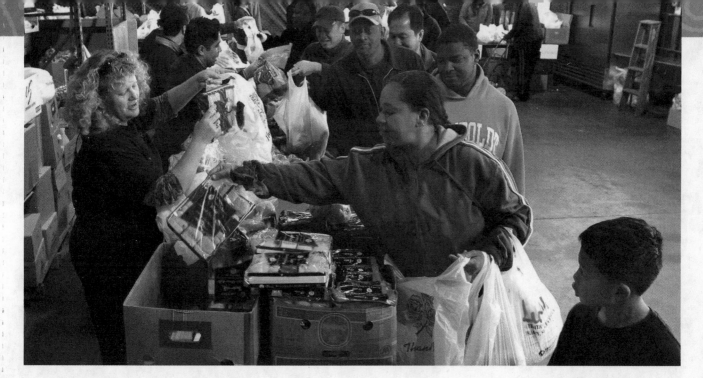

Volunteers provide a Thanksgiving meal for needy families.

Civic Engagement

Engaging, or participating, in civic life is another way to be a good citizen. **Civic** refers to the rights and responsibilities of citizens. Civic engagement includes voting and volunteering. It also includes paying taxes. A tax is money that the government collects. The government uses taxes to pay for community needs like schools, highways, and the police department.

Some people become very active in civic life. People who work to fix problems they see in society are called **activists**. Activists work hard for a certain cause, such as voting rights or the homeless. Large organizations can act as activists, too. Throughout the United States, there are many different civic organizations that work for different causes.

2. ✓ **Reading Check** Write how the photos in this lesson show good citizenship.

_____

_____

_____

The American Red Cross provides help to people in need in other countries.

Academic Vocabulary

issue • *n.*, an important public matter

aid • *n.*, help or support

Citizens of the Twenty-First Century

Civic engagement is changing in the twenty-first century. Technology has connected the world and made it easier to communicate. Citizens must understand what it means to be a good citizen in a digital world.

Voting remains an important right in civic life. Technology gives us more information about elections than ever before. Voters should learn about the **issues** before they vote. A responsible voter knows the facts and votes wisely.

Being a citizen today means learning how issues outside of your community affect you. For example, a flood in a faraway country could affect the price of goods sold in the United States. People living in that flooded country are likely to need **aid** from citizens all over the world.

The Internet has helped to make the world interconnected. People from different places can communicate online. It is important to be a good digital citizen. That means not being rude or disrespectful to others. You should also not be a cyberbully. **Cyberbullying** is sending mean messages online.

3.  **Identify** one way that civic engagement has changed in this century.

_____

_____

 **INTERACTIVITY**

Check your understanding of the key ideas of this lesson.

☑ Lesson 2 Check

4. **Main Idea and Details Describe** the role of a good citizen.

_____

_____

_____

_____

5. **Identify** an example of how you can participate in the civic life of your community.

_____

_____

6. **Understand the** *Quest* **Connections** Who in a community is helped by the work that volunteers do?

_____

_____

Word Wise

Prefixes A prefix is added to the beginning of a word. It changes that word's meaning. The prefix *inter-* means "between." What do you think *interconnected* means?

Ask and Answer Questions

One way to understand something you read is to ask and answer questions about the text. The kinds of questions you ask can vary. You may ask questions that can be answered by the text. Or, you might ask questions that can be answered by your own knowledge. Other times you might be curious about ideas in the text. You may need to do research to find an answer.

Read the paragraph and think of some questions you may have. Is there anything you do not understand? What are you curious about? Do you understand the meaning of all the words?

You are being a good citizen when you plant a tree. Trees help communities in many ways. They make communities more beautiful. They also give birds and squirrels a place to live. They provide shade and help cool off streets in the summer. Trees are also good for the environment because they supply oxygen to the air.

Your Turn!

1. Use the first two rows of the graphic organizer to answer the questions about the paragraph you read about planting trees. You may need to do research. In the third row, ask and answer your own question about the paragraph.

 **INTERACTIVITY**

Review and practice what you learned about asking and answering questions.

Questions	Answers
What is one way trees make a community better?	
What is oxygen?	

2. Go back to Lesson 2 and reread the section titled "Citizens of the Twenty-First Century." Write a question that you have about the text. Answer it using the text, an online resource, or your own knowledge.

_____

_____

_____

Taking Action for Our Rights

 INTERACTIVITY

Participate in a class discussion to preview the content of this lesson.

Unlock The BIG Question

I will know about people who fought for the rights and freedoms of our country's citizens.

Vocabulary

convention
suffrage
civil rights
segregate
delegate

Academic Vocabulary

convince
aware

In 1880, Susan B. Anthony spoke at a suffrage meeting in Chicago, Illinois.

Jumpstart Activity

Form a small group and choose a topic to discuss. For example, you might choose a movie, a band, a subject in school, or something important going on in your school, community, or state. Take turns standing up and giving your opinion about the topic.

Today, citizens have many rights and freedoms. But these rights and freedoms did not come easily. Throughout history, both famous leaders and ordinary people have worked hard to make sure everyone is treated equally.

JOIN THE NATIONAL WOMAN'S SUFFRAGE ASSOCIATION

JOIN THE NATIONAL WOMENS SUFFRAGE ASSOCIATION

Susan B. Anthony

Even after the Bill of Rights was added to the U.S. Constitution, women did not have the same rights as men. Susan B. Anthony wanted to change that. So she gave speeches about treating people fairly.

In 1848, Elizabeth Cady Stanton, Lucretia Mott, and other women organized a **convention**, or a large meeting. They wanted to discuss women's rights. A large group of people met in Seneca Falls, New York. One right the women wanted was **suffrage**, or the right to vote. It was the first time that women gathered in public to demand the right to vote. The Seneca Falls Convention was the start of the suffrage movement.

Then in 1851, Susan B. Anthony joined Elizabeth Cady Stanton in the suffrage movement. Together they formed the National American Woman Suffrage Association in 1869. Susan B. Anthony served as the president of this group for eight years.

In 1870, the Fifteenth Amendment to the United States Constitution was passed. It gave African American men the right to vote. Still, women could not vote. In 1872, Anthony voted in the election for United States president. This action was against the law, and she was arrested. She also had to pay $100 for breaking the law, but she refused to pay. She felt it was unfair.

After Anthony died in 1906, other women continued the fight. Finally, in 1920, the Nineteenth Amendment became law. Women had won the right to vote!

Women voted for the first time in 1920.

Winning attorneys of historic *Brown* v. *Board of Education* case in 1954 in front of the Supreme Court building. From left, George E. C. Hayes, Thurgood Marshall, and James Nabrit Jr.

Word Wise

Parts of Speech

Adjectives are describing words and provide extra information about nouns. Find *dangerous* in the paragraph. It describes a railroad track. Now look for the word *leaders* and find the adjective that describes *leaders*. What are some other adjectives that could also describe *leaders*?

Thurgood Marshall

Thurgood Marshall worked hard for civil rights. **Civil rights** are rights of all citizens to be treated equally under the law. Marshall believed that all citizens, not just some citizens, should have civil rights.

Marshall grew up in Baltimore, Maryland. He often debated at home with his father and brother. People who have different viewpoints often debate, or argue to convince others to agree with them. Marshall continued to debate in college and later became a lawyer. He began to argue in court to change unfair laws.

At this time, laws **segregated**, or separated, African American and white people in many places. These places included theaters, restaurants, and other public places. African American children and white children were segregated in colleges and schools, too. Marshall wanted to end segregation, especially in schools.

Reverend Oliver Brown, an African American, wanted his daughter, Linda, to attend a school for white students. The African American school was far from the Browns' home. Linda Brown had to cross a dangerous railroad track to get there. The white school was close to the Browns' home, but school leaders would not allow Linda to attend. Other African American families joined in the fight for civil rights.

Linda Brown's case was brought before the Supreme Court. Marshall argued this case, trying to **convince** the Supreme Court justices that school segregation was wrong. His debating skills helped him win the case. In 1954, all nine Supreme Court justices voted to end school segregation. This court case is known as *Brown* v. *Board of Education*.

Marshall continued to protect people's rights. In 1967, Marshall was chosen to be the first African American Supreme Court justice. He served on the Supreme Court for 24 years.

1. ☑ **Reading Check** A mother and daughter sit on the steps of the Supreme Court after segregation is made illegal. **Identify** and **circle** the part of the photograph that shows a change in civil rights.

Academic Vocabulary

convince • *v.*, to cause someone by the use of evidence to take a course of action or to believe something

Nettie Hunt explains *Brown* v. *Board of Education* to her daughter, Nickie.

The News

HIGH COURT BANS SEGREGATION IN PUBLIC SCHOOLS

Eleanor Roosevelt

Eleanor Roosevelt worked hard to improve people's lives. Roosevelt was the First Lady, or the wife of the president. Her husband, Franklin D. Roosevelt, was president from 1933 to 1945. While she was the First Lady, Roosevelt traveled all over the world to visit schoolchildren, sick people in hospitals, coal miners, and even people in jail. She told her husband everything she learned about these people. She was **aware** that all people need basic human rights.

In 1945, Eleanor Roosevelt had the opportunity to work as a leader for human rights. She was chosen to be the American delegate to the United Nations (U.N.). A **delegate** is a person chosen to act for others. The U.N. is an international peace organization. While at the U.N., Roosevelt led a group that worked for human rights. The group helped create the Universal Declaration of Human Rights. It recognized that all people in the world had the right to be treated equally under the law. They had the right to own property and the right to leave their country and then return.

Eleanor Roosevelt was a delegate to the United Nations.

2. ☑ **Reading Check** **Identify** some of the human rights that Eleanor Roosevelt worked for.

_____

_____

_____

_____

👆 **INTERACTIVITY**

Check your understanding of the key ideas of this lesson.

☑ **Lesson 3 Check**

3. **Make Connections** What was a common goal of the Nineteenth Amendment and the _Brown_ v. _Board of Education_ decision?

_____

_____

4. **Identify** one of the leaders you read about in this lesson. **Explain** why he or she is a good citizen.

_____

_____

_____

5. **Write** a word or phrase next to each person's name to tell what rights they fought for.

Susan B. Anthony: _____

Thurgood Marshall: _____

Eleanor Roosevelt: _____

American Heroes

Vocabulary

hero

risk

civil war

slavery

abolitionist

settlement house

advocate

Academic Vocabulary

despite

secure

Unlock **The BIG Question**

I will know about the lives of certain American heroes.

JumpStart Activity

When have you ever been brave? Talk with a partner and share stories of a time when you were brave.

Throughout American history, certain people have worked to protect our rights and freedoms. Many Americans call these people heroes. A **hero** is someone who has done special deeds and is a role model for others.

George Washington and Thomas Jefferson are among others who appear on Mount Rushmore because they were American heroes.

The Founding Fathers

People refer to the group of men who worked to shape the United States in its early years as the "Founding Fathers." You already read that long ago, Great Britain ruled what is now the United States. Many people were unhappy and wanted to be free from British rule. Each of the Founding Fathers played an important role in making the United States a free, independent country.

In 1776, a group of American leaders—the Continental Congress—decided what to do about British rule. Among them was Thomas Jefferson. You already learned that he helped write the Declaration of Independence. That document is the formal statement of freedom from British rule. When Jefferson and the Congress wrote and sent the Declaration to the British government, they were taking a risk. A **risk** is a dangerous chance. At that time, not everyone wanted to be free from British rule, and the British were firm about keeping control over America. The British and Americans were at war.

George Washington was the American military leader during the Revolutionary War. He was an excellent general and took many risks during the war. His leadership helped win the war.

After the war, the United States needed a constitution. Americans turned to many important leaders, including James Madison, to write that document. Madison was an important thinker. He helped plan the Constitution and the Bill of Rights. He has become known as the "Father of the Constitution" for his role. Both Washington and Madison went on to serve as presidents of the United States.

1. ☑ **Reading Check**
Identify and **underline** in the text one thing that each Founding Father accomplished for the United States.

Anne Hutchinson was told to leave Massachusetts.

Anne Hutchinson and Freedom of Religion

Some American heroes are known for standing up for what they believed in. Anne Hutchinson lived in England in the 1600s. She was not allowed to practice her religion there. She decided to move to Boston, Massachusetts, along with others who shared her beliefs.

In America, she began to form her own ideas about religion. Because her thoughts were different from the official religion, she risked her own safety. Later, religious leaders forced her to leave Massachusetts. She moved to an area that became the state of Rhode Island.

Freedom of religion has been important in America since early times. Other Americans have stood up for their religious rights. The idea was so important that freedom of religion became a key part of the Bill of Rights. This freedom is still important today.

Abraham Lincoln Ended Slavery

Abraham Lincoln was president of the United States during the Civil War. A **civil war** is fought between groups of people who live in the same country. The American Civil War was fought in the 1860s between southern states and mostly northern states. At the time, slavery was allowed in many states. **Slavery** was the practice of buying, selling, and owning people. Some southerners forced enslaved African Americans to work under brutal conditions. Many northerners were against slavery. As a result of this disagreement, the southern states joined together and broke away from the country. The Civil War began shortly after.

President Lincoln wrote a document called the Emancipation Proclamation. His purpose was to free all enslaved African Americans living in the southern states. Many Southerners believed it was their right to enslave people. This made it risky for Lincoln to issue the Proclamation. Slavery came to an official end when the northern states won the war in 1865.

Quest Connection

How do you think people who voted for Lincoln affected the issue of slavery?

INTERACTIVITY

Learn more about Abraham Lincoln and slavery.

Abraham Lincoln

Primary Source

All persons held as slaves within any State ... in rebellion against the United States, shall be then . . . and forever free.
—Abraham Lincoln, the Emancipation Proclamation, 1863

2. **☑ Reading Check** Turn to a partner, and **explain** how Abraham Lincoln helped free enslaved African Americans.

Clara Barton

Frederick Douglass

Academic Vocabulary

despite • *prep.*, without being affected by

Clara Barton Aided Soldiers

Clara Barton worked as a nurse during the Civil War. She also brought soldiers medicine and supplies on the battlefield. Later in life, she started an organization called the Red Cross. The Red Cross cares for soldiers and their families. It also helps people who are the victims of floods and other natural disasters.

Frederick Douglass Spoke Out Against Slavery

Frederick Douglass was an abolitionist. An **abolitionist** was someone who worked to abolish, or get rid of, slavery. Frederick Douglass was an enslaved person born in Maryland. He escaped to freedom as a young man and became a writer and speaker. Douglass spoke out about ending slavery. He traveled and spoke to people all over the United States. He was often attacked for his antislavery views. **Despite** the risk to his personal safety, Douglass continued to speak out.

Douglass's book, *Life and Times of Frederick Douglass,* is an important story of his escape from enslavement. He also wrote an antislavery newspaper called the *North Star*. By writing and speaking out against slavery, Douglass helped change others' opinions about slavery.

Harriet Tubman and the Underground Railroad

Like Douglass, Harriet Tubman was an African American hero born into slavery in Maryland. In the years before the Civil War, she escaped to Pennsylvania. There, she started working to help other enslaved African Americans become free.

Harriet Tubman worked with other abolitionists in the Underground Railroad. This was not an actual railroad. It was a secret system that helped enslaved African Americans living in southern states escape slavery. Tubman and other abolitionists risked their lives to **secure** others' freedom.

Academic Vocabulary

secure • *v.*, to make something safe and certain

3. ☑ **Reading Check** **Write** how Harriet Tubman worked to improve the lives of others.

_____

_____

The Underground Railroad helped enslaved African Americans escape to freedom.

213

Martin Luther King, Jr. Worked for Equal Rights

Well after the Civil War, the struggle for African American civil rights continued. Even though slavery had ended, African Americans did not have full civil rights. You read that segregation meant they had to go to schools that were separate from white people. They had to eat in separate areas in restaurants. Many were not allowed to vote.

Martin Luther King, Jr. gave his "I Have a Dream" speech in 1963.

Students celebrate
Martin Luther King, Jr.
Day at a parade.

Dr. Martin Luther King, Jr. believed that these rules were unfair. He gave speeches and organized peaceful protests in favor of civil rights. Some disagreed strongly with King. He and other activists faced violence. They risked their lives for their beliefs.

In 1963, King gave a speech declaring, "I have a dream." His dream, he said, was for children to be judged by who they are, and not by their skin color. As a result of the work of King and other leaders, two major civil rights laws were passed in 1964 and 1965.

Sadly, King was shot and killed in 1968. Years later, the U.S. government created a federal holiday to celebrate his life. The third Monday of each January, which is near King's birthday, is Martin Luther King, Jr. Day.

4. ☑ **Reading Check**
Cause and Effect
Identify and **underline** one effect of Martin Luther King, Jr.'s efforts to secure civil rights.

Jane Addams, Founder of Hull House

Jane Addams worked to improve life for the poor and for immigrants. She fought to change laws unfair to children, women, and factory workers. In 1881, Jane Addams and Ellen Gates Starr founded the settlement house, Hull House, in Chicago, Illinois. A **settlement house** was a community center located in a poor area of a city. At Hull House, children were cared for and could attend kindergarten. Immigrants learned English and got help finding jobs. People took classes in art, music, and drama. In addition to her role in social work, Addams was also an advocate for peace. An **advocate** is someone who fights on behalf of a cause. In 1931, she was awarded the Nobel Peace Prize.

Jane Addams with children at Hull House

Children learning pottery at Hull House

5. ☑ **Reading Check** **Describe** how Jane Addams helped children.

_____

_____

_____

INTERACTIVITY

Check your understanding of the key ideas of this lesson.

☑ **Lesson 4 Check**

6. **Main Idea and Details** **Identify** the risks George Washington took. Fill in the chart with supporting details.

Main Idea
George Washington took risks.

_____

_____

7. **Describe** why Frederick Douglass is considered to be a hero.

_____

_____

8. **Understand the** _Quest_ **Connections** If people had not voted for Abraham Lincoln to be president, what might have happened to enslaved African Americans?

_____

Fact and Opinion

A *fact* is a statement that can be proved true or false by doing research. "George Washington was the country's first president" is a fact. An *opinion* tells someone's feelings, beliefs, or ideas and cannot be proven. "George Washington was funny" is an opinion.

Read Caroline's letter aloud and look at the photo. Contrast the facts and opinions in the chart.

Hi Grandma,

I am excited to tell you what I learned about leaders in school. Thurgood Marshall was a lawyer. He always argued for good reasons. He worked to end school segregation. He became the first African American Supreme Court justice. He was the greatest!

Love,
Caroline

Thurgood Marshall

Facts	Opinions
• Marshall was a lawyer and he wore glasses.	• Marshall was the greatest.
• He worked to end school segregation.	• He always argued for good reasons.
• He became the first African American Supreme Court justice.	• He was handsome.

Your Turn!

INTERACTIVITY

Review and practice what you learned about fact and opinion.

Take turns **reading aloud** to a partner the letter that Caroline's grandmother wrote. Fill in the chart with facts and opinions based on what you hear and see in the photo.

Eleanor Roosevelt

Hi Caroline,

I agree with you. I think that Thurgood Marshall was special. I read about leaders in the library today. I read about Eleanor Roosevelt. She was another great leader. She was the First Lady from 1933 to 1945. Her husband, Franklin Delano Roosevelt, was president at that time. Mrs. Roosevelt wanted equal rights for all people. I think we will have a lot of fun learning about leaders when you visit.

With love,
Grandma

Facts	Opinions

Quality:
Problem Solving

Sylvia Mendez
Ending Segregation in Public Schools

When Sylvia Mendez was a little girl, there was one elementary school she wanted to attend more than any other. There was a problem, however. She was not allowed to go to that school. She was only allowed to go to a school for Mexican American girls and boys. Back in 1945, schools in much of the United States and in Orange County, California, where she lived, were segregated. White children went to certain schools, and Mexican American children went to other schools. The schools for Mexican American children were not as nice as the other schools in the country.

Sylvia's parents thought this was unfair. They believed that all children should be treated equally. They fought to allow Sylvia to go to her favorite school. In 1947, the Mendez family won a federal court case that allowed Sylvia to attend whatever school she wanted. The Mendez family's victory set an important example for other schools in the United States. By 1954, it was also against the law in the United States to separate schools by race.

Find Out More

1. What problem did Sylvia Mendez and her family solve?

_____

_____

_____

2. Research someone in your community who has been honored as a problem solver. Learn how the person improved the safety, welfare, and happiness of others.

Use these graphics to review some of the key terms, people, and ideas from this chapter.

	Example From Chapter	People and Groups From Chapter Who Illustrated This
Why do we follow rules and laws?	They keep our communities orderly and safe.	Police officers help keep our communities orderly and safe by making sure rules and laws are followed. 
How can we be good citizens at school?	Follow classroom rules; help fellow students.	Teachers help their students learn to be responsible citizens by the example they set. 
How can we be good citizens in our community?	Volunteer, do good deeds, be a role model, and engage in civic life.	People in the community and organizations such as the Red Cross help those in need. 
How can we be good citizens in the twenty-first century?	Be a good citizen in the digital world; no cyberbullying; help people in other countries.	Eleanor Roosevelt fought for the human rights of people all over the world. 

🎮 **GAMES**

Play the vocabulary game.

Vocabulary and Key Ideas

law, civil rights, volunteer, risk

1. Fill in the blank with the correct word from the word bank.

   a. to work without being paid _____

   b. an official rule _____

   c. rights of all citizens to be treated equally under

   the law _____

   d. a dangerous chance _____

abolitionist, advocate, Civil War, Emancipation Proclamation

2. **Identify** Fill in the blanks: Frederick Douglass was an
   _____ for enslaved African Americans. Like Harriet
   Tubman, he was an _____. That meant he wanted
   to get rid of slavery. An important step toward that goal came
   when Abraham Lincoln wrote the _____
   _____. Slavery was finally abolished when the
   northern states won the _____.

3. **Define** Fill in the circle next to the best answer.
   Which of the following shows good citizenship
   in today's world?

   Ⓐ Volunteering   Ⓒ Violating rules

   Ⓑ Cyberbullying   Ⓓ Being an abolitionist

Critical Thinking and Writing

4. **Identify** Look at the image. What is Susan B. Anthony most likely speaking about?

_____

5. **Main Idea and Details** How did what happened to Anne Hutchinson relate to the idea of freedom of religion?

_____

_____

_____

6. **Cause and Effect** What are the consequences of breaking a law or violating a rule?

_____

_____

_____

7. **Revisit the Big Question Describe** in detail two ways that people can participate in their community.

_____

_____

_____

_____

8. **Writing Workshop: Write Informative Text** What problem in your community do you think needs to be solved? On a separate sheet of paper, identify a problem and the kinds of things you can do to solve it.

Analyze Primary Sources

We do not have to become heroes overnight. Just a step at a time, meeting each thing that comes up, seeing it is not as dreadful as it appeared, discovering we have the strength to stare it down.

–Eleanor Roosevelt, *You Learn by Living*, 1960

9. What do you think Eleanor Roosevelt meant when she wrote "we do not have to become heroes overnight"?

_____

_____

_____

_____

Fact and Opinion

10. Read each statement. **Identify** if it is a fact or an opinion. Then write *fact* or *opinion* next to each statement.

_____ Eleanor Roosevelt worked for human rights.

_____ Thurgood Marshall was the best Supreme Court Justice.

_____ Susan B. Anthony was the most important woman in American history.

Quest Findings

Discuss Voting and Volunteering

You have read the lessons in this chapter and now you are ready to have your discussion. Remember that you are going to discuss whether voting or volunteering is more helpful to your community.

INTERACTIVITY

Use this activity to help you prepare your discussion.

1 Prepare to Discuss

Choose two facts that support each side of the discussion. Write them down on a separate piece of paper. Choose what you think is more important: voting or volunteering.

2 Write Your Opinion

Use your notes and your answers to the chapter's Quest Connections to prepare for your group discussion. Be prepared to use what you've written to support your opinion.

3 Have Your Discussion

Gather with your small group. Begin by discussing the importance of voting. Then talk about how volunteering helps others. Let all the students in your group have a chance to share their opinions.

4 Conclude

After your discussion, sum up what conclusions your group made. What did your group decide between voting and volunteering? Did your own opinion change or stay the same?

GO ONLINE FOR
DIGITAL RESOURCES

- ▶ VIDEO
- 👆 INTERACTIVITY
- 🔊 AUDIO
- 🎮 GAMES
- ☑ ASSESSMENT
- 📖 eTEXT

The **BIG** Question
▶ VIDEO

How does life change throughout history?

Lesson 1
New Ways to Travel

Lesson 2
A New Home in America

Lesson 3
New Ways to Communicate

Lesson 4
New Ideas

JumPstart Activity

👆 INTERACTIVITY

Look at the photo and then look around your classroom. In small groups, list ideas about how classrooms have changed.

_____

_____

_____

♪ **Rap** About It! ♪

 AUDIO

Times Were Changing

Preview the **chapter vocabulary** as you sing the rap:

As the nation grew, many things had to change,
Like travel—covered wagons and **wagon trains**.
Canals for boats, railroads for trains,
The Wright Brothers built and flew airplanes!

Immigrants came for a new life in the U.S.
And people looked for new land in the **frontier**
  out West.

With expansion moving fast in the United States,
People needed new ways to **communicate**.
New **inventions**, the telephone and **telegraph**,
Used wires to send and receive messages fast.

People worked for change and helped others
  fight,
For the same rights as others, or **equal rights**.

6 Quest
Project-Based Learning

Our Nation's Immigrants

Many people have moved to the United States over time. These people are known as immigrants. The immigrant experience is an important part of American history. Find out how and share what you learn with your class!

Quest Kick Off

Hello. You can make a 3-D model to tell about what life was like for an immigrant to the United States.

1 Ask Questions

What place will you show? What year will you represent?

....

....

....

....

2 Plan

INTERACTIVITY

Complete the interactivity to learn more about our nation's immigrants.

Talk with your teacher and others about where you can find information about your chosen place and time. What work do people do? Where do people live? How do people dress? How do they travel?

....

....

....

....

3 Look for Quest Connections

Begin looking for Quest Connections that will help you learn about our nation's immigrants.

4 Quest Findings
Share a 3-D Model

Use the Quest Findings page at the end of the chapter to help you make your 3-D exhibit.

Vocabulary

canal
wagon train
transcontinental
toll

Academic Vocabulary

continue
design

Unlock
The **BIG**
Question

I will know how new ways of traveling have changed people's lives.

JumpStart Activity

Work with a partner. List as many types of transportation as you can think of. Put a check mark by those you have used.

How do you travel from one place to another? You probably walk or ride in a car or bus. Long ago, explorers and settlers traveled by boat and by foot as they tried to learn about new lands.

Travel by Trails and Rivers

When Europeans arrived in North America in the 1500s, they knew nothing about the land. However, Native Americans knew the land well. They traveled by boat on rivers and by foot on trails they had made.

The Native Americans showed Europeans where to find what they needed. Later, explorers from Spain brought horses to North America. Horses made travel easier and faster.

Boats helped Lewis and Clark explore the West.

230

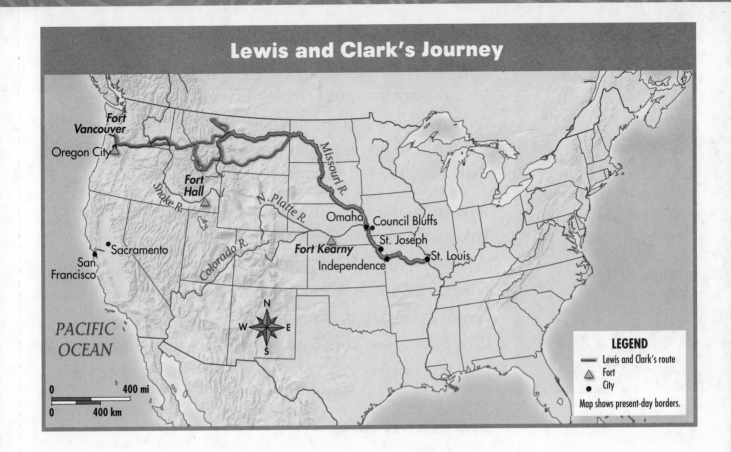

Lewis and Clark's Journey

As the country grew, many people wanted to explore the West. In 1803, President Thomas Jefferson hired Meriwether Lewis and William Clark to explore the land west of the Mississippi River. He asked them to learn about the Native Americans and the land in the West.

Lewis and Clark set out in 1804 with about 48 other men. Sacagawea (sak uh juh WEE uh) was a Lehmi Shoshone who helped them understand the language of the Native Americans they met.

It took two years for Lewis and Clark to finish their trip. The map shows where they went.

Their stories spurred a great deal of interest about the West. People heard about the huge open spaces and the chance of getting land they could farm. Because of Lewis and Clark, many white settlers traveled to the West and set up new communities.

Rivers and Canals

In the early 1800s, rivers were an important way to carry heavy goods. However, some rivers were too narrow or too fast for big boats. Sometimes a canal was built to let boats get through safely. A **canal** is a waterway that is dug by people.

In 1825, the Erie Canal helped connect the Great Lakes to New York City. Goods from what are now Wisconsin and Michigan were shipped over the Great Lakes. The goods were then carried down the Erie Canal to the Hudson River and then on to New York City. Soon, New York City became an important port. A port is a town or city that has a place for ships to land.

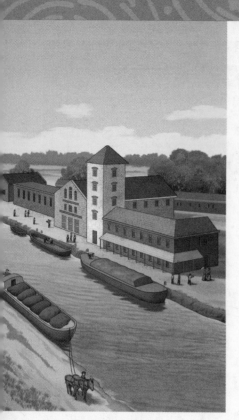

The Erie Canal improved transportation of goods and people.

Wagon Trains

Another form of transportation in the early 1800s was the covered wagon. Many people traveled to the West in wagon trains. A **wagon train** is a group of covered wagons that travels together for safety.

To make traveling west easier, Congress built the National Road. Many families began their trip on this paved road. It started in Maryland and ended in Illinois. From the end of the National Road, people traveled to the Oregon Trail, which began in Independence, Missouri. They followed this trail to Oregon.

The trip to Oregon took about six months. People faced harsh weather, sickness, and steep mountains. Although more than 12,000 people went west in the 1840s, a safer and faster way to travel was needed.

1. ☑ **Reading Check** **Identify** and underline ways in which people in communities met their needs for transportation.

The Oregon Trail and National Road

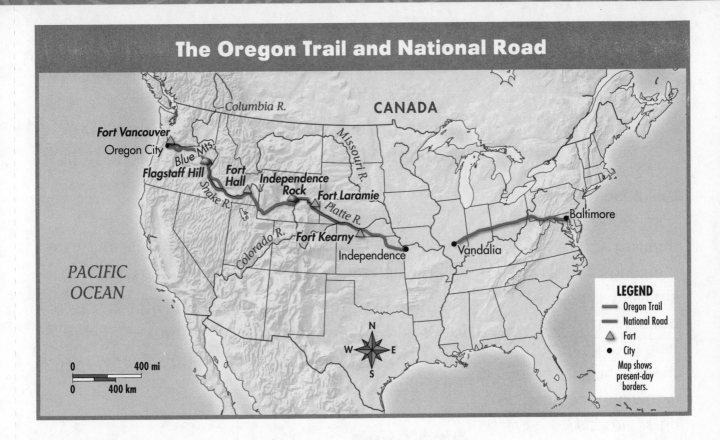

Railroads Cross the Country

The first steam locomotive was built in 1804. Steam locomotives are trains that run with steam engines. As improvements were made over the next ten years, they became powerful and could go long distances. Soon, people began planning railroads.

In 1863, two companies began building a railroad line across America. One company began east of the Mississippi River and one near the West Coast. On May 10, 1869, the two lines met in Promontory, Utah. The new railroad was called the transcontinental railroad. **Transcontinental** means "across the continent."

Railroads were a big improvement over slow canal boats, muddy roads, and narrow trails. Now, people could travel quickly and safely from Omaha, Nebraska, to Sacramento, California.

2. ☑ **Reading Check**
Underline the sentence that **identifies** what transcontinental means.

Highways Cross the Nation

Many new roads were built in the United States in the 1800s. These roads made travel easier.

Some landowners built toll roads on their land. A **toll** is money that is paid for using a road. Tolls helped pay for building and fixing roads.

The roads were used much less, though, after railroads were built. However, they became important again when many people started driving cars.

A huge highway system was finally built in the 1900s with money from the Federal-Aid Highway Act of 1956. At last, people could travel easily across the United States.

Airplanes

In the early 1900s, transportation **continued** to improve. Two brothers, Orville and Wilbur Wright, began building airplanes. On December 17, 1903, their first airplane flew. It stayed in the air for 12 seconds. Suddenly, people could fly!

The Wright brothers kept improving their **design**. The idea of traveling by airplane became popular.

Over the years, airplanes grew larger and more powerful. Today, jets carry people and items all over the world. A trip across the country, which once took months, now takes less than six hours.

3. **☑ Reading Check** **Draw Conclusions** **Explain** how travel changed in the 1900s.

_____

_____

INTERACTIVITY

Check your understanding of the key ideas of the lesson.

☑ Lesson 1 Check

4. **Draw Conclusions** **Analyze** each statement. Then write a conclusion you can draw about each statement.

   Railroads were a big improvement over muddy roads.

   _____

   _____

   Highways helped people travel across the United States.

   _____

   _____

5. **Explain** why wagon trains were the best way to travel across the country in the early 1800s.

   _____

   _____

   _____

6. Work in groups to **research** a mode of transportation. Use both print and digital sources. Use keyword searches, the table of contents, and the glossary or index to help you find information. Then **create** an advertisement for the mode of transportation as if it were brand new.

   _____

   _____

Compare Primary and Secondary Sources

Primary sources are documents, such as journals, photos, sketches, and maps, or artifacts from the time an event happened. Primary sources were written or used by someone who saw an event. Sometimes that person is called an eyewitness.

The written primary source that follows is from Meriwether Lewis. He describes coyotes. As you read, think about what this passage tells you about the past.

An artifact, like this compass, can be a primary source.

Primary Source

... the small woolf or burrowing dog of the praries are the inhabitants almost invariably of the open plains; they usually ascociate in bands of ten or twelve sometimes more and burrow near some pass or place much frequented by game; ... when a person approaches them they frequently bark, their note being precisely that of the small dog.

—Journal of Meriwether Lewis, May 5, 1805

The next passage also tells about Lewis and Clark's journey. But it was written by someone who did not see the events. It is a secondary source.

The members of Lewis and Clark's expedition saw many new plants and animals. They collected samples and wrote about what they found. They wanted people in the East to know about the West.

1. What does Meriwether Lewis's passage tell you about the past?

   _____

   _____

INTERACTIVITY

Review and practice what you have learned about comparing primary and secondary sources.

2. How are the words and spellings in Lewis's journal different from the way people write today?

   _____

   _____

3. **Compare** the journal entry and the secondary source. How are they alike and different?

   _____

   _____

   _____

   _____

   _____

INTERACTIVITY

Participate in a class discussion to preview the content of this lesson.

Vocabulary

immigrant
frontier
homestead
gold rush
exclusion

Academic Vocabulary

material
financial

Unlock The BIG Question

I will know how people's lives change when they move to a new country.

JumpStart Activity

In groups, think of family members or people you know who came to the United States from another country. Write a list. Share your list with the class. Find each country on a world map or globe.

People move to a new place for many reasons. Some need to find work. Some want religious freedom or a safe place to live. Some hope to earn more money. Some move to be closer to their family.

The Promise of America

People who move from one country to settle in a different country are called **immigrants**. Immigrants started coming to North America hundreds of years ago to start new lives.

Some of the first immigrants were people from Spain, France, and England. In the 1600s and 1700s, they crossed the Atlantic Ocean to come to North America. They settled in the Southeast, the Northeast, and even as far north as Canada.

In 1783, the United States won its independence from Great Britain. At that time, the nation was made up of 13 states, and all of the states were located in the East.

The West was a huge open land with many rivers and mountains. The soil was rich for farming, and gold could be found in the streams and rocks. While people were looking for gold, they also found other minerals, such as silver. People found many ways to earn money in the West.

In the mid-1800s, thousands of immigrants from Europe and Asia came to the United States. Most settled in cities along the East and West coasts where there were many jobs and places to live. Other immigrants bought or rented land to farm.

Most European immigrants sailed across the Atlantic Ocean and into New York Harbor. One of the first things they saw there was the Statue of Liberty. Even today, it welcomes immigrants.

The Statue of Liberty in New York Harbor has welcomed immigrants to the United States since 1886.

Americans Move West

As more immigrants came and cities became crowded, many people looked for more land in the American frontier. A **frontier** is a region that forms the edge of a settled area. People crossed steep mountains and wide rivers. The search for more land was dangerous. An explorer named Daniel Boone helped make this search easier.

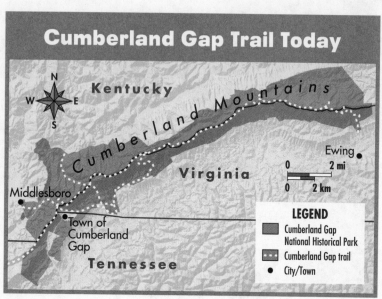

Cumberland Gap Trail Today

Kentucky

Cumberland Mountains

Virginia

Ewing

0   2 mi

0   2 km

Middlesboro

Town of Cumberland Gap

Tennessee

LEGEND

Cumberland Gap National Historical Park

Cumberland Gap trail

• City/Town

The Cumberland Gap trail had been used by American Indians for many years. It ran through the Cumberland Mountains. The map shows the Cumberland Gap trail today.

In 1775, Boone worked with 28 men to widen the Cumberland Gap trail and add new paths. This new road was called the Wilderness Road. Wagons could now travel through the mountains. As a result, thousands of settlers and explorers traveled west, beyond the Appalachian Mountains. In 1805, Zebulon Pike (ZEB yuh lun pyk) explored the Mississippi River. Davy Crockett began exploring present-day Tennessee in 1813.

1. ☑ **Reading Check** **Describe** how Daniel Boone changed the community by widening the Cumberland Gap trail.

_____

_____

The Homestead Act

The number of settlers moving west grew after 1862. In that year, the United States government passed the Homestead Act. A **homestead** is an area of land that includes a house and its buildings.

The Homestead Act allowed many Americans to get 160 acres of land for little money. The act helped people settle western lands. It helped the country add new states. Sadly, it also led to forced removal of American Indians from the land.

Families could buy land to start a new life in the West.

To be a homesteader, a person had to build a house and live on the land for five years. After that, the person owned the land. Thousands traveled west to find a new home. By the 1900s, there were 600,000 homesteaders in the West.

Many homesteaders were immigrants. Others had been enslaved in the South. By moving west, people started new lives. They farmed and fed their families. They started new communities and enjoyed religious freedom.

Life for homesteaders in the West was difficult. They built homes using any **materials** they could find. They carried water in buckets. They grew all of their food. Neighbors were far from each other, so it was difficult to get help. Many people returned home because life was harsh.

Academic Vocabulary

material • *n.*, an item that something is made of, such as stone, wood, grass, or mud

2. ☑ **Reading Check** **Draw Conclusions** **Identify** one detail that supports the conclusion that homesteaders started communities to fulfill a need for material well-being.

_____

_____

Immigrants From Asia

In 1848, people discovered gold in California. During the **gold rush**, thousands of people came from around the world to search for gold. Some of these people formed communities to meet their need for **financial** well-being.

Many immigrants came from China during the gold rush. At first, Americans welcomed them. However, some Americans thought that Chinese immigrants were taking too many jobs. In 1882, the United States government passed the Chinese Exclusion Act. **Exclusion** means "keeping people out of a place." This act stopped immigration from China for ten years.

In the 1880s, Japan started allowing workers to move to the United States. Many Japanese immigrants lived in California and in Hawaii, which was not yet a state. Most worked on farms or fished. Some owned small businesses.

Academic Vocabulary

financial • *adj.*, relating to matters of money

Quest Connection

Think about parts of an immigrant's daily life that you can show in your model.

👆 INTERACTIVITY

Take a closer look at the daily lives of immigrants to America.

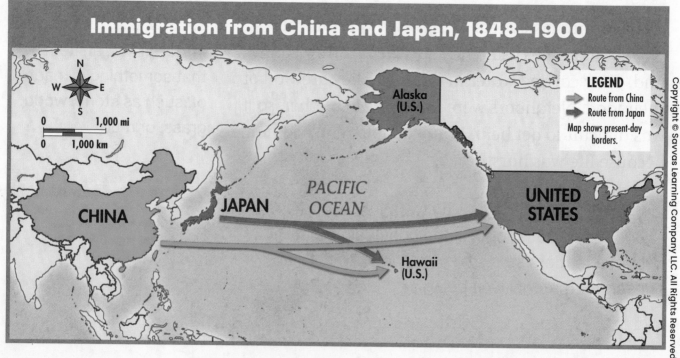

Immigration from China and Japan, 1848–1900

LEGEND
➡ Route from China
➡ Route from Japan
Map shows present-day borders.

CHINA
JAPAN
PACIFIC OCEAN
Alaska (U.S.)
Hawaii (U.S.)
UNITED STATES

0 1,000 mi
0 1,000 km

3. ☑ **Reading Check** Use the scale. **Measure** the distance in miles immigrants from China traveled to reach the continental United States.

_____

INTERACTIVITY

Check your understanding of the key ideas of the lesson.

☑ **Lesson 2 Check**

4. **Draw Conclusions** **Analyze** the lesson and draw a conclusion about how each of these events changed communities in the United States.

Wilderness Road: _____

_____

Homestead Act of 1862: _____

_____

Gold Rush: _____

_____

Chinese Exclusion Act of 1882: _____

_____

5. **Describe** what you think it was like to cross the Atlantic Ocean by ship in the 1800s.

_____

_____

6. **Understand the** _Quest_ **Connections** List answers to these questions about immigrants: How do people travel? What do people do? Where do they live?

_____

_____

Lesson 3
New Ways to Communicate

INTERACTIVITY

Participate in a class discussion to preview the content of this lesson.

Unlock The BIG Question

I will know the different ways people have communicated throughout history.

Vocabulary

communicate
invention
patent
telegraph

Academic Vocabulary

represent
introduce

JumpStart Activity

Think about ways you communicate each day. Share your ideas. Make a class chart showing ways you communicate beginning when you wake up until you go to sleep at night.

To learn about the world around us, we look and listen. We also use tools, such as telephones, radios, televisions, and computers. These tools help people communicate. When people **communicate**, they pass their thoughts or information to others.

The Pony Express

In the early 1800s, the only way to travel across the country was on horseback or by wagon train. Sending letters took anywhere from three weeks to two months.

As the country grew, the mail service had to improve. In 1860, a group of people had an idea. They set up the Pony Express. The Pony Express was a mail system that carried letters between St. Joseph, Missouri, and Sacramento, California. The map shows the route the mail traveled.

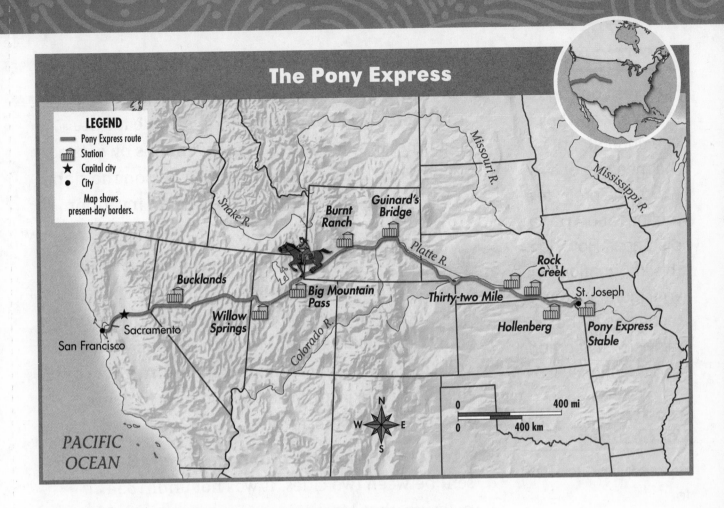

The Pony Express

LEGEND
- Pony Express route
- Station
- ★ Capital city
- • City

Map shows present-day borders.

Snake R.

Burnt Ranch

Guinard's Bridge

Platte R.

Rock Creek

Missouri R.

Mississippi R.

Bucklands

Big Mountain Pass

Thirty-two Mile

St. Joseph

Willow Springs

Hollenberg

Pony Express Stable

Colorado R.

Sacramento

San Francisco

PACIFIC OCEAN

N W E S

0 ——— 400 mi
0 ——— 400 km

Young men carried mailbags on horseback for 75 to 100 miles. Riders changed horses every ten miles at relay stations.

At the end of their part of the trip, riders waited at their last station for another rider coming from the opposite direction. Then they would pick up that rider's mailbag and ride home.

Pony Express riders rode through heavy snow and rain. They also kept away from American Indians, who did not want them on their land.

The Pony Express improved how people communicated. Now mail could reach the West Coast in only ten days. The Pony Express lasted only 18 months, as new systems began making communication even faster and easier.

Word Wise

Prefixes Looking at a prefix can help you understand the meaning of a word. The prefix *tele-* means "at or over a distance." How does this information help you figure out the meanings of the words *television, telegraph,* and *telephone*?

Academic Vocabulary

represent • *v.*, to stand for

introduce • *v.*, to use for the first time

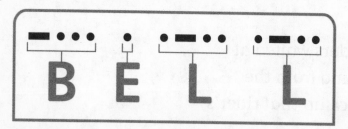

Dots and dashes represent letters in Morse code.

Telegraphs and Telephones

New inventions also improved communication. An **invention** is something that is made for the first time. People protect their inventions by getting patents on them. A **patent** gives a person the right to be the only one making or selling an invention.

In 1832, Samuel Morse began work to develop a telegraph. A **telegraph** is a machine that sends and receives signals through a thin wire. Six years later, he invented the Morse code. Look at the image showing an example of Morse code. The Morse code uses dots and dashes to **represent** letters and numbers. Telegraphs used Morse code to deliver messages almost instantly.

In 1844, the first telegraph message was sent between two cities. It was not until 1854, however, that Morse was given a patent for his invention.

Alexander Graham Bell liked the telegraph. He wondered, though, if he could send the human voice through wires. In 1876, Bell invented the telephone. For the first time, people could talk without seeing each other.

1. ☑ **Reading Check** **Identify** and underline the sentence that explains how the telephone changed the way people communicated. Then conduct research to find out how to write your name using Morse code.

Radio and Television

The telegraph and the telephone helped people communicate over long distances. However, these inventions used wires that were strung between buildings or cities. In 1896, Italian inventor Guglielmo Marconi (goo LYEL moh mahr KOH nee) found a way to send messages without wires.

Marconi patented a way for radio signals to travel through the air. People could now send and receive messages without telegraph wires.

In 1901, he received the first radio message sent across the Atlantic Ocean. Suddenly, people around the world could communicate instantly.

Many inventions were created by one person. However, some were developed by many people. The television was one of these inventions. The idea for the television is based on the work of Morse, Bell, Marconi, and many other scientists. Each one created parts of the new machine.

Although the creation of today's televisions took many years, most of the work was done in the 1920s and 1930s. In 1939, the television was **introduced** to a large audience at the World's Fair in New York. By the late 1940s, many Americans owned a television. These televisions showed black-and-white pictures. Since then, many scientists have improved the television. Today, almost every home in the United States has at least one television.

2. ☑ **Reading Check** Sequence Look at the pictures of communication tools. **Sequence** them 1–4 in the order they were invented.

Communication Tools

☐ **Radio**

☐ **Telephone**

☐ **Television**

☐ **Telegraph**

Satellites send and receive signals to make communication faster.

Communication Today

In the last 20 years, communication has changed even more. Satellites quickly send and receive signals for radios, televisions, cellular phones, and computers.

Computer technology has also improved communication. Technology is the scientific knowledge about how things work. When Bill Gates was young, computers were huge machines. No one had a computer at home. He helped to make personal computers possible. Today, people write e-mail messages that travel around the world in just a few seconds. They send photos and videos on cellular phones and computers. In the future, there will be new ways of communicating quickly.

3. ☑ **Reading Check** **Draw Conclusions** **Identify** and underline one impact of computers on your community. With a partner, **predict** and **discuss** how communication will change in the future.

☑ Lesson 3 Check

4. Draw Conclusions Analyze the lesson. Write a conclusion you can draw about how each invention has changed communities.

Cell phone

_____

_____

_____

Television

_____

_____

_____

Laptop computer

_____

_____

_____

5. Describe how people communicated with each other before the invention of the telephone. Tell how the telephone made communication easier.

_____

_____

_____

6. Summarize how personal computers affected the world.

_____

_____

_____

Draw Conclusions

A conclusion is a decision you make after you read facts and details. You use what you know and what you have learned to draw conclusions. Drawing conclusions helps you understand your reading.

Read the paragraph about homesteaders. Then look at the conclusion drawn from the details.

Homesteaders settled the West for many reasons. Some were farmers who could not get land in the East to farm. Some had been enslaved in the South. They wanted to make new lives for themselves and their families. Some homesteaders thought they could get rich by buying cheap land and farming it. Many found their lives in the West were difficult, but they enjoyed their freedom.

Homesteaders hoped for a better life.

Settling the West

Details	Conclusion
1. Farmers had no land in the East. 2. People who had been enslaved wanted to start new lives. 3. People wanted to get rich.	People became homesteaders in the West because they wanted a better life.

Your Turn!

 INTERACTIVITY

Review and practice what you have learned about drawing conclusions.

1. Analyze the passage about the Pony Express. Then fill in the chart with two more details about the Pony Express riders. Last, write a conclusion you can draw from the details.

> The Pony Express was created during the Civil War to help people find out what was happening around the country. Before the Pony Express, the mail had been carried by stagecoach and by boat.
>
> Pony Express riders risked their lives to deliver the mail. They rode as fast as they could, and they did not rest very often.
>
> Mail delivery was much faster with the Pony Express, but it was not safe enough or fast enough. The Pony Express went out of business after the telegraph was invented.

The Pony Express Riders

Details

1. Riders risked their lives.

2. _____

   _____

3. _____

   _____

Conclusion

_____

_____

_____

_____

Vocabulary

equal rights
assembly line
vaccine

Academic Vocabulary

provide
protect

Unlock The BIG Question

I will know how new ideas and machines changed people's lives throughout history.

Jumpstart Activity

Act out an invention from the past. When your classmates guess correctly, say why you think the invention was important.

Throughout history, new ideas have changed lives. Some ideas involve making new things, such as cars. Others involve new ways to live.

Seeking Equal Rights

In the late 1800s and early 1900s, more people began to work to give all Americans equal rights. When people have **equal rights**, they have the same rights as others.

Women wanted the right to vote. African Americans wanted their children to have the right to go to the same schools as white children. Workers wanted rules to keep them safe. Many Americans worked to turn these ideas into laws.

In the early 1900s, many schools were segregated. White and African American students went to separate schools. Sometimes no schools were available for African American children.

Some people thought this was wrong. They wanted all children to have equal educations. In 1904, Mary McLeod Bethune opened a school for African American girls in Florida.

New Inventions

In the 1900s, the lives of Americans changed in other ways, too. One big change was caused by the invention of the first practical, or useful, light bulb. In 1879, Thomas Edison had invented a light bulb that was cheap and reliable. It **provided** light without needing to light a fire or a candle.

It took years for electrical wires to be put in and power stations to be built. However, by the 1900s, factories and offices could stay open at night. People could walk safely on well-lit streets, too.

Today, inventions are still changing people's lives. Cameras and computers have changed the way people communicate, shop for goods, and gather information about the world.

Academic Vocabulary

provide • *v.*, to give, to supply

Employees of the Edison Electric Lighting Company march in an 1884 parade. The marchers have light bulbs on their helmets. Wires up their sleeves send electricity to the bulbs.

Henry Ford rides in his car, the Model T.

Quest Connection

Think about new ideas and machines that you can show in your model.

INTERACTIVITY

Take a closer look at new ideas and machines.

1. ☑ **Reading Check**
Identify and underline the sentence that tells the type of new business that Henry Ford started in the early 1900s.

New Machines and New Businesses

In 1831, Cyrus Hall McCormick invented a machine that cut grain. It was called a reaper. Before, people cut crops by hand. The reaper made cutting grain faster and easier. Today, machines help farmers use more land and grow more crops.

One of the most important inventions of the late 1800s was the automobile, or car. In 1903, Henry Ford opened a business that built and sold cars. At that time, most people could not afford a car.

Ford wanted to build a car that everyone could afford. This led him to invent the assembly line. On an **assembly line**, each worker does only one part of a job. Ford's assembly line idea was used in factories around the world.

Assembly lines helped Ford make a car called the Model T, which cost less than other cars. Now, millions of people could afford to buy cars. People like Ford who started new businesses shaped communities in the past. New businesses provided jobs and products for people to buy.

New Ideas in Medicine

In the 1700s, a disease called smallpox killed millions of people. No one knew what caused it. There was no cure.

Then in 1796, Edward Jenner found a way to **protect** people from this terrible disease. He gave them a vaccine made from a very weak virus. A **vaccine** helps people's bodies fight off disease. Jenner's vaccine helped people fight off smallpox.

Polio was another terrible disease. In the 1950s, a Jewish American doctor named Jonas Salk used Jenner's ideas to invent a vaccine against polio. Salk gave people a dead form of the polio virus. Salk's vaccine helped people's bodies learn how to fight off the polio virus. The vaccine saved many lives.

Louis Pasteur (LOO ee pas TOOR) discovered that many diseases are caused by germs. In the 1860s, he invented a way to kill germs by heating foods and cooling them quickly. This process is called pasteurization. Today, most milk we drink is pasteurized.

2. ☑ **Reading Check** Main Idea and Details **Identify** the impact of pasteurization.

_____

_____

_____

Academic Vocabulary

protect • _v._, to keep from harm, keep safe

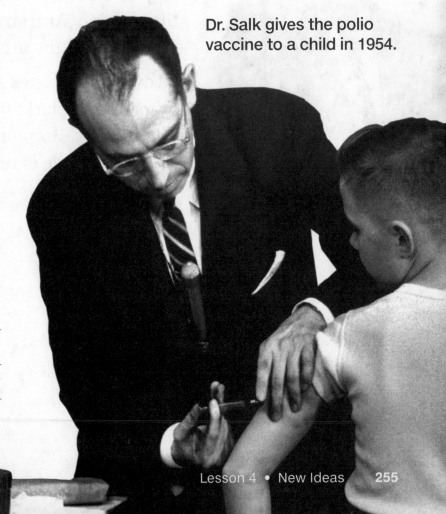

Dr. Salk gives the polio vaccine to a child in 1954.

Martha Graham

Jacob Lawrence

New Ideas in the Arts

New forms of artistic expression developed in the early 1900s. Traditional forms of dance, art, and music were transformed as artists explored innovative styles.

Martha Graham is often considered the founder of modern dance. In contrast to the graceful flow of movements of classical ballet, she used a dance style that focused on emotions and human experiences. She started her own dance company in 1926. She continued influencing the dance world both in the United States and abroad until her death in 1991.

Jacob Lawrence was an African American painter. In 1941 he gained fame when he was 25 years old with his 60-panel *Migration Series*. Using words and paintings, these pieces told the story of the Great Migration. This was a period starting in 1916 when thousands of African Americans moved from the rural south to the urban north.

Lawrence depicted African American life and history using blacks and browns with contrasting bright colors. His paintings portrayed everyday life in a unique style of realism.

Another change came to the music world with the development of jazz. Louis Armstrong was one of the most influential musicians of this style. He transformed jazz by highlighting a soloist instead of the ensemble. Armstrong was also a singer, popularizing "scat" singing, ad-libbing nonsense syllables in the vocals. Using energetic improvisation, he helped jazz move from novelty into fine art.

Louis Armstrong

3. 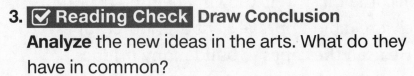 **Draw Conclusion**
Analyze the new ideas in the arts. What do they have in common?

_____

_____

☑ **Lesson 4 Check**

👆 **INTERACTIVITY**

Check your understanding of the key ideas of the lesson.

4. **Make Connections** What do Graham and Lawrence draw their inspiration from?

_____

_____

5. Think about someone in the early 1900s driving a Model T Ford. **Describe** how that trip might be different from a trip you take in a car today.

_____

6. **Understand the** *Quest* Connections What new ideas, machines, and inventions can you show in your model?

_____

_____

John Roebling and the Brooklyn Bridge

John Roebling was an engineer. He bought land in Pennsylvania and moved to the United States from Germany in 1831. Many transportation projects were underway in the United States.

Roebling worked on canals and railroads, but it was bridge building for which he became most well known. Roebling began to make wire ropes. These were a big improvement over other ropes that did not last long. He used the ropes to build many bridges.

In 1867, Roebling started to design the Brooklyn Bridge, which crossed the East River from Manhattan to Brooklyn in New York City. Roebling died before the bridge was finished, but his son and daughter-in-law finished his work in 1883.

Using a Primary Source

Study the image of the Brooklyn Bridge. It is a primary source because it was created during the time the bridge was being built.

1. Circle the steel ropes that held up the bridge.
2. The Brooklyn Bridge still stands today. Why do you think this is so?

_____

_____

Wrap It Up

Look at the photo of another bridge from today. How are the Brooklyn Bridge and this bridge alike?

_____

_____

_____

Quality:
Leadership

Mary McLeod Bethune
Champion of Education

The fifteenth of 17 children, Mary McLeod Bethune was the only one in her family to go to school. As a child, she thought that the biggest difference between white and Black children was the ability to read. She wanted to learn to read and to teach others. After walking miles to and from school each day, she came home and taught her sisters and brothers what she had learned.

As an adult, she felt the best way to help people was to educate women because women taught entire families. She opened a school for girls in Florida. Later, she led voter registration drives. Her schools also trained people to work in defense plants during World War II. She was a high-ranking official in the government of President Franklin Roosevelt.

Find Out More

1. How did Mary McLeod Bethune show leadership?

_____

_____

_____

2. People can show leadership in many ways. One way to lead is by helping others improve by teaching them new skills. Share with a partner your ideas about what you can teach others.

Use this word web to review some of the key terms and ideas from this chapter.

Communication
telegraph, telephone, radio, TV, satellites

Travel
cars, railroads, canals, wagon trains, highways, airplanes

Inventions
cameras, computers, light bulb, assembly line, cars

NEW

Medicine
vaccines, pasteurization

Places to Live
western lands, East/West coasts, homesteads, California

Human Rights
equal education, activism, equal rights for all

GAMES

Play the vocabulary game.

Vocabulary and Key Ideas

Complete each sentence with one of these four words: vaccine, immigrant, transcontinental, communicate.

1. The _____ railroad ran from the Mississippi River to the West Coast.

2. A(n) _____ is a person who comes to a new country to live.

3. New ways to _____ in the 1800s included using telegraphs and telephones.

4. A(n) _____ helps people's bodies learn to fight off a disease.

Critical Thinking and Writing

5. **Describe** how the transcontinental railroad changed the United States.

   _____

   _____

6. **Identify** the types of jobs Japanese immigrants did after they arrived in the United States in the 1800s.

   _____

   _____

7. Write the idea or invention of each person beside their name in the second column. In the third column, write either *science, business,* or *technology* to categorize each invention.

Name	Invention	Category
Jonas Salk	polio vaccine	science
Henry Ford		
Cyrus Hall McCormick		
Edward Jenner		
Louis Pasteur		

8. Revisit the Big Question: How has life changed throughout history?

_____

_____

_____

9. Writing Workshop: Write Informative Text On a separate sheet of paper, **describe** how landforms and geography affected the way people traveled and how new technology improved travel.

A smile or a tear has not nationality; joy and sorrow speak alike to all nations, and they, above all the confusion of tongues, proclaim the brotherhood of man.

—Frederick Douglass, "Our Composite Nationality" speech, 1869

10. Summarize this quotation in your own words.

_____

_____

_____

Compare Primary and Secondary Sources

11. Circle the sentence that is a primary source.

The ears are large erect and pointed the head long . . . more like that of the fox; tale long.

A historian writes about the experiences of Lewis and Clark's expedition.

Quest Findings

INTERACTIVITY

Use this activity to help you prepare your model to share.

Share a 3-D Model

In this chapter, you have read about our nation's immigrants. Now you are ready to make a 3-D model or exhibit that tells an immigrant story.

1 Prepare Your Model

On separate paper, draw a sketch of what you want to include in your 3-D model. You might want to show machines, inventions, methods of transportation, or people.

2 Gather Supplies

You can use a cardboard base, paint, clay, markers, construction paper, or other supplies.

3 Label the Objects

Use index cards (cut into smaller sizes) to label the parts of your model. Explain the time and place. Tell who the people are.

4 Share With the Class

Describe your model to the class. Tell what the new home and the new land were like. Explain the importance of what your model shows. Invite people to ask questions.

Chapter 7

Celebrating Our Communities

GO ONLINE FOR DIGITAL RESOURCES

- ▶ VIDEO
- 👆 INTERACTIVITY
- 🔊 AUDIO
- 🎮 GAMES
- ☑ ASSESSMENT
- 📖 ETEXT

The BIG Question   How is culture shared?

▶ VIDEO

Lesson 1

What Makes a Community?

Lesson 2

Three Types of Communities

Lesson 3

People and Cultures

Lesson 4

Culture Through the Arts

Lesson 5

Cultural Celebrations

Lesson 6

Our Nation's Diversity

JumpStart Activity    INTERACTIVITY

Write a short poem that tells about a time when people have come together in your community. Your poem might tell about a cultural festival, a holiday, a sports event, or some other gathering. Share your poem with a partner.

Rap About It!

🔊 AUDIO

Celebrating Community

Preview the chapter **vocabulary** as you sing the rap.

In a **community**, people live, work, and play.
They have laws and rules to keep people safe.
Many communities have **diverse cultures** too,
Where they celebrate the way of life
  of different groups.

You'll find **rural** communities in countrysides,
Many of these people live a farming life.
In **suburban** communities outside cities
Many houses with yards line the streets.

Urban communities are found
  in large city locations
And have tall buildings and public transportation.
Those who share similar culture live in
  culture regions,
Adapting the way they live based
  on climate and seasons.

Look At My Community!

Your community is a great place to live or visit! The people may come from different cultures and participate in many festivals or other celebrations. One way to tell people about all your community has to offer is to create an advertisement.

Quest Kick Off

Hi there! I live in a great community, and I bet you do, too! Your Quest is to create an advertisement to describe why people like your community. Tell people about your community's cultures and activities.

1 Ask Questions

What type of community do you live in? What cultures and kinds of activities are found in your community?

....

....

....

....

2 Plan

Look up information about your community on the Internet or at the library. Interview family members and others. What activities are done in your community? What do they tell about it?

....

....

....

....

👆 INTERACTIVITY

Complete the activities to get started on your advertisement.

3 Look for Quest Connections

Begin looking for Quest Connections that will help you create your advertisement.

4 Quest Findings
Create Your Advertisement

Use the Quest Findings page at the end of the chapter to help you create your advertisement.

What Makes a Community?

👆 **INTERACTIVITY**

Participate in a class discussion to preview the content of this lesson.

Unlock The BIG Question

I will know ways in which communities are the same and different.

Vocabulary

community
location
natural resource
mineral
diverse
culture

Academic Vocabulary

produce
participate

JumpStart Activity

When you think of where you live, what are the first ideas that come to your mind? Make a list of words to describe where you live. Include words that tell about its location, streets, buildings, places, and people. Share your list with a partner.

Where do you live? That's easy! You live in a community. A **community** is a place where people live, work, and have fun together.

A street found in the center of a community is convenient for all residents. These "main streets" are similar to others found throughout the United States.

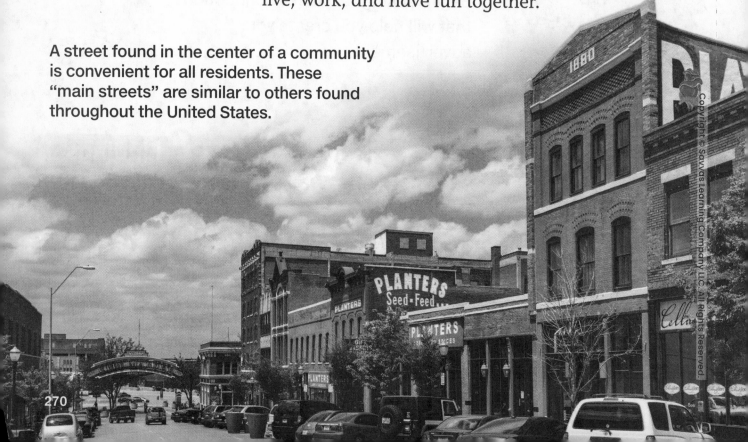

Communities are alike in many ways. People in communities help each other. They care about the safety of their communities. They follow laws, or rules, to make their communities safe places to live, work, and play. Many people have jobs or businesses. For fun, people join clubs and sports teams, go shopping, and see movies.

Why Communities Are Formed

People have settled in communities for many reasons. Some communities were formed so that people could be safe and have rules to follow. As new areas of our country were settled, people created laws and set up governments. Austin was formed to be the capital of the Republic of Texas. Other communities were formed so that people could be free to practice their religion. The Pilgrims came to this land to practice their religion freely.

People have also formed communities looking for material well-being, or the chance to live comfortably. Some settlers settled communities because of their **location**, or where they were. They chose areas with good **natural resources**, or something in nature that is useful to people. Having bodies of water nearby offered food and enjoyment. Farmers settled where there was good soil to help them grow crops and raise animals.

Trees were also an important land resource. People used trees for building homes, schools, and stores. As people kept building, their communities continued to grow. All of these things contributed to their material well-being.

People enjoy spending time outdoors in their communities.

A mountain community during the fall

Communities in Regions

Communities have been settled in all 50 states of the United States. You already learned about the five regions of the United States: the Northeast, the Southeast, the Midwest, the Southwest, and the West. There are different groups of states located in each region.

You probably remember that some states in the Northeast and West are located where there are many mountains. The Rocky Mountains in the West are some of the highest in the United States. The Appalachian Mountains in the eastern United States are the oldest mountains in the country. People like to settle near mountains because of the activities they can enjoy there. They can ski and sled in winter. In summer, they can go camping, hiking, or mountain climbing.

Beach communities are found in some regions along the shoreline, near the coasts. Some people settle there because they enjoy swimming or surfing. Others settle near the shoreline for job opportunities including fishing, food service, and tourism.

Some regions have communities located near mineral resources such as coal or iron. A **mineral** is a resource that does not come from an animal or a plant. Businesses that **produce** items made with minerals are located in these communities.

Academic Vocabulary

produce • *v.*, to make or create

People in Communities

People all over the world form communities. Many people in communities have jobs to earn money. Some work as doctors, teachers, or police officers. When people are not working, they enjoy different activities. People might **participate** in their favorite activities, such as gardening, riding bicycles, or playing a sport. Others might try activities they have never done before.

Many communities have **diverse**, or different, cultures. **Culture** is the way of life of a group of people. Some communities hold cultural festivals, parades, and fairs. Naperville, Illinois, for example, is a diverse community. Every year it hosts the Midwest SOARRING Foundation Harvest Powwow. This celebrates American Indian culture through food, dancing, and the arts.

Academic Vocabulary

participate • *v.*, to take part in

A dance from American Indian culture

1. ☑ **Reading Check** Fill in the chart with examples that **describe** your community.

My Community			
Land Resources	**Water Resources**	**Work**	**Activities**

Communities Change Over Time

Homophones are words that are pronounced the same way but have different spellings and meanings. Find the word *their* in the second paragraph. *Their* and *there* are homophones. Write the meaning of each word.

Communities change over time. What was once an open field may be a parking lot. A small town could grow into a big city as more people settle there. New and different businesses open. A shop that sold farm supplies may now sell computers.

One thing has not changed over time: people want to make their community a better place. They might work at food banks or pick up litter.

You can find out how your community was settled and how it has changed. Read about it. Compare and contrast past and present images and maps. Interview people who have lived in your community for a long time.

2. ☑ **Reading Check Compare** the maps. Turn to a partner and **discuss** what may have caused the Capitol area to change.

Capitol Square, Austin, Texas

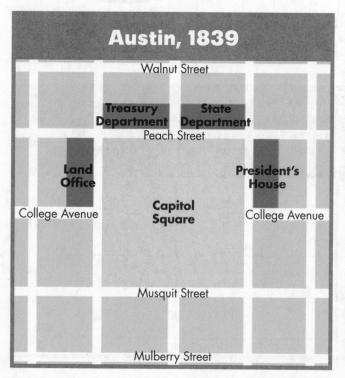

Capitol Complex, Austin, Texas

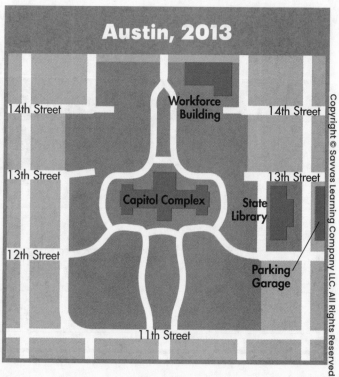

INTERACTIVITY

Check your understanding of the key ideas of this lesson.

Lesson 1 Check

3. Main Idea and Details Describe two ways that communities can grow and change over time.

_____

_____

_____

_____

4. Identify three jobs people in your community have to earn money. Describe how these jobs make your community a better place.

_____

_____

_____

5. Explain two reasons why communities have been formed. Then tell why you think your community was formed.

_____

_____

_____

_____

Generalize

A generalization is a broad statement that tells how different ideas or facts are alike in some way. Look at the chart and read the three facts. Each fact tells a way people use different natural resources to meet their needs. Now read the generalization. The generalization is a statement made about all of the facts. It tells how the facts are alike: people use natural resources to meet their needs.

Fact

People use wood to build houses.

Fact

People use water for drinking.

Fact

People buy vegetables at markets.

Generalization
People depend on natural resources.

Your Turn!

Read the newspaper article about Maple City.
Then answer the questions.

Maple City News

Soccer season starts this Saturday in Maple City! The town just finished building a new soccer field. Now there are two large soccer fields: one for the girls' team and one for the boys' team. Since there are two fields, each team has enough time to practice. People in the community also raised money to pay for new equipment and uniforms for both teams. Maple City is a great place to play soccer!

A soccer game in Maple City

1. **Identify** and **underline** two facts about soccer in Maple City.

2. **Identify** and **circle** the generalization in the article that tells how these facts are alike.

3. Write three facts to support this generalization: My community is a great place to live.

_____

_____

_____

_____

Three Types of Communities

INTERACTIVITY

Participate in a class discussion to preview the content of this lesson.

Unlock The BIG Question

I will know what rural, suburban, and urban communities are like.

Vocabulary

rural
urban
suburban

Academic Vocabulary

reside
obtain

JumPstart Activity

With a group, make signs that say "in a city," "near a city," and "in the countryside."

Then take turns describing one of these places while others try to guess the place. Use sentence starters such as, *I see _____, I hear _____, I smell _____, I like _____.* A group member should point to the correct sign as soon as he or she figures it out.

What kind of community do you live in? Is it a rural, urban, or suburban community?

A rural community

278

A **rural** community is found in the countryside where there is plenty of open space. An **urban** community is one that is in a large city. A **suburban** community is a community near a large city.

Rural Communities

Belle Plaine, Iowa, is a rural community about 40 miles southwest of Cedar Rapids, Iowa. Today about 3,000 people live in Belle Plaine. They like to get together and have fun during the year. On the Fourth of July, there are fireworks, music, and a parade. One special kind of parade is a tractorcade. More than 500 tractors parade through Belle Plaine and other rural communities in Iowa!

A tractorcade moves through a community.

Rural communities have their own mayors and other government officials to make and enforce laws, or rules, for their community. Local governments also provide services, such as schools, for their towns. Some towns have their own schools, while others share schools. Many rural communities have the technology to connect to the Internet quickly or use cell phones, but there are still some that may not. People in these communities may use slower dial-up phone lines to connect to the Internet. Rural communities have local newspapers that share information.

Some people in rural communities are farmers. Farmers grow crops like corn that people in larger towns and cities depend on.

People in rural communities depend on other communities, too. They travel to suburban or urban communities to buy what they need. People may travel by bus or drive their cars.

Suburban Communities

Alamo Heights, Texas, is a suburban community. It is surrounded by the city of San Antonio. Today almost 8,000 people live in Alamo Heights.

In Alamo Heights and other suburban communities, there are many houses with yards lining the streets. You might also expect to see a library, a post office, schools, stores, a movie theater, and parks there. Take a short drive, and you will find a large shopping mall.

Suburban communities have their own governments to make their local laws. People in suburban communities are often proud of where they **reside**. When there is litter on the streets of Alamo Heights, for example, people help clean it up. They cut the grass and clean streets, just like people in other suburban communities do.

Academic Vocabulary

reside • *v.*, to live in or have a permanent home at

People live in neighborhoods in different suburban communities.

There are plenty of activities for children in suburban communities. They can swim at the community pool or play basketball in a local park. They can also join a soccer or baseball team.

People in suburban communities **obtain** news about their town from local newspapers, on the Internet, or on television.

Many people who live in suburban communities work in a nearby city. Some people who live in Alamo Heights work in San Antonio. While some drive their cars or trucks on busy highways, others choose to take an express bus to work.

People began moving to suburban communities to get away from the crowded cities. As new highways were built to help people get to the city quickly, suburban living became more popular.

Academic Vocabulary

obtain • *v.*, to acquire or get

People in suburbs use highways to get to and from the city.

1. ☑ **Reading Check** **Generalize Write** two facts that support this generalization: There are many activities that children in suburban communities can enjoy.

_____

_____

_____

Quest Connection

Think about the type of community you live in. What does it have to offer its residents?

INTERACTIVITY

Explore different types of communities.

Atlanta

Urban Communities

Many people live, work, and play in urban communities like Atlanta, Georgia. About 4.5 million people live in Atlanta. Most live in apartments or high-rise condominiums. A condo is housing owned by the people who live there and may be part of a larger building.

In Atlanta and other cities, people work in tall buildings, or skyscrapers. Many people from suburban communities travel to cities to work. Once inside the city, people can use public transportation to get around. The city of Atlanta has a rapid transit rail system, streetcars, and buses. Cities such as New York have underground subways. San Francisco has cable cars.

There are many things to do for fun in a city. People can shop in stores or visit museums. In urban areas, people have access to technology. Internet and cell phones help make communication easier.

Features of Communities

	Rural	Suburban	Urban
Location	in the countryside	near a large city	in a large city
Population	small population	medium-sized population	large population
Buildings	farmhouses, barns	houses, shopping malls	apartment buildings, row houses, skyscrapers

Like other communities, an urban community has its own local government and schools. In a city, a mayor and a city council are elected to make laws.

2. ☑ **Reading Check** **Compare and Contrast**
   Analyze the Features of Communities chart. Then **underline** the words in the chart that show how the population in each type of community is different.

INTERACTIVITY

Check your understanding of the key ideas of this lesson.

☑ **Lesson 2 Check**

3. **Generalize** Write a generalization about transportation in an urban community. Then **identify** two facts to support your generalization.

_____

_____

_____

_____

4. **Describe** the type of community you live in. **Explain** how your community is similar to and different from one of the other types of communities.

_____

_____

_____

_____

5. **Understand the** *Quest* Connections **Write** two reasons why people might like to live in your community.

_____

_____

_____

Copyright © Savvas Learning Company LLC. All Rights Reserved.

👆 **INTERACTIVITY**

Participate in a class discussion to preview the content of this lesson.

Unlock The BIG Question

I will know how culture is shaped by people and climate.

Vocabulary

cultural region
recreation

Academic Vocabulary

construct
layer

Chinatown in New York is an example of a cultural region.

JumpStart Activity

Look at a 12-month calendar with a partner. Turn to the current month. Then go to the next month. Make predictions about that month. What will the weather be like? What kind of clothing will you wear? What holidays will you celebrate? What special foods might you eat? Then answer the same questions for two other months at different times of the year.

Today, the United States is a nation of many different cultures. Culture includes a group's language, religion, holidays, clothing, and food. People who share a similar culture may live in a **cultural region**. The United States has many cultural regions.

Cultural Regions

Every cultural region is shaped by the people who settled there. For example, Native American groups lived in North America and South America long ago. Then in the 1400s and 1500s, European explorers arrived. They brought their own cultures, which were different from those of the Native Americans.

Soon, more Europeans came to settle in the Americas. The map shows where in North America they settled. Europeans and Native Americans often lived near one another. Both groups learned about each other's cultural heritage. For example, in Jamestown, Virginia, the Native Americans taught English settlers new ways to plant crops. The English settlers taught the Native Americans to use the tools that the settlers had brought with them.

Many places throughout North America and South America were settled by Europeans hundreds of years ago. These places have kept some of the culture that the Europeans brought.

Settlements in North America, 1700–1750

800 mi

800 km

St. Lawrence River

New France

Nez Percé

Mandan

Iroquois

Miami

Thirteen Colonies

Pomo

Shosone

Pawnee

New Spain

Hopi

Louisiana

ATLANTIC OCEAN

Navajo

Comanche

Rio Grande

Mississippi River

Calusa

Gulf of Mexico

Caribbean Sea

LEGEND
English
French
Spanish
Group   American Indian group

Cultures in Warm and Cold Climates

Did you know that climate shapes a cultural region? Climate affects the type of shelters people build, their forms of recreation, the foods they eat, and the clothing they wear. **Recreation** is a way of enjoying yourself.

Academic Vocabulary

construct • *v.*, to build

People who live in regions with warm climates, such as tropical Central America, often **construct** shelters that help them to stay cool. They may build houses in shaded areas or with powerful air conditioners. In a cold climate region, people's homes are built to hold in the heat. They may also have large windows to let in sunlight.

Climate also affects recreation. People who live in warm climates near water can swim, fish, or go boating many months of the year. In cold climates, the water may be frozen for many months.

What you eat for dinner tonight may also depend on climate. For example, if you live near rich soil in a temperate climate, you might grow your own vegetables and fruits. If you live near the coast, you might eat some fresh fish. Although foods can be transported from all over the world, many people still eat the foods that are grown in their own region.

Fishing in cold climates is not easy.

In Mexico, people make and sell clothing to wear in the warm climate there.

Quest Connection

What forms of recreation are found in your community?

INTERACTIVITY

Explore different forms of recreation and entertainment.

Climate also helps people choose what kind of clothing to wear. In the warm climates of the southeastern United States, people wear light clothing. These may include shorts and short-sleeved shirts, and hats to protect their skin from the sun. People also wear sandals to help their feet stay cool.

In cold climates, such as in parts of Canada, people need to stay warm. They wear **layers** of clothes under heavy coats. They wear gloves on their hands and thick hats to keep their heads warm. Places in cold climates are often wet with snow. People wear boots that keep their feet warm and dry.

Academic Vocabulary

layer • *n.*, a single covering

1. ☑ **Reading Check** **Identify** two ways people adapt to a cold climate.

_____

_____

Tibet

Egypt

Climates and World Cultures

The climates in Tibet and Egypt affect the cultural heritage of their people. Tibet is a cultural region in Asia. Egypt is a country in Africa. The climate of Tibet is mostly cold and can be dry. In Egypt, the climate is warm and dry. In fact, Egypt receives less rain than any country in the world!

The Tibetan people live on a plateau covered with grasslands. Mount Everest, the tallest mountain in the world, is nearby. Many people raise animals, including sheep and yaks. They eat cheese and butter made from the milk these animals produce. In some places, people live in tents made from the thick hair of yaks, which helps keep the tents warm inside.

In Egypt, most people live near the Nile River so they can get water for drinking, bathing, and watering crops. Since much of the land is desert, those who do not live near the river often still rely on it for water. These people may farm by bringing water in from the Nile River or raise animals. Many people build homes with bricks made from the nearby resources of mud and straw. On hot nights, people sleep on the flat rooftops to stay cool.

2. ☑ **Reading Check Compare and Contrast Explain** ways the cultures in Tibet and Egypt are similar and different.

_____

_____

_____

● **INTERACTIVITY**

Check your understanding of the key ideas of this lesson.

☑ Lesson 3 Check

3. Compare and Contrast Categorize the recreation and shelter that can be found in regions with warm climates and regions with cold climates.

	Warm Climate Region	Cold Climate Region
Recreation		
Shelter		

4. Write two facts about what you can do in the climate where you live. Then **write** a generalization that relates to the two facts.

_____

_____

_____

5. Understand the _Quest_ **Connections** How are the climate and recreation in your community related?

_____

_____

_____

INTERACTIVITY

Participate in a class discussion to preview the content of this lesson.

Vocabulary

arts
anthem
cultural heritage

Academic Vocabulary

assist
perform

Unlock The BIG Question

I will know how people share culture through the arts.

JumpStart Activity

Everyone has a talent. Maybe you paint, play an instrument, or dance. Are you good at sports? Perhaps you write great poems or stories. Stand up and act out what your talent is for a partner. Then tell why you enjoy taking part in your talent.

You can learn many things about a culture from the art that people create. Most people think of the **arts** as paintings and sculptures, but the arts can also include songs, poems, stories, and dances.

In 1931, "The Star-Spangled Banner" became the national anthem of the United States.

Songs, Poems, and Culture

People write songs and poetry about people, ideas, places, or events. Our national **anthem**, "The Star-Spangled Banner," was a poem that Francis Scott Key wrote about a War of 1812 battle. An anthem is a song of loyalty to a nation. Key shares his pride at seeing the flag victorious over Fort McHenry.

Primary Source

Oh, say can you see by the dawn's early light
What so proudly we hailed at the twilight's
last gleaming?
Whose broad stripes and bright stars through
the perilous fight,
O'er the ramparts we watched were so gallantly
streaming?

—"The Star Spangled Banner,"
Francis Scott Key, 1812

Phillis Wheatley was taken from Africa and brought to Boston when she was eight. She wrote poems about her faith, slavery, famous people, and current events. Wheatley wrote this poem at the outbreak of the American Revolution.

Phillis Wheatley published her first poem when she was just 12 years old.

Primary Source

Proceed, great chief, with virtue on thy side,
Thy ev'ry action let the Goddess guide.
A crown, a mansion, and a throne that shine,
With gold unfading, WASHINGTON! Be thine.

—"To His Excellency General Washington,"
Phillis Wheatley, 1776

Stories and Culture

People all over the world tell stories to share their history, their ideas, and what is important to them. Some stories are written, while others are spoken. Some stories celebrate the cultural heritage of different groups. **Cultural heritage** describes the traditions, customs, and artifacts of a cultural group. Some examples of cultural heritage are stories, dance, art, and buildings.

Laura Ingalls Wilder was an author who wrote about her family and life during the pioneer days. The *Little House Books* show the harsh conditions that people who settled on the frontier dealt with. Today, the town where Wilder was born hosts a festival that celebrates Wilder and her family.

Patricia McKissack was an author who wrote more than one hundred books. McKissack wrote about African American heroes like Sojourner Truth and players in the Negro Baseball Leagues. She said that she hoped to "build bridges with books."

Tomie dePaola is an author and an artist. His stories and pictures often show dePaola's cultural heritage—half Italian and half Irish. In *Patrick: Patron Saint of Ireland,* dePaola retells the legend of St. Patrick making the snakes leave Ireland.

Tomie dePaola writes many stories that celebrate his cultural heritage.

1. ☑ **Reading Check** **Explain** why Tomie dePaola's work is significant to the Irish and Italian communities.

_____

_____

Sculptures, Paintings, and Culture

Looking at art is another way to learn about different cultures. Some artists use natural resources that are important to their culture to create works of art. In the mountains of South Dakota, artists and workers are carving a sculpture of the Lakota leader Crazy Horse into the rock. Sculptor Korczak Ziolkowski designed this memorial and also **assisted** with Mount Rushmore.

Some artists show details of their culture in paintings. Carmen Lomas Garza is a Chicana native artist who was born in South Texas. Garza creates paintings and other works of art that celebrate the Mexican American culture and experience and illustrate daily life.

Kadir Nelson is an American artist. Some of his paintings are of historical figures. He has painted images of Nelson Mandela, Frederick Douglass, and Dr. Martin Luther King, Jr. In 2008, Nelson published his first children's book, called *We Are the Ship: The Story of Negro League Baseball*.

Crazy Horse Memorial

Academic Vocabulary

assist • *v.*, to provide help or support

2. ☑ **Reading Check** **Draw Conclusions** **Explain** why the paintings of Kadir Nelson are significant to both the African American and international communities.

_____

_____

_____

_____

perform • *v.*, to present
to an audience

Hula dancers

Ballet dancers

Dance and Culture

Dance is an important part of a group's culture. In Hawaii, the hula was **performed** long ago for chiefs, kings, or queens. Hula dancers move their arms and hips in smooth and flowing movements. Island flowers were used for necklaces called leis. Today, the hula is performed for all people.

Near the Appalachian Mountains in the eastern United States, people do folk dances. Folk dances are dances that have been passed down from one generation to another. Square dancing is a type of folk dance. Dancers stand in a "square" with two people on each side of the square. A singer calls out the instructions for each movement such as to move in a circle.

In ballet, dancers make smooth movements. They may jump, spin, or dance on their toes. Many ballet dancers wear costumes and pointed shoes. Russian ballet dancers are well known throughout the world. In France and Russia, ballet dancing was first performed only for kings and queens. Today, however, people all over the world enjoy ballet.

3. ☑ Reading Check Compare and Contrast

Compare the hula dance and ballet.

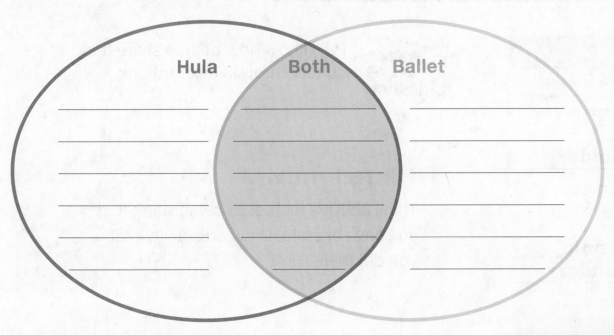

Hula   Both   Ballet

☑ Lesson 4 Check

 **INTERACTIVITY**

Check your understanding of the key ideas of this lesson.

4. **Compare and Contrast** Choose two authors and artists. **Explain** how their work is alike and why it is important.

_____

_____

5. **Describe** what some of the arts in your community tell about its culture.

_____

_____

6. **Generalize Write** a generalization based on the following facts: Songs, poems, and stories tell about a group's culture. Other art forms show culture through paintings, sculpture, or dance.

_____

Cultural Celebrations

INTERACTIVITY

Participate in a class discussion to preview the content of this lesson.

Vocabulary

ethnic group

harvest

Academic Vocabulary

observe

typically

Unlock The BIG Question

I will know how people share their culture through celebrations.

JumpStart Activity

Think about a festival or celebration that you have been to. Draw an activity that you did there.

Families and communities celebrate many different holidays and special traditions. These celebrations help people remember important people or events and are part of a cultural heritage.

An Independence Day celebration

Culture Through Traditions

People often have traditions that they follow on holidays. People in a culture learn these traditions from older family members or from people in their community. The traditions are part of the holiday each year.

Traditions can include eating a certain food, such as turkey on Thanksgiving. Other traditions include certain activities, such as watching fireworks on Independence Day. On some holidays, there is a tradition to wear a certain color. On St. Patrick's Day, many people wear the color green.

Days to Honor Leaders

Some celebrations honor people. Martin Luther King, Jr. was an important leader. He worked to get African Americans the same civil rights as other Americans. He wanted to bring about change peacefully, without force. People celebrate his life on Martin Luther King, Jr. Day, a national holiday in January. Many schools and offices close. It is a day for service to others. People have also created statues to honor King.

King followed the ideas of Mohandas Gandhi from India. Gandhi believed that people should not use violence. He worked for change in his home country of India. He used peaceful ways and did not harm people. People in India celebrate Gandhi's birthday on October 2. On that day, people do not go to school or work. Instead, families do special works of service for others.

A statue honors
Martin Luther King, Jr.

Celebrating Freedom

Academic Vocabulary

observe • *v.*, to celebrate in an accepted way

typically • *adv.*, usually or in most cases

Around the world people celebrate their freedom in different ways. People in the United States celebrate Independence Day on the Fourth of July. Many Americans **observe** this holiday with their family and their friends. They hold parades, fly flags, picnic, and watch fireworks.

Many symbols and landmarks of the United States are part of Independence Day celebrations. People gather at landmarks such as the Liberty Bell in Philadelphia.

In India, people celebrate their independence from British rule on August 15. People fly colorful kites and watch the raising of the Indian flag. The prime minister, or government leader, of India speaks about India's accomplishments each year.

On May 5, people in both Mexico and the United States celebrate Mexico's victory against French troops. The victory was a step forward on Mexico's path to freedom. This holiday is called Cinco de Mayo, which means "Fifth of May." On Cinco de Mayo, people **typically** watch parades, listen to music, and eat traditional Mexican foods.

Colorful dresses, music, and dance are part of many Cinco de Mayo celebrations.

1. ☑ **Reading Check** Compare and Contrast **Compare** India's independence celebration with the United States'.

_____

_____

_____

Ethnic Celebrations

Ethnic groups often celebrate important events and traditions. An **ethnic group** includes people who share the same language, culture, and way of life.

Juneteenth is an ethnic celebration honoring an important event. June 19, 1865, is the day that African Americans in Galveston, Texas, learned that slavery had ended. Today, Juneteenth is a holiday in more than 40 states. Communities celebrate with parades, music, and speeches. Families celebrate with reunions and picnics.

Juneteenth is celebrated in honor of Black American freedom and achievement.

In New York City, Puerto Rican Day is celebrated with a big parade. This day celebrates Puerto Rican traditions. People of Puerto Rican descent express pride by waving Puerto Rican flags. Puerto Rican music rings through the streets. People dance and enjoy traditional Puerto Rican foods.

Irish traditions are celebrated in many communities across the country. For example, in Dublin, Ohio, the Dublin Irish Festival is held in late August. It features Celtic music and workshops in cultural skills such as making soda bread. Ethnic celebrations provide everyone opportunities to learn about different cultures.

2. ☑ **Reading Check** **Generalize** **Describe** an ethnic celebration in your local community. Then **write** a generalization about it.

_____

_____

_____

Word Wise

Multiple Meanings
Some words have more than one meaning. To determine the meaning that is intended, you need to read the sentence. Use a dictionary to look up the word *ring*. Read all its meanings. Then reread the third paragraph. What do you think the word *rings* means in the sentence?

Quest Connection

Talk with a partner about how people celebrate their culture in your community.

👆 **INTERACTIVITY**

Explore different kinds of celebrations.

Harvest Celebrations

People throughout the world celebrate harvests. A **harvest** is the crops gathered at the end of the growing season. In the United States, some communities' festivals celebrate corn, cranberry, and even strawberry harvests.

In Japan, people celebrate in hopes of a good rice harvest. They plant rice seedlings in the fields, sing, and dance. Later in the year, another celebration gives thanks for the rice harvest.

Thanksgiving began as a harvest celebration when English settlers gathered with American Indians to celebrate their harvest and to give thanks. Today, Thanksgiving is in November. Families and friends eat a special meal and celebrate what they are thankful for.

Kwanzaa is also a celebration that was based on a harvest festival held in parts of Africa. Today, Black Americans celebrate Kwanzaa to honor important values.

During Kwanzaa families light candles and share their values.

3. ☑ **Reading Check** **Identify** and **underline** the harvest celebrations that take place in the United States.

☑ **Lesson 5 Check**

INTERACTIVITY

Check your understanding of the key ideas of this lesson.

4. **Compare and Contrast** **Compare** two independence celebrations you read about.

_____

_____

_____

_____

_____

5. **Write** about a cultural celebration that you share with your community. **Explain** its significance.

_____

_____

6. **Understand the** **Quest** **Connections** What special foods, activities, music, or dance are part of ethnic and other celebrations in your community?

_____

_____

_____

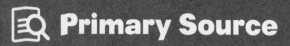
Photographs: Cultures in the United States

Photographs can be primary sources if they show important information about an event or a group of people. For example, photographs might provide details about how people live today. They may let viewers learn about other cultures. They may show what a culture's traditional food, art, or clothing looks like. You can look at multiple primary source photographs to make comparisons.

Look at the photographs. They show details about the various cultural groups of the United States.

Close Reading

1. Circle the images that show people performing.

2. Based on the photographs, what different activities take place at cultural festivals?

_____

_____

_____

Wrap It Up

How do these photographs demonstrate that cultural diversity is important in the United States?

_____

_____

_____

INTERACTIVITY

Participate in a class discussion to preview the content of this lesson.

Vocabulary

ancestor

powwow

Academic Vocabulary

converse

property

Unlock The BIG Question

I will know how people share and express their culture.

JumPstart Activity

Your classroom is likely made up of students of different cultures or backgrounds. Stand up and share one thing you have learned from a classmate about another culture. Then share one thing about your culture.

The United States is home to millions of people from other countries. Some have come to be safe, to find religious freedom, and for opportunity.

People from all over the world live in urban environments in the United States.

Since so many people have come to live in the United States, this gives the country diversity. This diversity offers people in communities in each region the chance to build friendships with people from other cultures.

Susan From Seattle, Washington

Susan lives with her family in Seattle, Washington, in the West region of the United States. Susan's **ancestors**, or relatives who lived long ago, came to Seattle from the country of Japan. They came to the United States in the 1800s in search of gold. Susan lives in downtown Seattle. She lives in the urban area many people call the International District.

In the International District, there are people from all over the world, including Japan and China. Near her home, Susan shops with her mother for rice and spices from Asia that they use to make traditional Japanese meals. Many of these meals include rice and vegetables.

When Susan is at home, she speaks Japanese with her parents and her grandmother. At school, Susan speaks English like the rest of her classmates. Susan enjoys playing with friends and taking care of her family's garden. One of her favorite places to visit is the Japanese Garden in Seattle. It reminds her of all the cherry trees she saw on her last visit to Japan. In Japan, people celebrate when the cherry trees bloom.

Enjoying a Japanese garden

Charlie enjoys seeing other Comanches wearing traditional dress at a powwow in New Mexico.

Charlie From Comanche Nation

Charlie lives in the Southwest region of the United States. Charlie's family are members of the Comanche Nation. His ancestors have lived on the same land for hundreds of years.

Charlie and his family attend gatherings called **powwows**. At the powwows, Charlie and his family sing and dance. They meet with other American Indians to celebrate their cultures.

Manuel From Chicago, Illinois

Manuel is from Chicago, Illinois, a city in the Midwest region of the United States. Many people from Mexico, Central America, and South America have settled in his neighborhood. In Manuel's community, most people speak Spanish at home.

Manuel's family came from Mexico to Chicago three years ago. They came to start a better life. Today, Manuel has many relatives in his neighborhood. Each Sunday, they go to a Catholic church because religion is an important part of their culture.

1. ☑ **Reading Check** **Main Idea and Details**
Identify and **underline** characteristics of Manuel's and Charlie's cultural heritage.

Sam From Long Island, New York

Sam lives on a farm on Long Island in the Northeast region of the United States. Sam's ancestors came from Italy. They traveled by ship and arrived at Ellis Island in the 1880s. Ellis Island was a center where newcomers came before they could enter the United States. His ancestors moved to Long Island to be farmers. Today, Sam lives on the same farm where his ancestors lived.

Since Sam was first learning to speak, his parents taught him to speak Italian. They want him to be able to **converse** with their relatives who still live in Italy. They also sing many Italian songs that his parents learned when they were young.

Eating together is important to Sam's family. On the weekends, they gather in the middle of the day to eat a large meal. Sam's grandmother cooks many different Italian foods. Sam's favorite is ravioli! Sam loves to help his grandmother make and arrange the noodles.

Sam helps his father sell their crops at the local farmers' market.

Academic Vocabulary

converse • *v.*, to talk back and forth

2. ☑ **Reading Check** **Compare and Contrast** **Explain** how Sam's and Charlie's cultures are similar and different.

_____

_____

_____

_____

_____

_____

Abby likes to read different types of books at the library.

Abby From Atlanta, Georgia

Abby lives in Atlanta in the Southeast region of the United States. Atlanta is the largest city in Georgia. It is also a city with great diversity.

Abby is a Black American. Her ancestors were brought to Georgia from West Africa. They were forced to work on large farms called plantations with no pay. After the American Civil War, her ancestors were set free and they began to farm their own **property**.

Today, Abby's father works in the public library. He helps people learn about the history of the city and the history of Black Americans. When Abby's father was young, his family began to celebrate Kwanzaa. Today, Abby's family has continued this tradition. During Kwanzaa, Abby likes to discuss the seven symbols and values that are part of the celebration.

3. ☑ **Reading Check Compare** Abby's celebration of Kwanzaa with Charlie's celebration at a powwow. How are they the same?

_____

_____

_____

_____

Academic Vocabulary

property • *n.*, a piece of land owned by someone

✔ Lesson 6 Check

4. **Compare and Contrast Analyze** the information in this lesson about Manuel and Susan. Fill in the Venn diagram to compare and contrast their cultures.

Manuel's Mexican Culture   **Susan's Japanese Culture**

Both

5. **Identify** reasons people might choose to form diverse communities.

_____

_____

_____

6. Based on the facts in the lesson, **write** a generalization about the benefits of diversity.

_____

_____

Take Informed Action

When you take informed action, you actively work to solve a problem. For example, your community might have statues that only honor one culture. You can take action to help solve this problem.

First, gather information about the problem. You can:

• Read newspapers and look at Web sites.

• Talk to others who know about the issue.

Then ask yourself how strongly the issue matters to you.

Next, you can take action to help solve a problem. Here are some ways:

• Write a letter to a newspaper and make signs.

• Ask others to sign a petition and to send messages to decision makers.

• Participate in meetings about the problem.

• Volunteer to help solve the problem directly.

Please sign our petition.

Let's build a house for people in our community!

INTERACTIVITY

Review and practice what you learned about taking informed action.

1. Read the information in the box. Then answer the questions.

> Some people think they do not know enough about your community's cultures. They want to solve the problem.

   How might you find out more information about the problem?

   _____

2. The community thinks a cultural museum might help solve the problem. What can you do to help get the museum built?

   _____

   _____

3. What effect do you think your help might have?

   _____

   _____

   _____

I have a question to ask.

Signs can send a powerful message.

HONOR ALL OUR HEROES

Marian Anderson
Entertainer

Quality:
Commitment

Marian Anderson was a woman with an outstanding singing voice. She was committed to being the best singer that she could be. Anderson made it her goal to overcome obstacles such as poverty and discrimination. In this way, she served as a model for Black Americans striving for equal rights.

In 1939, Anderson was not allowed to perform at Constitution Hall in Washington, D.C. The group called Daughters of the American Revolution (DAR) said no to her because of the color of her skin. Many people were upset. One such person was First Lady Eleanor Roosevelt. She invited Anderson to sing at the Lincoln Memorial. Thousands of fans showed up in support. Many more tuned in on the radio.

Find Out More

1. Why was it important that so many people attended Anderson's concert at the Lincoln Memorial? Talk with a partner about your answer.

_____

_____

_____

2. Research to find out at least two awards that Marian Anderson received. Write their names.

_____

_____

_____

Use these graphics to review some of the key terms, people, and ideas from this chapter.

Kinds of Communities
- urban
- rural
- suburban

Parts of a Community
- laws
- people
- buildings
- things to do

Cultures and Art
- songs and poems
- stories
- art
- dance

Celebrating Our Community

¡Hola!

People and Cultures
- languages and religions
- cultural regions
- adapting to climates

Our Nation's Diversity
- ancestors
- cultural diversity
- acceptance and respect

Celebrations
- traditions
- leaders
- freedom
- harvests

GAMES

Play the vocabulary game.

Vocabulary and Key Ideas

1. Draw a line from each term to its correct definition.

urban   a way of enjoying yourself

ethnic   a place where people live, work,
group   and have fun together

recreation   people who share the same
                              language, culture, and way of life

ancestor   describes a large city

anthem   a relative who lived long ago

community   a song of loyalty to a nation

2. **Identify** and **contrast** things you could find in a home in a hot region and a home in a cold region.

_____

_____

_____

3. **Describe** Fill in the circle next to the best answer. What is one way people in communities meet their need for laws?

   (A) highways

   (B) local government

   (C) schools

   (D) local newspapers

Critical Thinking and Writing

4. **Contrast** How are the books of Laura Ingalls Wilder and Patricia McKissack different?

5. **Cause and Effect** What led to the growth of suburban communities? Why have they become more popular?

6. **Identify** What is an example of a tradition that is part of America's cultural heritage?

7. **Revisit the Big Question** What are three ways that people share their culture with others?

8. **Writing Workshop: Write Informative Text** On a separate sheet of paper, identify the type of community you live in. Write about the people in your community who work to make it a better place to live. Explain why these people are important to your community.

Analyze Primary Sources

We all should know that diversity makes for a rich tapestry, and we must understand that all the threads of the tapestry are equal in value no matter their color; equal in importance no matter their texture.

—Maya Angelou, "Rainbow in the Cloud: The Wisdom and Spirit of Maya Angelou," 2014

9. A tapestry is a cloth with different colorful designs or pictures. What do you think Maya Angelou meant when she wrote "diversity makes for a rich tapestry"?

_____

_____

_____

_____

Take Informed Action

10. When citizens take informed action, how are they contributing to their community? What is one way you can take informed action to contribute to your community?

_____

_____

_____

_____

_____

_____

_____

Quest Findings

⏺ **INTERACTIVITY**

Complete the activities to get started on your advertisement.

Create Your Advertisement

You have read the lessons in this chapter, and now you are ready to create your advertisement. It can be a print ad or a video ad. Remember that your goal is to tell people about all the wonderful things your community has to offer.

1 Prepare to Write

Decide on three reasons why people like to live in your community. Make a few notes about each reason. Consider the type of community, its cultures and arts, and its forms of recreation, celebrations, or other events.

3 Share With a Partner

Trade advertisements with a partner. Check that your partner's ad has both text and pictures that tell about the community. Share ideas to make the ad better.

2 Create Your Advertisement

Use your notes and write a short ad in which you tell others what your community has to offer. Include pictures related to your community, its cultures, arts, and events.

4 Present Your Ad

Present your ad to your classmates. Make sure you look at your audience and show them the pictures about your community. If your ad is a video, ask an adult to help you film it beforehand using a camera.

The Declaration of Independence

In Congress, July 4, 1776
The Unanimous Declaration of the Thirteen
United States of America

The first part of the Declaration of Independence is called the Preamble. A preamble is an introduction, or the part that comes before the main message. The Preamble states why the Declaration was written.

When in the Course of human events it becomes necessary for one people to dissolve the political bands which have connected them with another, and to assume among the powers of the earth, the separate and equal station to which the Laws of nature and of nature's God entitle them, a decent respect to the opinions of mankind requires that they should declare the causes which impel them to the separation.

The second paragraph lists the basic rights that all people should have. The founders called these **unalienable** rights, meaning that these rights cannot be taken or given away. If a government cannot protect these rights, the people must change the government or create a new one.

We hold these truths to be self-evident, that all men are created equal, that they are endowed by their Creator with certain unalienable Rights, that among these are Life, Liberty and the Pursuit of Happiness. That to secure these rights, Governments are instituted among Men, deriving their just powers from the consent of the governed; That whenever any Form of Government becomes destructive of these ends it is the Right of the People to alter or to abolish it, and to institute new Government, laying its foundation on such principles and organizing its powers in such form, as to them shall seem most likely to effect their Safety and Happiness. Prudence, indeed, will dictate that Governments long established should not be changed for light and transient causes; and accordingly all experience hath shown, that mankind are more disposed to suffer, while evils are sufferable, than to right themselves by abolishing the forms to which they are accustomed. But when a long train of abuses and usurpations, pursuing invariably the same Object evinces a design to reduce them under absolute Despotism, it is their right, it is their duty, to throw off such Government, and to provide new Guards for their future security.

1. According to the Declaration, what are three "unalienable rights"? Circle these words in the text.

Such has been the patient sufferance of these Colonies; and such is now the necessity which constrains them to alter their former Systems of Government. The history of the present King of Great Britain is a history of repeated injuries and usurpations, all having in direct object the establishment of an absolute Tyranny over these States. To prove this, let Facts be submitted to a candid world.

The third paragraph introduces the List of Grievances. Each part of this list begins with the words, "He has…." These words refer to King George III's actions in the colonies. To prove that the king had abused his power over the colonies, this list of 27 complaints described how the British government and the king had treated the colonists.

He has refused his Assent to Laws, the most wholesome and necessary for the public good.

He has forbidden his Governors to pass Laws of immediate and pressing importance, unless suspended in their operation till his

Assent should be obtained; and when so suspended, he has utterly neglected to attend to them.

He has refused to pass other Laws for the accommodation of large districts of people, unless those people would relinquish the right of Representation in the Legislature, a right inestimable to them and formidable to tyrants only.

He has called together legislative bodies at places unusual, uncomfortable, and distant from the depository of their Public Records, for the sole purpose of fatiguing them into compliance with his measures.

He has dissolved Representative Houses repeatedly, for opposing with manly firmness his invasions on the rights of the people.

He has refused for a long time, after such dissolutions, to cause others to be elected; whereby the Legislative powers, incapable of Annihilation, have returned to the People at large for their exercise; the State remaining in the mean time exposed to all the dangers of invasions from without, and convulsions within.

He has endeavored to prevent the population of these States; for that purpose obstructing the Laws for Naturalization of Foreigners; refusing to pass others to encourage their migration hither, and raising the conditions of new Appropriations of Lands.

He has obstructed the Administration of Justice, by refusing his Assent to Laws for establishing Judiciary powers.

He has made Judges dependent on his Will alone for the tenure of their offices, and the amount and payment of their salaries.

He has erected a multitude of New Offices, and sent hither swarms of Officers to harass our people and eat out their substance.

He has kept among us in time of peace, Standing Armies, without the Consent of our legislatures.

He has affected to render the Military independent of, and superior to, the Civil Power.

He has combined with others to subject us to a jurisdiction foreign to our constitutions, and unacknowledged by our laws; giving his Assent to their Acts of pretended Legislation:

For quartering large bodies of armed troops among us;

For protecting them, by a mock Trial, from punishment for any Murders which they should commit on the Inhabitants of these States;

In the List of Grievances, the colonists complain that they have no say in choosing the laws that govern them. They say that King George III is not concerned about their safety and happiness. They list the times when the king denied them the right to representation. The colonists also state that the king has interfered with judges, with the court system, and with foreigners who want to become citizens.

2. There are many words in the Declaration that may be unfamiliar to you. Circle three words you do not know. Look the words up in the dictionary. Write one word and its meaning on the lines below.

_____

_____

_____

_____

_____

_____

_____

This page continues the colonists' long List of Grievances.

3. In your own words, briefly sum up three grievances.

_____

_____

_____

4. Match each word from the Declaration with its meaning. Use a dictionary if you need help with a word.

abolishing   tried to achieve

plundered   changing

suspending   doing away with

altering   stopping for a time

endeavored   robbed

Statement of Independence
After listing their many grievances, the signers begin their statement of independence. Because the king has refused to correct the problems, he is an unfair ruler. Therefore, he is not fit to rule the free people of America.

For cutting off our Trade with all parts of the world;

For imposing Taxes on us without our Consent;

For depriving us, in many cases, of the benefits of Trial by Jury;

For transporting us beyond Seas to be tried for pretended offenses;

For abolishing the free System of English Laws in a neighboring Province, establishing therein an Arbitrary government, and enlarging its Boundaries so as to render it at once an example and fit instrument for introducing the same absolute rule into these Colonies;

For taking away our Charters, abolishing our most valuable Laws, and altering fundamentally the Forms of our Governments;

For suspending our own Legislatures, and declaring themselves invested with Power to legislate for us in all cases whatsoever.

He has abdicated Government here, by declaring us out of his Protection, and waging War against us.

He has plundered our seas, ravaged our Coasts, burned our towns, and destroyed the lives of our people.

He is at this time transporting large Armies of foreign mercenaries to complete the works of death, desolation and tyranny, already begun with circumstances of Cruelty and perfidy scarcely paralleled in the most barbarous ages, and totally unworthy the Head of a civilized nation.

He has constrained our fellow Citizens taken Captive on the high Seas to bear Arms against their Country, to become the executioners of their friends and Brethren, or to fall themselves by their Hands.

He has excited domestic insurrections amongst us, and has endeavored to bring on the inhabitants of our frontiers the merciless Indian Savages whose known rule of warfare, is an undistinguished destruction of all ages, sexes, and conditions.

In every stage of these Oppressions We have Petitioned for Redress in the most humble terms. Our repeated Petitions have been answered only by repeated injury. A Prince, whose character is thus marked by every act which may define a Tyrant, is unfit to be the ruler of a free People.

Nor have We been wanting in attentions to our British brethren. We have warned them from time to time of attempts by their legislature to extend an unwarrantable jurisdiction over us. We have reminded them of the circumstances of our emigration and settlement here. We have appealed to their native justice and magnanimity, and we have conjured them by the ties of our common kindred to disavow these usurpations, which, would inevitably interrupt our connections and correspondence. They too have been deaf to the voice of justice and of consanguinity. We must, therefore, acquiesce in the necessity, which denounces our Separation, and hold them, as we hold the rest of mankind, Enemies in War, in Peace Friends.

We, therefore, the Representatives of the United States of America, in General Congress, Assembled, appealing to the Supreme Judge of the world for the rectitude of our intentions, do, in the Name, and by the Authority of the good People of these Colonies, solemnly publish and declare, That these United Colonies are, and of right ought to be Free and Independent States; that they are Absolved from all Allegiance to the British Crown, and that all political connection between them and the State of Great Britain, is and ought to be totally dissolved, and that as Free and Independent States, they have full Power to levy War, conclude Peace, contract Alliances, establish Commerce, and to do all other Acts and Things which Independent States may of right do. And for the support of this Declaration, with a firm reliance on the protection of Divine Providence, we mutually pledge to each other our Lives, our Fortunes, and our sacred Honor.

New Hampshire:
Josiah Bartlett
William Whipple
Matthew Thornton

Massachusetts Bay:
John Hancock
Samuel Adams
John Adams
Robert Treat Paine
Elbridge Gerry

Rhode Island:
Stephan Hopkins
William Ellery

Connecticut:
Roger Sherman
Samuel Huntington
William Williams
Oliver Wolcott

New York:
William Floyd
Philip Livingston
Francis Lewis
Lewis Morris

New Jersey:
Richard Stockton
John Witherspoon
Francis Hopkinson
John Hart
Abraham Clark

Delaware:
Caesar Rodney
George Read
Thomas M'Kean

Maryland:
Samuel Chase
William Paca
Thomas Stone
Charles Carroll of
    Carrollton

Virginia:
George Wythe
Richard Henry Lee
Thomas Jefferson
Benjamin Harrison
Thomas Nelson, Jr.
Francis Lightfoot Lee
Carter Braxton

Pennsylvania:
Robert Morris
Benjamin Rush
Benjamin Franklin
John Morton
George Clymer
James Smith
George Taylor
James Wilson
George Ross

North Carolina:
William Hooper
Joseph Hewes
John Penn

South Carolina:
Edward Rutledge
Thomas Heyward, Jr.
Thomas Lynch, Jr.
Arthur Middleton

Georgia:
Button Gwinnett
Lyman Hall
George Walton

In this paragraph, the signers point out that they have asked the British people for help many times. The colonists hoped the British would listen to them because they have so much in common. The British people, however, paid no attention to their demand for justice. This is another reason for why the colonies must break away from Great Britain.

In the last paragraph, the members of the Continental Congress declare that the thirteen colonies are no longer colonies. They are now a free nation with no ties to Great Britain. The United States now has all the powers of other independent countries.

5. List three powers that the signers claim the new nation now has.

_____

_____

_____

_____

_____

6. The signers promised to support the Declaration of Independence and each other with their lives, their fortunes, and their honor. On a separate sheet of paper, tell what you think this means. Then explain why it was a brave thing to do.

United States Constitution

This **Preamble** gives the reasons for writing and having a Constitution. The Constitution will form a stronger and more united nation. It will lead to peace, justice, and liberty and will defend American citizens. Finally, it will improve the lives of people.

Section 1. Congress
The legislative branch of government makes the country's laws. Called the Congress, it has two parts, or houses: the House of Representatives and the Senate.

Section 2. The House of Representatives
Members of the House of Representatives are elected every two years. Representatives must be 25 years old and United States citizens. They must also live in the states that elect them.

The number of Representatives for each state is based on the population, or number of people who live there.

1. Why do some states have more Representatives in Congress than other states?

_____

_____

_____

_____

Over the years, the Constitution has been altered, or changed. These altered parts are shown here in gray type.

PREAMBLE

We the People of the United States, in Order to form a more perfect Union, establish Justice, insure domestic Tranquility, provide for the common defense, promote the general Welfare, and secure the Blessings of Liberty to ourselves and our Posterity, do ordain and establish this Constitution for the United States of America.

ARTICLE I

Section 1.
All legislative Powers herein granted shall be vested in a Congress of the United States, which shall consist of a Senate and House of Representatives.

Section 2.
1. The House of Representatives shall be composed of Members chosen every second Year by the People of the several States, and the Electors in each State shall have the Qualifications requisite for Electors of the most numerous Branch of the State Legislature.

2. No Person shall be a Representative who shall not have attained to the age of twenty-five Years, and been seven Years a Citizen of the United States, and who shall not, when elected, be an Inhabitant of that State in which he shall be chosen.

3. Representatives and direct Taxes shall be apportioned among the several States which may be included within this Union, according to their respective Numbers, which shall be determined by adding to the whole Number of free Persons, including those bound to Service for a Term of Years and excluding Indians not taxed, three fifths of all other Persons. The actual Enumeration shall be made within three Years after the first Meeting of the Congress of the United States, and within every subsequent Term of ten Years, in such Manner as they shall by Law direct. The Number of Representatives shall not exceed one for every thirty Thousand, but each State shall have at Least one Representative; and, until such enumeration shall be made, the State of New Hampshire shall be entitled to choose three, Massachusetts eight, Rhode Island and Providence Plantations one, Connecticut five, New York six, New Jersey four, Pennsylvania eight, Delaware one, Maryland six, Virginia ten, North Carolina five, South Carolina five, and Georgia three.

4. When vacancies happen in the Representation from any State, the Executive Authority thereof shall issue Writs of Election to fill such Vacancies.
5. The House of Representatives shall choose their Speaker and other Officers; and shall have the sole Power of Impeachment.

Section 3.

1. The Senate of the United States shall be composed of two Senators from each State chosen by the Legislature thereof for six Years; and each Senator shall have one Vote.
2. Immediately after they shall be assembled in Consequences of the first Election, they shall be divided, as equally as may be, into three Classes. The Seats of the Senators of the first Class shall be vacated at the Expiration of the second Year; of the second Class, at the Expiration of the fourth Year; and of the third Class, at the Expiration of the sixth Year; so that one-third may be chosen every second Year; and if Vacancies happen by Resignation, or otherwise, during the Recess of the Legislature of any State, the Executive thereof may make temporary Appointments until the next Meeting of the Legislature, which shall then fill such Vacancies.
3. No Person shall be a Senator who shall not have attained to the Age of thirty Years, and been nine Years a Citizen of the United States, and who shall not, when elected, be an Inhabitant of that State for which he shall be chosen.
4. The Vice President of the United States shall be President of the Senate but shall have no Vote, unless they be equally divided.
5. The Senate shall choose their other Officers, and also a President pro tempore, in the Absence of the Vice President, or when he shall exercise the Office of President of the United States.
6. The Senate shall have the sole Power to try all Impeachments. When sitting for that Purpose, they shall be on Oath or Affirmation. When the President of the United States is tried, the Chief Justice shall preside: And no Person shall be convicted without the Concurrence of two thirds of the Members present.
7. Judgment in Cases of Impeachment shall not extend further than to removal from Office, and disqualification to hold and enjoy any Office of honor, Trust, or Profit under the United States: but the Party convicted shall nevertheless be liable and subject to Indictment, Trial, Judgment and Punishment, according to Law.

A state governor calls a special election to fill an empty seat in the House of Representatives.

Members of the House of Representatives choose their own leaders. They also have the power to impeach, or accuse, government officials of crimes.

Section 3. Senate
Each state has two Senators. A Senator serves a six-year term.

At first, each state legislature elected its two Senators. The Seventeenth Amendment changed that. Today, the voters of each state elect their Senators.

Senators must be 30 years old and United States citizens. They must also live in the states they represent.

2. How is the length of a Senator's term different from a Representative's term?

_____

_____

The Vice President is the officer in charge of the Senate but only votes to break a tie. When the Vice President is absent, a temporary leader (President Pro Tempore) leads the Senate.

The Senate holds impeachment trials. When the President is impeached, the Chief Justice of the Supreme Court is the judge. A two-thirds vote is needed to convict. Once convicted, an official can be removed from office. Other courts of law can impose other punishments.

Section 4. Elections and Meetings of Congress

The state legislatures determine the times, places, and method of holding elections for senators and representatives.

Section 5. Rules for Congress

The Senate and House of Representatives judge the fairness of the elections and the qualifications of its own members. At least half of the members must be present to do business. Each house may determine the rules of its proceedings and punish its member for disorderly behavior. Each house of Congress shall keep a record of its proceedings and from time to time publish the record.

3. Why is it important for Congress to publish a record of what they do?

_____

_____

_____

_____

Section 6. Rights and Restrictions of Members of Congress

The Senators and Representatives shall receive payment for their services to be paid out of the Treasury of the United States. Members of Congress cannot be arrested during their attendance at the session of Congress, except for a very serious crime, and they cannot be arrested for anything they say in Congress. No person can have a government job while serving as a member of Congress.

Section 4.

1. The Times, Places and Manner of holding Elections for Senators and Representatives, shall be prescribed in each State by the Legislature thereof; but the Congress may at any time by law make or alter such Regulations, except as to the Places of choosing Senators.

2. The Congress shall assemble at least once in every Year, and such Meeting shall be on the first Monday in December, unless they shall by Law appoint a different Day.

Section 5.

1. Each House shall be the Judge of the Elections, Returns and Qualifications of its own Members, and a Majority of each shall constitute a Quorum to do Business; but a smaller Number may adjourn from day to day, and may be authorized to compel the Attendance of absent Members, in such Manner, and under such Penalties, as each House may provide.

2. Each House may determine the Rules of its Proceedings, punish its Members for disorderly Behavior, and, with the Concurrence of two thirds, expel a Member.

3. Each House shall keep a Journal of its Proceedings, and from time to time publish the same, excepting such Parts as may in their Judgment require Secrecy; and the Yeas and Nays of the Members of either House on any question shall, at the Desire of one fifth of those Present, be entered on the Journal.

4. Neither House, during the Session of Congress, shall, without the Consent of the other, adjourn for more than three days, nor to any other Place than that in which the two Houses shall be sitting.

Section 6.

1. The Senators and Representatives shall receive a Compensation for their Services, to be ascertained by Law, and paid out of the Treasury of the United States. They shall in all Cases, except Treason, Felony, and Breach of the Peace, be privileged from Arrest during their Attendance at the Session of their respective Houses, and in going to and returning from the same; and for any Speech or Debate in either House, they shall not be questioned in any other Place.

2. No Senator or Representative shall, during the Time for which he was elected, be appointed to any civil Office under the Authority of the United States, which shall have been created, or the Emoluments whereof shall have been increased during such time; and no Person holding any Office under the United States, shall be a Member of either House during his Continuance in Office.

Section 7.

1. All Bills for raising Revenue shall originate in the House of Representatives; but the Senate may propose or concur with amendments as on other Bills.

2. Every Bill which shall have passed the House of Representatives and the Senate, shall, before it become a law, be presented to the President of the United States: If he approve, he shall sign it, but if not he shall return it, with his Objections to that House in which it shall have originated, who shall enter the Objections at large on their Journal, and proceed to reconsider it. If after such Reconsideration two thirds of the House shall agree to pass the Bill, it shall be sent, together with the Objections, to the other House, by which it shall likewise be reconsidered, and if approved by two thirds of that House, it shall become a Law. But in all such Cases the Votes of both Houses shall be determined by Yeas and Nays, and the Names of the Persons voting for and against the Bill shall be entered on the Journal of each House respectively. If any Bill shall not be returned by the President within ten Days (Sunday excepted) after it shall have been presented to him, the Same shall be a law, in like Manner as if he had signed it, unless the Congress by their Adjournment, prevent its Return, in which Case it shall not be a Law.

3. Every Order, Resolution, or Vote to which the Concurrence of the Senate and House of Representatives may be necessary (except on a question of adjournment) shall be presented to the President of the United States; and before the Same shall take Effect, shall be approved by him, or, being disapproved by him, shall be repassed by two thirds of the Senate and House of Representatives, according to the Rules and Limitations prescribed in the Case of a Bill.

Section 8.

The Congress shall have Power

1. To lay and collect Taxes, Duties, Imposts and Excises to pay the Debts and provide for the common Defense and general Welfare of the United States; but all Duties, Imposts and Excises, shall be uniform throughout the United States;

2. To borrow Money on the credit of the United States;

3. To regulate Commerce with foreign Nations, and among the several States, and with the Indian Tribes;

4. To establish an uniform Rule of Naturalization, and uniform Laws on the subject of Bankruptcies throughout the United States;

Section 7. How Laws are Made

All bills for raising money shall begin in the House of Representatives. The Senate may suggest or agree with amendments to these tax bills, as with other bills.

Every bill which has passed the House of Representatives and the Senate must be presented to the President of the United States before it becomes a law. If the President approves of the bill, the President shall sign it. If the President does not approve, then the bill may be vetoed. The President then sends it back to the house in which it began, with an explanation of the objections. That house writes the objections on their record and begins to reconsider it. If two thirds of each house agrees to pass the bill, it shall become a law. If any bill is neither signed nor vetoed by the President within ten days, (except for Sundays) after it has been sent to the President, the bill shall be a law. If Congress adjourns before ten days have passed, the bill does not become a law.

Section 8. Powers of Congress

Among the powers of Congress listed in Section 8 are:

- establish and collect taxes on imported and exported goods and on goods sold within the country. Congress also shall pay the debts and provide for the defense and general welfare of the United States. All federal taxes shall be the same throughout the United States.
- borrow money on the credit of the United States;
- make laws about trade with other countries, among the states, and with the American Indian tribes;
- establish one procedure by which a person from another country can become a legal citizen of the United States;
- protect the works of scientists, artists, authors, and inventors;
- create federal courts lower than the Supreme Court;

- declare war;
- establish and support an army and navy;
- organize and train a National Guard and call them up in times of emergency;
- govern the capital and military sites of the United States; and
- make all laws necessary to carry out the powers of Congress.

4. The last clause of Section 8 is called "the elastic clause" because it stretches the power of Congress. Why do you think it was added to the Constitution?

_____

_____

_____

_____

_____

_____

_____

5. To coin Money, regulate the Value thereof, and of foreign Coin, and fix the Standard of Weights and Measures;

6. To provide for the Punishment of counterfeiting the Securities and current Coin of the United States;

7. To establish Post Offices and post Roads;

8. To promote the Progress of Science and useful Arts, by securing, for limited Times to Authors and Inventors the exclusive Right to their respective Writings and Discoveries;

9. To constitute Tribunals inferior to the supreme Court;

10. To define and punish Piracies and Felonies committed on the high Seas, and Offences against the Law of nations;

11. To declare War, grant Letters of Marque and Reprisal, and make Rules concerning Captures on Land and Water;

12. To raise and support Armies; but no Appropriation of Money to that Use shall be for a longer Term than two Years;

13. To provide and maintain a Navy;

14. To make Rules for the Government and Regulation of the land and naval Forces;

15. To provide for calling forth the Militia to execute the Laws of the Union, suppress Insurrections and repel Invasions;

16. To provide for organizing, arming, and disciplining the Militia, and for governing such Part of them as may be employed in the Service of the United States, reserving to the States respectively the Appointment of the Officers, and the Authority of training the Militia according to the discipline prescribed by Congress;

17. To exercise exclusive Legislation in all Cases whatsoever, over such District (not exceeding ten Miles square) as may, by Cession of Particular States, and the Acceptance of Congress, become the Seat of the Government of the United States, and to exercise like Authority over all Places purchased by the Consent of the Legislature of the State in which the Same shall be, for the Erection of Forts, Magazines, Arsenals, Dockyards and other needful Buildings;—And

18. To make all Laws which shall be necessary and proper for carrying into Execution the foregoing Powers and all other Powers vested by this Constitution in the Government of the United States, or in any Department or Officer thereof.

Section 9.

1. The Migration or Importation of such Persons as any of the States now existing shall think proper to admit, shall not be prohibited by the Congress prior to the Year one thousand eight hundred and eight, but a Tax or duty may be imposed on such Importation, not exceeding ten dollars for each Person.

2. The Privilege of the Writ of Habeas Corpus shall not be suspended, unless when in Cases of Rebellion or Invasion the public safety may require it.

3. No Bill of Attainder or ex post facto Law shall be passed.

4. No Capitation, or other direct, Tax shall be laid, unless in Proportion to the Census of Enumeration herein before directed to be taken.

5. No Tax or Duty shall be laid on Articles exported from any State.

6. No Preference shall be given by any Regulation of Commerce or Revenue to the Ports of one State over those of another: nor shall Vessels bound to, or from, one State, be obliged to enter, clear or pay Duties in another.

7. No Money shall be drawn from the Treasury, but in Consequence of Appropriations made by Law; and a regular Statement and Account of the Receipts and Expenditures of all public Money shall be published from time to time.

8. No Title of Nobility shall be granted by the United States: And no Person holding any Office of Profit or Trust under them, shall, without the Consent of the Congress, accept of any present, Emolument, Office, or Title, of any kind whatever, from any King, Prince, or foreign State.

Section 10.

1. No State shall enter into any Treaty, Alliance, or Confederation; grant Letters of Marque and Reprisal; coin Money; emit Bills of Credit; make any Thing but gold and silver Coin a Tender in Payment of Debts; pass any Bill of Attainder, ex post facto Law, or Law impairing the Obligation of Contracts, or grant any Title of Nobility.

2. No State shall, without the Consent of the Congress, lay any Imposts or Duties on Imports or Exports, except what may be absolutely necessary for executing its inspection Laws; and the net Produce of all Duties and Imposts, laid by any State on Imports or Exports, shall be for the Use of the Treasury of the United States; and all such Laws shall be subject to the Revision and Control of the Congress.

Section 9: Powers Denied to Congress

Congress cannot

- stop slaves from being brought into the United States until 1808;
- arrest and jail people without charging them with a crime, except during an emergency;
- punish a person without a trial; punish a person for something that was not a crime when he or she did it;
- pass a direct tax, such as an income tax, unless it is in proportion to the population;
- tax goods sent out of a state;
- give the seaports of one state an advantage over another state's ports; let one state tax the ships of another state;
- spend money without passing a law to make it legal; spend money without keeping good records;
- give titles, such as king and queen, to anyone; allow federal workers to accept gifts or titles from foreign governments.

5. Why do you think the writers included the last clause of Section 9?

_____

_____

_____

_____

_____

_____

Section 10: Powers Denied to the States

After listing what Congress is not allowed to do, the Constitution tells what powers are denied to the states.

State governments do not have the power to
- make treaties with foreign countries; print money; do anything that Section 9 of the Constitution says the federal government cannot;
- tax goods sent into or out of a state unless Congress agrees;
- keep armed forces or go to war; make agreements with other states or foreign governments unless Congress agrees.

6. What problems might arise if one state went to war with a foreign country?

_____

_____

_____

_____

_____

Article 2 describes the executive branch.

Section 1. Office of President and Vice President

The President has power to execute, or carry out, the laws of the United States.

Electors from each state choose the President. Today, these electors are called the Electoral College and are chosen by the voters.

Before 1804, the person with the most electoral votes became President. The person with the next-highest number became Vice President. The Twelfth Amendment changed this way of electing Presidents.

3. No State shall, without the Consent of Congress, lay any Duty of Tonnage, keep Troops, or Ships of War in time of Peace, enter into any Agreement or Compact with another State, or with a foreign Power, or engage in War, unless actually invaded, or in such imminent Danger as will not admit of delay.

ARTICLE II

Section 1.

1. The executive Power shall be vested in a President of the United States of America. He shall hold his Office during the Term of four Years, and, together with the Vice President, chosen for the same Term, be elected as follows:

2. Each State shall appoint, in such Manner as the Legislature thereof may direct, a Number of Electors, equal to the whole Number of Senators and Representatives to which the State may be entitled in the Congress: but no Senator or Representative, or Person holding an Office of Trust or Profit, under the United States, shall be appointed an Elector.

3. The Electors shall meet in their respective States, and vote by Ballot for two Persons, of whom one at least shall not be an Inhabitant of the same State with themselves. And they shall make a List of all the Persons voted for, and of the Number of Votes for each; which List they shall sign and certify, and transmit sealed to the Seat of the Government of the United States, directed to the President of the Senate. The President of the Senate shall, in the Presence of the Senate and House of Representatives, open all the Certificates, and the Votes shall then be counted. The Person having the greatest Number of Votes shall be the President, if such Number be a majority of the whole Number of Electors appointed; and if there be more than one who have such Majority, and have an equal Number of Votes, then, the House of Representatives shall immediately choose by Ballot one of them for President; and if no Person have a Majority, then from the five highest on the List the said House shall in like Manner choose the President. But in choosing the President, the Votes shall be taken by States, the Representatives from each State having one Vote; a quorum for this Purpose shall consist of a Member or Members from two thirds of the States, and a Majority of all the States shall be necessary to a Choice. In every Case, after the Choice of the President, the Person having the greatest Number of Votes of the Electors shall be the Vice President. But if there should remain two or more who have equal Votes, the Senate shall choose from them by Ballot the Vice President.

4. The Congress may determine the Time of choosing the Electors, and the Day on which they shall give their Votes; which Day shall be the same throughout the United States.

5. No Person except a natural born Citizen, or a Citizen of the United States, at the time of the Adoption of this Constitution, shall be eligible to the Office of President; neither shall any person be eligible to that Office who shall not have attained to the Age of thirty-five Years, and been fourteen Years a Resident within the United States.

6. In Case of the Removal of the President from Office, or of his Death, Resignation, or Inability to discharge the Powers and Duties of the said Office, the Same shall devolve on the Vice President, and the Congress may by Law provide for the Case of Removal, Death, Resignation or Inability, both of the President and Vice President, declaring what Officer shall then act as President, and such Officer shall act accordingly, until the Disability be removed, or a President shall be elected.

7. The President shall, at stated Times, receive for his Services, a Compensation, which shall neither be increased nor diminished during the Period for which he shall have been elected, and he shall not receive within that Period any other Emolument from the United States, or any of them.

8. Before he enter on the Execution of his Office, he shall take the following Oath or Affirmation: "I do solemnly swear (or affirm) that I will faithfully execute the Office of President of the United States, and will to the best of my Ability, preserve, protect and defend the Constitution of the United States."

Section 2.

1. The President shall be Commander in Chief of the Army and Navy of the United States, and of the Militia of the several States, when called into the actual Service of the United States; he may require the Opinion, in writing, of the principal Officer in each of the executive Departments, upon any Subject relating to the Duties of their respective Offices, and he shall have Power to Grant Reprieves and Pardons for Offences against the United States, except in Cases of Impeachment.

Congress decides when electors are chosen and when they vote for President. Americans now vote for the electors on Election Day, the Tuesday after the first Monday in November.

To become President, a person must be born in the United States and be a citizen. Presidents also have to be at least 35 years old and have lived in the United States for at least 14 years.

If a President dies or leaves office for any reason, the Vice President becomes President. If there is no Vice President, Congress decides on the next President. (In 1967, the Twenty-fifth Amendment changed how these offices are filled.)

7. Why is it important to agree on how to replace the President or Vice President if one should die or leave office?

_____

_____

_____

_____

The President's salary cannot be raised or lowered while he is in office. The President cannot accept other money or gifts while in office. Before taking office, the President must swear to preserve, protect, and defend the Constitution.

Section 2. Powers of the President

The President controls the armed forces and National Guard, and can ask for advice of those who run government departments. (These advisers to the President are members of the Cabinet.) The President can pardon, or free, people convicted of federal crimes.

The President can make treaties, but two thirds of the Senate must approve them. The President, with Senate approval, can name Supreme Court judges, ambassadors, and other important officials.

8. What is the Senate's ability to approve or reject treaties an example of?

_____

_____

Section 3. Duties of the President

From time to time, the President must talk to Congress about the condition of the nation. (Today, we call this speech the State of the Union address. It is given once a year in late January.) In an emergency, the President can call on Congress to meet. The President also meets with foreign leaders, makes sure the nation's laws are carried out, and signs the orders of military officers.

Section 4. Removal From Office

The President, Vice President, and other high officials can be impeached. If proved guilty, they are removed from office.

2. He shall have Power, by and with the Advice and Consent of the Senate, to make Treaties, provided two thirds of the Senators present concur; and he shall nominate, and by and with the Advice and Consent of the Senate, shall appoint Ambassadors, other public Ministers and Consuls, Judges of the supreme Court, and all other Officers of the United States, whose Appointments are not herein otherwise provided for, and which shall be established by Law: but the Congress may by Law vest the Appointment of such inferior Officers, as they think proper, in the President alone, in the Courts of Law, or in the Heads of Departments.

3. The President shall have Power to fill up all Vacancies that may happen during the Recess of the Senate, by granting Commissions which shall expire at the End of their next Session.

Section 3.

He shall from time to time give to the Congress Information of the State of the Union, and recommend to their Consideration such Measures as he shall judge necessary and expedient; he may, on extraordinary Occasions, convene both Houses, or either of them, and in Case of Disagreement between them, with Respect to the Time of Adjournment, he may adjourn them to such Time as he shall think proper; he shall receive Ambassadors and other public Ministers; he shall take Care that the Laws be faithfully executed, and shall Commission all the Officers of the United States.

Section 4.

The President, Vice President and all Civil Officers of the United States, shall be removed from Office on Impeachment for and Conviction of, Treason, Bribery, or other high Crimes and Misdemeanors.

ARTICLE III

Article 3 deals with the judicial branch.

Section 1.

The judicial Power of the United States, shall be vested in one supreme Court, and in such inferior Courts as the Congress may from time to time ordain and establish. The Judges, both of the supreme and inferior Courts, shall hold their Offices during good Behavior, and shall, at stated Times, receive for their Services, a Compensation, which shall not be diminished during their Continuance in Office.

Section 1. Federal Courts

The judges of the Supreme Court and other federal courts have the power to make decisions in courts of law. If they act properly, federal judges hold their offices for life.

9. Do you think it's a good idea that federal judges hold their offices for life? Why?

_____

_____

_____

_____

_____

_____

Section 2.

1. The judicial Power shall extend to all Cases, in Law and Equity, arising under this Constitution, the Laws of the United States, and Treaties made, or which shall be made, under their Authority;— to all Cases affecting Ambassadors, other public ministers, and Consuls;— to all Cases of Admiralty and maritime Jurisdiction;— to Controversies to which the United States shall be a Party;— to Controversies between two or more States;— between a State and Citizens of another State;— between Citizens of different States;— between Citizens of the same State claiming Lands under Grants of different States, and between a State, or the Citizens thereof, and foreign States, Citizens, or Subjects.

2. In all Cases affecting Ambassadors, other public Ministers and Consuls, and those in which a State shall be a Party, the supreme Court shall have original Jurisdiction. In all the other Cases before mentioned, the supreme Court shall have appellate Jurisdiction, both as to Law and Fact, with such Exceptions, and under such Regulations as the Congress shall make.

3. The trial of all Crimes, except in Cases of Impeachment, shall be by Jury; and such Trial shall be held in the State where the said Crimes shall have been committed; but when not committed within any State, the Trial shall be at such Place or Places as the Congress may by Law have directed.

Section 2. Powers of Federal Courts

Federal Courts have legal power over
- laws made under the Constitution
- treaties made with foreign nations
- cases occurring at sea
- cases involving the federal government
- cases involving states or citizens of different states
- cases involving foreign citizens or governments

Only the Supreme Court can judge cases involving ambassadors, government officials, or states. Other cases begin in lower courts, but they can be appealed, or reviewed, by the Supreme Court. In criminal cases other than impeachment, trials are held in the state in which the crime took place. A jury decides the case.

Section 3. Treason

Treason is waging war against the United States or helping its enemies. To be found guilty of treason, a person must confess to the crime; or, two people must have seen the crime committed.

10. Name the three branches of federal government described in Articles 1–3.

_____

_____

_____

Congress decides the punishment for a traitor. The traitor's family cannot be punished if innocent.

Article 4 deals with relationships between the states.

Section 1. Recognition by Each State

Each state must respect the laws and court decisions of the other states.

Section 2. Rights of Citizens in Other States

Citizens keep all their rights when visiting other states.

A person charged with a crime who flees to another state must be returned to the state in which the crime took place.

A slave who escapes to another state must be returned to his or her owner. (The Thirteenth Amendment outlawed slavery.)

Section 3. New States

Congress may let new states join the United States. New states cannot be formed from the land of existing states unless Congress approves.

Congress has the power to make laws to govern territories of the United States.

Section 3.

1. Treason against the United States shall consist only in levying War against them, or in adhering to their Enemies, giving them Aid and Comfort. No Person shall be convicted of Treason unless on the Testimony of two Witnesses to the same overt Act, or on Confession in open Court.

2. The Congress shall have Power to declare the Punishment of Treason, but no Attainder of Treason shall work Corruption of Blood, or Forfeiture except during the Life of the Person attainted.

ARTICLE IV

Section 1.

Full Faith and Credit shall be given in each State to the public Acts, Records, and judicial Proceedings of every other State. And the Congress may by general Laws prescribe the Manner in which such Acts, Records and Proceedings shall be proved, and the Effect thereof.

Section 2.

1. The Citizens of each State shall be entitled to all Privileges and Immunities of Citizens in the several States.

2. A Person charged in any State with Treason, Felony, or other Crime, who shall flee from justice, and be found in another State, shall on Demand of the executive Authority of the State from which he fled, be delivered up, to be removed to the State having Jurisdiction of the Crime.

3. No Person held to Service or Labor in one State, under the Laws thereof, escaping into another, shall, in Consequence of any Law or Regulation therein, be discharged from Service or Labor, but shall be delivered up on Claim of the Party to whom such Service or Labor may be due.

Section 3.

1. New States may be admitted by the Congress into this Union; but no new State shall be formed or erected within the Jurisdiction of any other State; nor any State be formed by the Junction of two or more States, or Parts of States, without the Consent of the Legislatures of the States concerned as well as of the Congress.

2. The Congress shall have Power to dispose of and make all needful Rules and Regulations respecting the Territory or other Property belonging to the United States; and nothing in this Constitution shall be so construed as to Prejudice any Claims of the United States, or of any particular State.

Section 4.

The United States shall guarantee to every State in this Union a Republican Form of Government, and shall protect each of them against Invasion; and on Application of the Legislature, or of the Executive (when the Legislature cannot be convened) against domestic Violence.

ARTICLE V

The Congress, whenever two thirds of both Houses shall deem it necessary, shall propose Amendments to this Constitution, or, on the Application of the Legislatures of two thirds of the several States, shall call a Convention for proposing Amendments, which, in either Case, shall be valid to all Intents and Purposes, as Part of this Constitution, when ratified by the Legislatures of three fourths of the several States, or by Conventions in three fourths thereof, as the one or the other Mode of Ratification may be proposed by the Congress; Provided that no Amendment which may be made prior to the Year One thousand eight hundred and eight shall in any Manner affect the first and fourth Clauses in the Ninth section of the first Article; and that no State, without its Consent, shall be deprived of its equal Suffrage in the Senate.

ARTICLE VI

Section 1.

All Debts contracted and Engagements entered into, before the Adoption of this Constitution, shall be as valid against the United States under this Constitution, as under the Confederation.

Section 2.

This Constitution, and the Laws of the United States which shall be made in Pursuance thereof; and all Treaties made, or which shall be made, under the Authority of the United States, shall be the supreme Law of the Land; and the Judges in every State shall be bound thereby, anything in the constitution or Laws of any State to the Contrary notwithstanding.

Section 4. Guarantees to the States
The federal government guarantees that each state has the right to elect its leaders. The federal government will also protect the states from invasion and violent disorders.

11. There were only thirteen states when the Constitution was written. Do you think the framers expected the United States to grow in size? Why?

_____

_____

_____

_____

_____

Article 5 describes the two ways the Constitution can be amended. Two thirds of the Senate and House of Representatives can suggest an amendment, or two thirds of the state legislatures can have a special convention to suggest an amendment. Once an amendment has been suggested, three fourths of the state legislatures or three fourths of the special conventions must approve the amendment.

Article 6 deals with national law and the national debt. The federal government promises to pay all its debts and keep all agreements made under the Articles of Confederation.

The Constitution and federal laws are the highest laws in the land. If state laws disagree with them, the federal laws must be obeyed.

Section 3. Supporting the Constitution

Federal and state officials must promise to support the Constitution. A person's religion cannot disqualify him or her from holding office. Nine of the thirteen states must approve the Constitution for it to become the law of the land.

Article 7 deals with ratifying the Constitution. On September 17, 1787, twelve years after the Declaration of Independence, everyone at the Constitutional Convention agreed that the Constitution was complete.

The delegates to the Constitutional Convention signed their names below the Constitution to show they approved of it.

12. "The power under the Constitution will always be in the people," wrote George Washington in 1787. Explain what you think he meant.

_____

_____

_____

_____

_____

_____

Section 3.

The Senators and Representatives before mentioned, and the Members of the several State legislatures, and all executive and judicial Officers, both of the United States and of the several States, shall be bound by Oath or Affirmation, to support this Constitution; but no religious Test shall ever be required as a Qualification to any Office or public Trust under the United States.

ARTICLE VII

The ratification of the Conventions of nine States, shall be sufficient for the Establishment of this Constitution between the States so ratifying the same.

Done in Convention by the Unanimous Consent of the States present the Seventeenth Day of September in the Year of our Lord one thousand seven hundred and Eighty-seven and of the Independence of the United States of America the twelfth. In witness whereof We have hereunto subscribed our Names.

Attest:
William Jackson,
Secretary
George Washington,
President and Deputy from Virginia

New Hampshire
John Langdon
Nicholas Gilman

Massachusetts
Nathaniel Gorham
Rufus King

Connecticut
William Samuel
   Johnson
Roger Sherman

New York
Alexander Hamilton

New Jersey
William Livingston
David Brearley
William Paterson
Jonathan Dayton

Pennsylvania
Benjamin Franklin
Thomas Mifflin
Robert Morris
George Clymer
Thomas FitzSimons
Jared Ingersoll
James Wilson
Gouverneur Morris

Delaware
George Read
Gunning Bedford, Jr.
John Dickinson
Richard Bassett
Jacob Broom

Maryland
James McHenry
Dan of St. Thomas
   Jenifer
Daniel Carroll

Virginia
John Blair
James Madison, Jr.

North Carolina
William Blount
Richard Dobbs
   Spaight
Hugh Williamson

South Carolina
John Rutledge
Charles
   Cotesworth Pinckney
Charles Pinckney
Pierce Butler

Georgia
William Few
Abraham Baldwin

AMENDMENTS

Amendment 1

Congress shall make no law respecting an establishment of religion, or prohibiting the free exercise thereof, or abridging the freedom of speech, or of the press; or the right of the people peaceably to assemble, and to petition the Government for a redress of grievances.

Amendment 2

A well-regulated Militia being necessary to the security of a free State, the right of the people to keep and bear Arms, shall not be infringed.

Amendment 3

No Soldier shall, in time of peace be quartered in any house, without the consent of the Owner, nor, in time of war, but in a manner to be prescribed by law.

Amendment 4

The right of the people to be secure in their persons, houses, papers, and effects, against unreasonable searches and seizures, shall not be violated, and no Warrants shall issue, but upon probable cause, supported by Oath or affirmation, and particularly describing the place to be searched, and the persons or things to be seized.

Amendment 5

No person shall be held to answer for a capital, or otherwise infamous crime, unless on a presentment or indictment of a Grand Jury, except in cases arising in the land or naval forces, or in the Militia, when in actual service in time of War, or public danger; nor shall any person be subject for the same offence to be twice put in jeopardy of life or limb; nor shall be compelled in any criminal case to be a witness against himself, nor be deprived of life, liberty, or property, without due process of law; nor shall private property be taken for public use, without just compensation.

The first ten amendments to the Constitution are called the Bill of Rights.

First Amendment—1791
Freedom of Religion and Speech

Congress cannot set up an official religion or stop people from practicing a religion. Congress cannot stop people or newspapers from saying what they want. People can gather peacefully to complain to the government.

Second Amendment—1791
Right to Have Firearms

People have the right to own and carry guns.

Third Amendment—1791
Right Not to House Soldiers

During peacetime, citizens do not have to house soldiers.

Fourth Amendment—1791
Search and Arrest Warrant

People or homes cannot be searched without reason. A search warrant is needed to search a house.

Fifth Amendment—1791
Rights of People Accused of Crimes

Only a grand jury can accuse people of a serious crime. No one can be tried twice for the same crime if found not guilty. People cannot be forced to testify against themselves.

13. Write the amendment number that protects each right.

_____ to speak freely

_____ to be protected against unreasonable searches

_____ to not be put on trial twice for the same crime

Sixth Amendment—1791
Right to a Jury Trial

People have the right to a fast trial by a jury and to hear the charges and evidence against them. They also have the right to a lawyer and to call witnesses in their own defense.

Seventh Amendment—1791
Right to a Jury Trial in a Civil Case

In a civil, or noncriminal case, a person also has the right to a trial by jury.

Eighth Amendment—1791
Protection From Unfair Punishment

A person accused of a crime cannot be forced to pay a very high bail. A person convicted of a crime cannot be asked to pay an unfairly high fine or be punished in a cruel or unusual way.

Ninth Amendment—1791
Other Rights

People have other rights that are not specifically mentioned in the Constitution.

Tenth Amendment—1791
Powers of the States and the People

Some powers are not given to the federal government or denied to states. These rights belong to the states or to the people.

Eleventh Amendment—1795
Limits on Rights to Sue States

People from another state or foreign country cannot sue a state.

Amendment 6

In all criminal prosecutions, the accused shall enjoy the right to a speedy and public trial, by an impartial jury of the State and district wherein the crime shall have been committed, which district shall have been previously ascertained by law, and to be informed of the nature and cause of the accusation; to be confronted with the witnesses against him; to have compulsory process for obtaining witnesses in his favor, and to have the Assistance of Counsel for his defense.

Amendment 7

In Suits at common law, where the value in controversy shall exceed twenty dollars, the right of trial by jury shall be preserved, and no fact tried by a jury, shall be otherwise re-examined in any Court of the United States, than according to the rules of the common law.

Amendment 8

Excessive bail shall not be required, nor excessive fines imposed, nor cruel and unusual punishment inflicted.

Amendment 9

The enumeration in the Constitution, of certain rights, shall not be construed to deny or disparage others retained by the people.

Amendment 10

The powers not delegated to the United States by the Constitution, nor prohibited by it to the States, are reserved to the States respectively, or to the people.

Amendment 11

The Judicial power of the United States shall not be construed to extend to any suit in law or equity, commenced or prosecuted against one of the United States by Citizens of another State, or by Citizens or Subjects of any Foreign State.

Amendment 12

The Electors shall meet in their respective States and vote by ballot for President and Vice President, one of whom, at least, shall not be an inhabitant of the same State with themselves; they shall name in their ballots the person voted for as President, and in distinct ballots the person voted for as Vice President, and they shall make distinct lists of all persons voted for as President, and of all persons voted for as Vice President, and of the number of votes for each, which lists they shall sign and certify, and transmit sealed to the seat of the government of the United States, directed to the President of the Senate;— The President of the Senate shall, in the presence of the Senate and the House of Representatives, open all the certificates and the votes shall then be counted;— the person having the greatest Number of votes for President shall be the President, if such number be a majority of the whole number of Electors appointed; and if no person have such a majority, then, from the persons having the highest numbers not exceeding three on the list of those voted for as President, the House of Representatives shall choose immediately, by ballot, the President. But in choosing the President, the votes shall be taken by States, the representation from each State having one vote; a quorum for this purpose shall consist of a member or members from two thirds of the States, and a majority of all the States shall be necessary to a choice. And if the House of Representatives shall not choose a President whenever the right of choice shall devolve upon them, before the fourth day of March next following, then the Vice President shall act as President, as in case of death or other constitutional disability of the President. The person having the greatest number of votes as Vice President, shall be the Vice President, if such number be a majority of the whole number of Electors appointed, and if no person have a majority, then from the two highest numbers on the list, the Senate shall choose the Vice President; a quorum for the purpose shall consist of two thirds of the whole number of Senators, a majority of the whole number shall be necessary to a choice. But no person constitutionally ineligible to the office of President shall be eligible to that of Vice-President of the United States.

Twelfth Amendment—1804
Election of President and Vice President

This amendment changed the way the Electoral College chooses the President and Vice President. Before this amendment, candidates for President and Vice President ran separately, and each elector had two votes—one for President and one for Vice President. The candidate receiving the most votes became President, and the runner-up became Vice President.

Under this amendment, a candidate for President and a candidate for Vice President must run together. Each elector has only one vote, and the pair of candidates that receives more than half the electoral votes become the President and Vice President. If no one receives a majority of the electoral votes, the House of Representatives votes for the President from a list of the top three vote getters. In this situation, each state has one vote, and the candidate must receive more than half of the votes to become President.

If the Representatives fail to elect a President by March 4 (later changed to January 20), the Vice President serves as President. If no candidate receives at least half the electoral votes for Vice President, the names of the two top vote getters are sent to the Senate. The Senators then vote on the names, and the person receiving more than half the votes becomes Vice President.

Thirteenth Amendment—1865
Abolition of Slavery

The United States outlaws slavery. Congress can pass any laws that are needed to carry out this amendment.

Fourteenth Amendment—1868
Rights of Citizens

People born in the United States are citizens of both the United States and of the state in which they live. States must treat their citizens equally. States cannot deny their citizens the rights outlined in the Bill of Rights.

This section of the amendment made former slaves citizens of both the United States and their home state.

Based on its population, each state has a certain number of Representatives in Congress. The number of Representatives from a state might be lowered, however, if the state does not let certain citizens vote.

This section tried to force states in the South to let former slaves vote.

14. Why would a state not want to have its number of Representatives in Congress cut?

_____

_____

_____

_____

_____

Amendment 13

Section 1. Neither slavery nor involuntary servitude, except as a punishment for crime whereof the party shall have been duly convicted, shall exist within the United States, or any place subject to their jurisdiction.

Section 2. Congress shall have power to enforce this article by appropriate legislation.

Amendment 14

Section 1. All persons born or naturalized in the United States and subject to the jurisdiction thereof, are citizens of the United States and of the State wherein they reside. No State shall make or enforce any law which shall abridge the privileges or immunities of citizens of the United States; nor shall any State deprive any person of life, liberty, or property, without due process of law; nor deny to any person within its jurisdiction the equal protection of the laws.

Section 2. Representatives shall be apportioned among the several States according to their respective numbers, counting the whole number of persons in each State, excluding Indians not taxed. But when the right to vote at any election for the choice of electors for President and Vice President of the United States, Representatives in Congress, the Executive and Judicial officers of a State, or the members of the Legislature thereof, is denied to any of the male inhabitants of such State, being twenty-one years of age and citizens of the United States, or in any way abridged, except for participation in rebellion, or other crime, the basis of representation therein shall be reduced in the proportion which the number of such male citizens shall bear to the whole number of male citizens twenty-one years of age in such State.

Section 3. No person shall be a Senator or Representative in Congress, or elector of President and Vice President, or hold any office, civil or military, under the United States, or under any State, who, having previously taken an oath, as a member of Congress, or as an officer of the United States, or as a member of any State legislature, or as an executive or judicial officer of any State, to support the Constitution of the United States, shall have engaged in insurrection or rebellion against the same, or given aid or comfort to the enemies thereof. But Congress may, by a vote of two thirds of each House, remove such disability.

Section 4. The validity of the public debt of the United States, authorized by law, including debts incurred for payment of pensions and bounties for services in suppressing insurrection or rebellion, shall not be questioned. But neither the United States nor any State shall assume or pay any debt or obligation incurred in aid of insurrection or rebellion against the United States, or any claim for the loss or emancipation of any slave; but all such debts, obligations and claims shall be held illegal and void.

Section 5. The Congress shall have power to enforce, by appropriate legislation, the provisions of this article.

Amendment 15

Section 1. The right of citizens of the United States to vote shall not be denied or abridged by the United States or by any State on account of race, color, or previous condition of servitude.

Section 2. The Congress shall have power to enforce this article by appropriate legislation.

Officials who took part in the Civil War against the United States cannot hold federal or state office. Congress can remove this provision by a two-thirds vote.

The United States will pay back the money it borrowed to fight the Civil War. The money that the South borrowed to fight the Civil War will not be paid back to lenders. The former owners of slaves will not be paid for the slaves that were set free. Congress can pass any necessary laws to enforce this article.

15. List two ways in which the Fourteenth Amendment tended to punish those who rebelled against the United States.

_____

_____

_____

_____

_____

_____

_____

_____

Fifteenth Amendment—1870 Voting Rights
The federal and state government cannot stop people from voting based on race or color. Former slaves must be allowed to vote.

Sixteenth Amendment—1913
Income Tax
Congress has the power to collect an income tax regardless of the population of a state. (Originally, Section 9 of Article 1 had denied this power to Congress.)

Seventeenth Amendment—1913
Direct Election of Senators
The voters of each state will elect their Senators directly. (Originally, Article 1, Section 3 said state legislatures would elect Senators.)

A state can hold a special election to fill an empty Senate seat. Until then, the governor can appoint a Senator to fill an empty seat.

Eighteenth Amendment—1919
Prohibition
Making, importing, or selling alcoholic drinks is illegal in the United States. This was called Prohibition because the amendment prohibited, or outlawed, alcohol.

Congress and the states can make any laws to prohibit alcohol.

This amendment becomes part of the Constitution if it is approved within seven years.

This amendment was repealed, or cancelled, in 1933 by the Twenty-first Amendment.

16. Write the amendment number that did each of the following:

_____ let the Federal Government collect income tax

_____ guaranteed voting rights for African Americans

_____ outlawed the sale of alcohol

_____ abolished slavery

_____ let voters elect their Senators

Amendment 16

The Congress shall have power to lay and collect taxes on incomes, from whatever source derived, without apportionment among the several States, and without regard to any census or enumeration.

Amendment 17

The Senate of the United States shall be composed of two Senators from each State, elected by the people thereof, for six years; and each Senator shall have one vote. The electors in each State shall have the qualifications requisite for electors of the most numerous branch of the State legislatures.

When vacancies happen in the representation of any State in the Senate, the executive authority of such State shall issue writs of election to fill such vacancies: Provided, That the legislature of any State may empower the executive thereof to make temporary appointments until the people fill the vacancies by election as the legislature may direct.

This amendment shall not be so construed as to affect the election or term of any Senator chosen before it becomes valid as part of the Constitution.

Amendment 18

Section 1. After one year from the ratification of this article the manufacture, sale, or transportation of intoxicating liquors within, the importation thereof into, or the exportation thereof from the United States and all territory subject to the jurisdiction thereof for beverage purposes is hereby prohibited.

Section 2. The Congress and the several States shall have concurrent power to enforce this article by appropriate legislation.

Section 3. This article shall be inoperative unless it shall have been ratified as an amendment to the Constitution by the legislatures of the several States, as provided in the Constitution, within seven years of the date of the submission hereof to the States by Congress.

Amendment 19

The right of citizens of the United States to vote shall not be denied or abridged by the United States or by any State on account of sex.

Congress shall have power to enforce this article by appropriate legislation.

Amendment 20

Section 1. The terms of the President and Vice President shall end at noon on the 20th day of January, and the terms of Senators and Representatives at noon on the 3d day of January, of the years in which such terms would have ended if this article had not been ratified; and the terms of their successors shall then begin.

Section 2. The Congress shall assemble at least once in every year, and such meeting shall begin at noon on the 3d day of January, unless they shall by law appoint a different day.

Section 3. If, at the time fixed for the beginning of the term of the President, the President elect shall have died, the Vice President elect shall become President. If a President shall not have been chosen before the time fixed for the beginning of his term, or if the President-elect shall have failed to qualify, then the Vice President elect shall act as President until a President shall have qualified; and the Congress may by law provide for the case wherein neither a President elect nor a Vice President elect shall have qualified, declaring who shall then act as President, or the manner in which one who is to act shall be selected, and such person shall act accordingly until a President or Vice President shall have qualified.

Section 4. The Congress may by law provide for the case of the death of any of the persons from whom the House of Representatives may choose a President whenever the right of choice shall have devolved upon them, and for the case of the death of any of the persons from whom the Senate may choose a Vice President whenever the right of choice shall have devolved upon them.

Section 5. Sections 1 and 2 shall take effect on the 15th day of October following the ratification of this article.

Section 6. This article shall be inoperative unless it shall have been ratified as an amendment to the Constitution by the legislatures of three fourths of the several States within seven years from the date of its submission.

Nineteenth Amendment—1920
Women's Right to Vote

No government can stop people from voting because of their sex. Congress can pass necessary laws to carry out this amendment.

Twentieth Amendment—1933
Terms of Office

The term of a new President begins on January 20. This date is called Inauguration Day. Members of Congress take office on January 3. (Originally their terms began on March 4.)

Congress must meet at least once a year. They should first meet on January 3, unless they choose a different day.

If a candidate for President does not win a majority of votes in the Electoral College and dies while the election is being decided in the House, Congress has the power to pass laws to resolve the problem. Congress has similar power if a candidate for Vice President dies while the election is being decided in the Senate.

Sections 1 and 2 of this amendment take effect on the fifteenth day of October after the amendment becomes part of the Constitution. This amendment has to be approved by three fourths of the states within seven years.

17. How long was
the Eighteenth
Amendment in effect
in the United States?

_____

18. Do you think a
President should be
limited to just two
terms in office? Why or
why not?

_____

_____

_____

_____

_____

_____

Amendment 21

Section 1. The eighteenth article of amendment to the Constitution of the United States is hereby repealed.

Section 2. The transportation or importation into any State, Territory, or possession of the United States for delivery or use therein of intoxicating liquors, in violation of the laws thereof, is hereby prohibited.

Section 3. This article shall be inoperative unless it shall have been ratified as an amendment to the Constitution by conventions in the several States, as provided in the Constitution, within seven years from the date of the submission hereof to the States by the Congress.

Amendment 22

Section 1. No person shall be elected to the office of the President more than twice, and no person who has held the office of President, or acted as President, for more than two years of a term to which some other person was elected President shall be elected to the office of the President more than once. But this Article shall not apply to any person holding the office of President, when this Article was proposed by the Congress, and shall not prevent any person who may be holding the office of President, or acting as President, during the term within which this Article becomes operative from holding the office of President or acting as President during the remainder of such term.

Section 2. This article shall be inoperative unless it shall have been ratified as an amendment to the Constitution by the legislatures of three fourths of the several states within seven years from the date of its submission to the States by the Congress.

Amendment 23

Section 1. The District constituting the seat of Government of the United States shall appoint in such manner as the Congress may direct:

A number of electors of President and Vice President equal to the whole number of Senators and Representatives in Congress to which the District would be entitled if it were a State, but in no event more than the least populous State; they shall be in addition to those appointed by the States, they shall be considered, for the purposes of the election of President and Vice President, to be electors appointed by a State; and they shall meet in the District and perform such duties as provided by the twelfth article of amendment.

Amendment 24

Section 1. The right of citizens of the United States to vote in any primary or other election for President or Vice President, for electors for President or Vice President, or for Senator or Representative in Congress, shall not be denied or abridged by the United States or any State by reason of failure to pay any poll tax or other tax.

Section 2. The Congress shall have power to enforce this article by appropriate legislation.

Amendment 25

Section 1. In case of the removal of the President from office or of his death or resignation, the Vice President shall become President.

Section 2. Whenever there is a vacancy in the office of the Vice President, the President shall nominate a Vice President who shall take office upon confirmation by a majority vote of both Houses of Congress.

Section 3. Whenever the President transmits to the President pro tempore of the Senate and the Speaker of the House of Representatives his written declaration that he is unable to discharge the powers and duties of his office, and until he transmits to them a written declaration to the contrary, such powers and duties shall be discharged by the Vice President as Acting President.

Twenty-third Amendment—1961 Presidential Elections for District of Columbia

People living in Washington, D.C., have the right to vote in presidential elections. Washington, D.C., can never have more electoral votes than the state with the smallest number of people.

Twenty-fourth Amendment—1964 Outlawing of Poll Tax

No one can be stopped from voting in a federal election because he or she has not paid a poll tax or any other kind of tax.

Congress can make laws to carry out this amendment.

Twenty-fifth Amendment—1967 Presidential Succession

If the President dies or resigns, the Vice President becomes President. If the office of Vice President is empty, the President appoints a new Vice President.

When the President is unable to carry out the duties of the office, Congress should be informed. The Vice President then serves as Acting President. The President may resume the duties of the office after informing Congress.

If the Vice President and half the President's top advisers, or Cabinet, inform Congress that the President cannot carry out his or her duties, the Vice President becomes Acting President. If the President informs Congress that he or she is able to carry out these duties, the President returns to office. However, after four days, if the Vice President and half the Cabinet again tell Congress that the President cannot carry out his or her duties, the President does not return to office. Instead, Congress must decide within 21 days whether the President is able to carry out his or her duties. If two thirds of Congress votes that the President cannot continue in office, the Vice President becomes Acting President. If two thirds do not vote in this way, the President remains in office.

19. Write the number of the amendment that:

_____ gave votes to women

_____ gave votes to citizens in Washington, D.C.

_____ gave votes to 18-year-old people

_____ outlawed taxes that blocked voting

Section 4. Whenever the Vice President and a majority of either the principal officers of the executive departments or of such other body as Congress may by law provide, transmit to the President pro tempore of the Senate and the Speaker of the House of Representatives their written declaration that the President is unable to discharge the powers and duties of his office, the Vice President shall immediately assume the powers and duties of the office as Acting President.

Thereafter, when the President transmits to the President pro tempore of the Senate and the Speaker of the House of Representatives his written declaration that no inability exists, he shall resume the powers and duties of his office unless the Vice President and a majority of either the principal officers of the executive department or of such other body as Congress may by law provide, transmit within four days to the President pro tempore of the Senate and the Speaker of the House of Representatives their written declaration that the President is unable to discharge the powers and duties of his office. Thereupon Congress shall decide the issue, assembling within forty-eight hours for that purpose if not in session. If the Congress, within twenty-one days after receipt of the latter written declaration, or, if Congress is not in session, within twenty-one days after Congress is required to assemble, determines by two-thirds vote of both Houses that the President is unable to discharge the powers and duties of his office, the Vice President shall continue to discharge the same as Acting President; otherwise, the President shall resume the powers and duties of his office.

Amendment 26

Section 1. The right of citizens of the United States, who are eighteen years of age or older, to vote shall not be denied or abridged by the United States or by any State on account of age.

Section 2. The Congress shall have the power to enforce this article by appropriate legislation.

Amendment 27

No law varying the compensation for the services of the Senators and Representatives, shall take effect, until an election of Representatives shall have intervened.

The United States of America, Political

New Hampshire

Vermont

Maine

Augusta

Montpelier

Concord

Massachusetts

Boston

Albany

Providence

New York

Hartford

Rhode Island

Connecticut

Pennsylvania

New Jersey

Harrisburg

Trenton

Annapolis

Dover

Delaware

Columbus

West Virginia

Maryland

Indianapolis

Charleston

Virginia

Washington, D.C.

Richmond

Frankfort

Kentucky

Raleigh

Nashville

North Carolina

Tennessee

Columbia

Arkansas

South Carolina

Little Rock

Alabama

Atlanta

Mississippi

Georgia

Louisiana

Montgomery

Jackson

Baton Rouge

Tallahassee

Florida

Minnesota

St. Paul

Wisconsin

Michigan

Madison

Lansing

Iowa

Des Moines

Illinois

Indiana

Ohio

Springfield

Jefferson City

Missouri

LEGEND

⭐ National capital

★ State capital

N

W   E

S

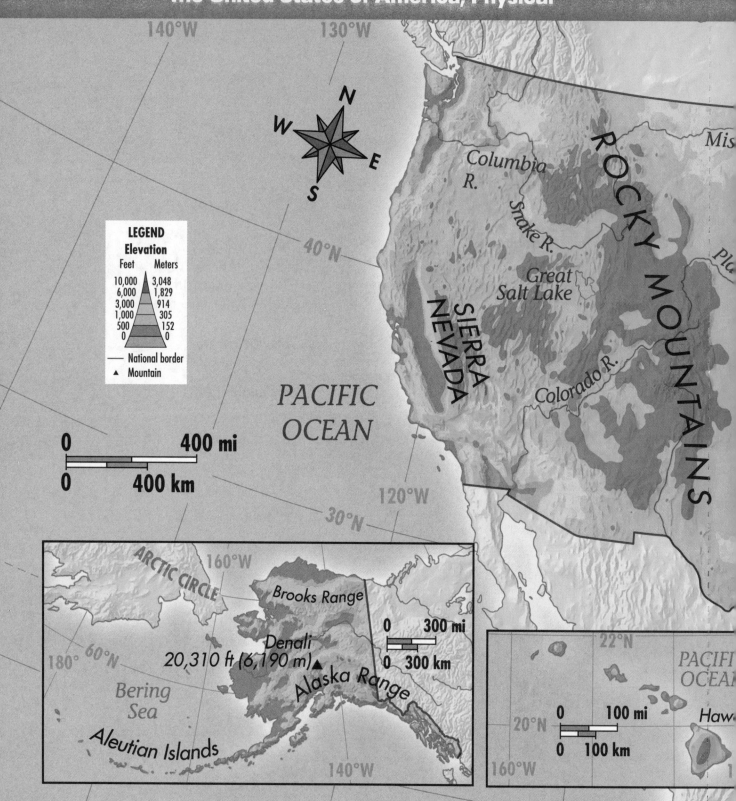

140°W

130°W

N
W   E
S

Columbia R.

Snake R.

ROCKY MOUNTAINS

Mis

40°N

LEGEND
Elevation

Feet	Meters
10,000	3,048
6,000	1,829
3,000	914
1,000	305
500	152
0	0

— National border
▲ Mountain

SIERRA NEVADA

Great Salt Lake

Pla

Colorado R.

PACIFIC OCEAN

0   400 mi

0   400 km

120°W

30°N

ARCTIC CIRCLE   160°W

Brooks Range

0   300 mi

0   300 km

Denali
20,310 ft (6,190 m)▲

Alaska Range

180°   60°N

Bering Sea

Aleutian Islands

140°W

22°N

PACIFI
OCEAN

20°N

0   100 mi

0   100 km

Haw

160°W

Missouri R.

GREAT PLAINS

Platte R.

Red R.

Rio Grande

Lake
Superior

Great Lakes

Lake
Huron

Lake
Ontario

Lake
Michigan

Lake Erie

CENTRAL
PLAINS

APPALACHIAN MOUNTAINS

Ohio R.

Mississippi R.

COASTAL PLAIN

ATLANTIC
OCEAN

80°W

70°W

Gulf of Mexico

90°W

TROPIC OF CANCER

20°N

PACIFIC
OCEAN

Hawaii

154°W

map
area

North America, Political

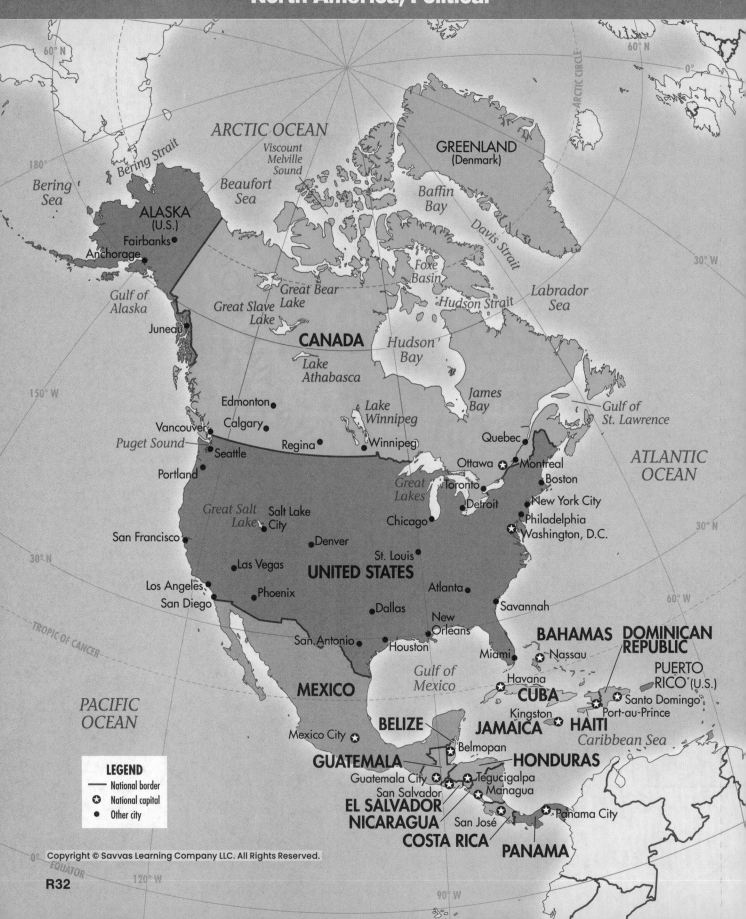

LEGEND
— National border
✪ National capital
• Other city

ARCTIC OCEAN

Bering Strait

Bering Sea

ALASKA (U.S.)

Fairbanks •
Anchorage •

Gulf of Alaska

Juneau •

Viscount Melville Sound

Beaufort Sea

GREENLAND (Denmark)

Baffin Bay

Davis Strait

Foxe Basin

Great Bear Lake

Great Slave Lake

CANADA

Hudson Strait

Labrador Sea

Hudson Bay

Lake Athabasca

James Bay

Gulf of St. Lawrence

ATLANTIC OCEAN

Edmonton •
Calgary •

Lake Winnipeg

Vancouver •
Puget Sound
Seattle •
Portland •

Regina •

Winnipeg •

Quebec •
Ottawa ✪ Montreal •
Toronto •
Detroit •
Boston •
New York City •
Philadelphia •
Washington, D.C. ✪

Great Lakes

Great Salt Lake

Salt Lake City •

San Francisco •

Denver •

Chicago •

St. Louis •

UNITED STATES

Las Vegas •

Los Angeles •
San Diego •

Phoenix •

Dallas •

Atlanta •

Savannah •

San Antonio •

Houston •

New Orleans •

Miami •

60° W

30° N

TROPIC OF CANCER

MEXICO

Gulf of Mexico

BAHAMAS
Nassau •

DOMINICAN REPUBLIC

PUERTO RICO (U.S.)

Havana ✪

CUBA

Santo Domingo ✪
Port-au-Prince ✪

PACIFIC OCEAN

Mexico City ✪

BELIZE

Belmopan ✪

Kingston ✪
JAMAICA

HAITI

Caribbean Sea

GUATEMALA

Guatemala City ✪

San Salvador ✪

HONDURAS
Tegucigalpa ✪
Managua ✪

EL SALVADOR
NICARAGUA
COSTA RICA

San José ✪

Panama City ✪
PANAMA

North America, Physical

ARCTIC OCEAN

Bering Strait

Point Barrow

Viscount Melville Sound

Ellesmere Island

Greenland

60° N

60° N

0°

ARCTIC CIRCLE

Bering Sea

Beaufort Sea

Banks Island

Queen Elizabeth Islands

Melville I. Devon I.

Baffin Bay

Brooks Range

Aleutian Islands

Denali 20,310 ft (6,190 m)

Alaska Range

Yukon River

Victoria Island

Baffin Island

Davis Strait

Cape Farewell

30° W

Alaska Peninsula

Kodiak Island

Mt. Logan 19,524 ft (5,951 m)

Gulf of Alaska

Yukon Plateau

Mackenzie R.

Great Bear Lake

Foxe Basin

Labrador Sea

ATLANTIC OCEAN

Liard R.

Great Slave L.

Hudson Strait

Haida Qwaii (Queen Charlotte Islands)

Coast Mountains

Peace R.

Athabasca R.

Lake Athabasca

Hudson Bay

Labrador

Newfoundland

CANADIAN SHIELD

James Bay

St. Lawrence R.

Gulf of St. Lawrence

Vancouver Island

Saskatchewan R.

Lake Winnipeg

Great Lakes

Nova Scotia

Puget Sound

Cascade Range

ROCKY MOUNTAINS

GREAT

APPALACHIAN MOUNTAINS

Bay of Fundy

Cape Cod

Long Island

Coast Ranges

Snake R.

Mississippi R.

Missouri R.

Black Hills

INTERIOR PLAINS

Ohio R.

Cape Hatteras

Great Salt Lake

Sierra Nevada

GREAT BASIN

Platte R.

Arkansas

Ozark Plateau

PLAINS

COASTAL PLAIN

Mt. Whitney 14,495 ft (4,418 m)

Colorado R.

30° N

Death Valley (lowest point in N.A.) −282 ft (−86 m)

Baja California

Sonoran Desert

Sierra Madre Occidental

Rio Grande

Sierra Madre Oriental

Gulf of Mexico

Bahamas

Puerto Rico

Lesser Antilles

60° W

TROPIC OF CANCER

Cuba

Greater Antilles

Hispaniola

LEGEND

Elevation

Feet	Meters
10,000	3,048
6,000	1,829
3,000	914
1,000	305
500	152
0	0

▲ Peak

▼ Below sea level

Yucatán Peninsula

Citlaltépetl ▲ 18,701 ft (5,700 m)

Jamaica

Caribbean Sea

Isthmus of Panama

PACIFIC OCEAN

Lake Nicaragua

R33

0° EQUATOR

120° W

90° W

The World, Political

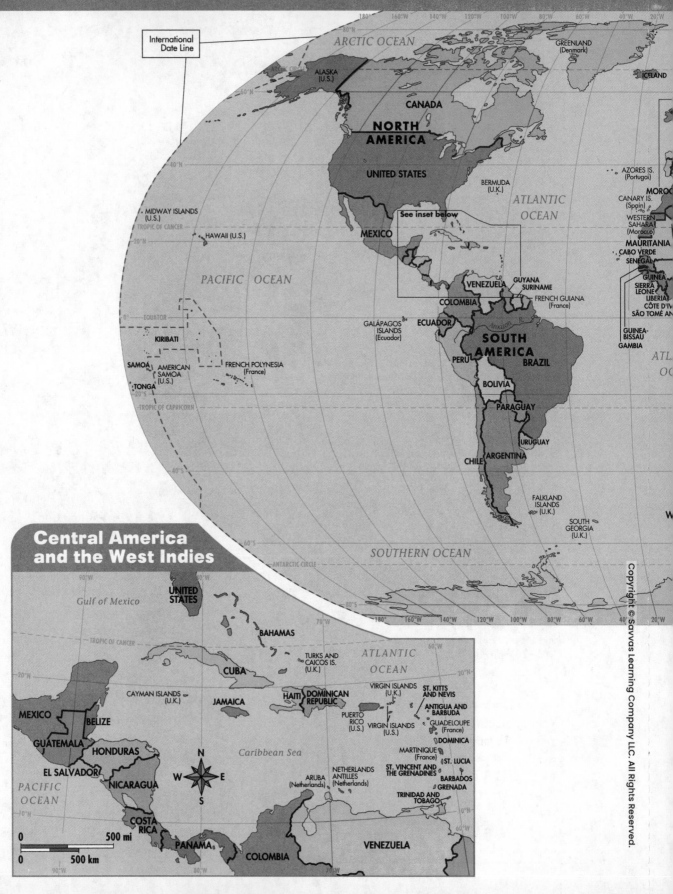

International Date Line

ARCTIC OCEAN

GREENLAND
(Denmark)

ICELAND

ALASKA
(U.S.)

CANADA

NORTH
AMERICA

UNITED STATES

BERMUDA
(U.K.)

ATLANTIC
OCEAN

AZORES IS.
(Portugal)

CANARY IS.
(Spain)

MOROC

WESTERN
SAHARA
(Morocco)

MAURITANIA

MIDWAY ISLANDS
(U.S.)

TROPIC OF CANCER

HAWAII (U.S.)

MEXICO

See inset below

CABO VERDE

SENEGAL

GUINEA

SIERRA
LEONE

LIBERIA

CÔTE D'IV

SÃO TOMÉ AN

GUINEA-
BISSAU

GAMBIA

PACIFIC OCEAN

VENEZUELA

GUYANA
SURINAME

FRENCH GUIANA
(France)

COLOMBIA

EQUATOR

GALÁPAGOS
ISLANDS
(Ecuador)

ECUADOR

KIRIBATI

Amazon

SOUTH
AMERICA

ATL.
OC

SAMOA

AMERICAN
SAMOA
(U.S.)

FRENCH POLYNESIA
(France)

PERU

BRAZIL

TONGA

BOLIVIA

TROPIC OF CAPRICORN

PARAGUAY

URUGUAY

CHILE

ARGENTINA

FALKLAND
ISLANDS
(U.K.)

SOUTH
GEORGIA
(U.K.)

W

SOUTHERN OCEAN

ANTARCTIC CIRCLE

Central America and the West Indies

UNITED
STATES

Gulf of Mexico

BAHAMAS

TROPIC OF CANCER

TURKS AND
CAICOS IS.
(U.K.)

ATLANTIC
OCEAN

CUBA

CAYMAN ISLANDS
(U.K.)

JAMAICA

HAITI

DOMINICAN
REPUBLIC

VIRGIN ISLANDS
(U.K.)

ST. KITTS
AND NEVIS

ANTIGUA AND
BARBUDA

MEXICO

BELIZE

PUERTO
RICO
(U.S.)

VIRGIN ISLANDS
(U.S.)

GUADELOUPE
(France)

GUATEMALA

HONDURAS

Caribbean Sea

DOMINICA

MARTINIQUE
(France)

ST. LUCIA

EL SALVADOR

NICARAGUA

N
W   E
S

NETHERLANDS
ANTILLES
(Netherlands)

ST. VINCENT AND
THE GRENADINES

BARBADOS

PACIFIC
OCEAN

ARUBA
(Netherlands)

GRENADA

TRINIDAD AND
TOBAGO

COSTA
RICA

PANAMA

COLOMBIA

VENEZUELA

0   500 mi

0   500 km

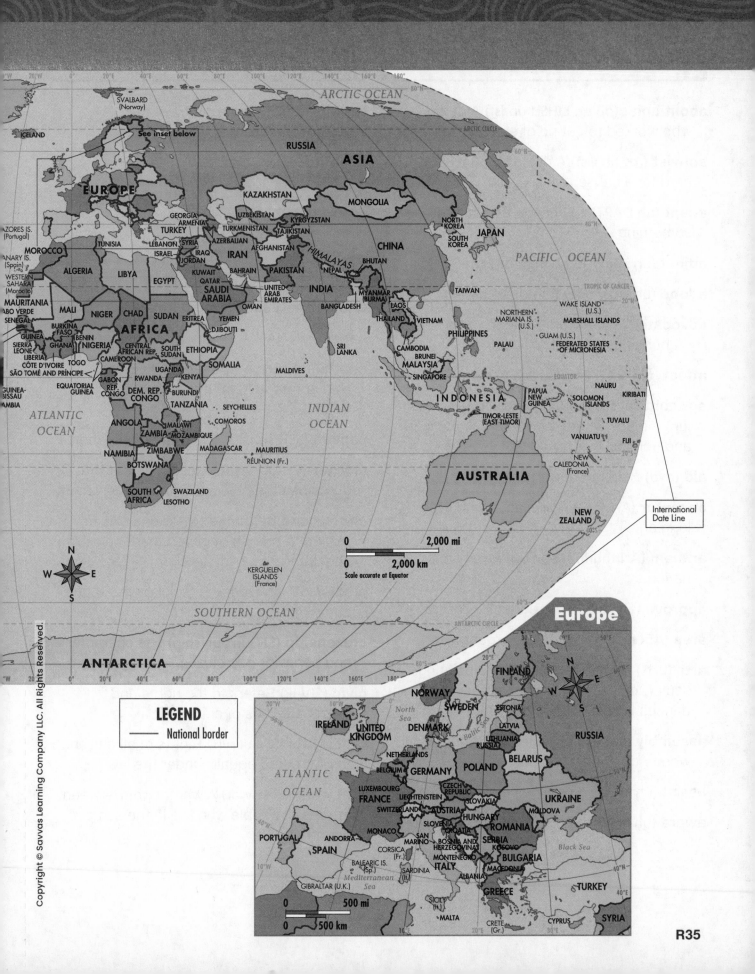

ARCTIC OCEAN

SVALBARD
(Norway)

See inset below

ICELAND

RUSSIA

ASIA

ARCTIC CIRCLE

EUROPE

KAZAKHSTAN

MONGOLIA

AZORES IS.
(Portugal)

GEORGIA
ARMENIA
TURKEY

UZBEKISTAN
TURKMENISTAN   KYRGYZSTAN

TAJIKISTAN

NORTH
KOREA

JAPAN

PACIFIC OCEAN

TUNISIA

LEBANON
ISRAEL   SYRIA

AZERBAIJAN

AFGHANISTAN

CHINA

SOUTH
KOREA

MOROCCO

IRAQ
JORDAN

IRAN

HIMALAYAS

BHUTAN

TAIWAN

CANARY IS.
(Spain)

ALGERIA

LIBYA

EGYPT

KUWAIT
QATAR

BAHRAIN

PAKISTAN

NEPAL

MYANMAR
(BURMA)

TROPIC OF CANCER

WESTERN
SAHARA
(Morocco)

SAUDI
ARABIA

UNITED
ARAB
EMIRATES

INDIA

BANGLADESH

LAOS

WAKE ISLAND
(U.S.)

MAURITANIA

MALI

NIGER

CHAD

SUDAN

OMAN

YEMEN

ERITREA

THAILAND

VIETNAM

NORTHERN
MARIANA IS.
(U.S.)

MARSHALL ISLANDS

CABO VERDE
SENEGAL

BURKINA
FASO

AFRICA

DJIBOUTI

SRI
LANKA

CAMBODIA

PHILIPPINES

GUAM (U.S.)

GUINEA
SIERRA
LEONE
LIBERIA

GHANA

BENIN
NIGERIA

CENTRAL
AFRICAN REP.

SOUTH
SUDAN

ETHIOPIA

SOMALIA

PALAU

FEDERATED STATES
OF MICRONESIA

CÔTE D'IVOIRE
SÃO TOMÉ AND PRÍNCIPE

TOGO

CAMEROON

UGANDA
KENYA

MALDIVES

MALAYSIA

BRUNEI

SINGAPORE

GUINEA-
BISSAU
GAMBIA

EQUATORIAL
GUINEA

GABON
REP.
CONGO

RWANDA
BURUNDI

DEM. REP.
CONGO

TANZANIA

SEYCHELLES

INDIAN
OCEAN

INDONESIA

PAPUA
NEW
GUINEA

SOLOMON
ISLANDS

NAURU

KIRIBATI

EQUATOR

ATLANTIC
OCEAN

ANGOLA

ZAMBIA

MALAWI
MOZAMBIQUE

COMOROS

TIMOR-LESTE
(EAST TIMOR)

TUVALU

NAMIBIA

ZIMBABWE

BOTSWANA

MADAGASCAR

MAURITIUS
RÉUNION (Fr.)

VANUATU

FIJI

AUSTRALIA

NEW
CALEDONIA
(France)

SOUTH
AFRICA

SWAZILAND

LESOTHO

N
W   E
S

2,000 mi

International
Date Line

KERGUELEN
ISLANDS
(France)

2,000 km

Scale accurate at Equator

NEW
ZEALAND

SOUTHERN OCEAN

ANTARCTIC CIRCLE

ANTARCTICA

LEGEND
— National border

Europe

NORWAY

FINLAND

N
W   E
S

IRELAND

UNITED
KINGDOM

North
Sea

SWEDEN

DENMARK

Baltic Sea

ESTONIA

LATVIA

LITHUANIA

RUSSIA

RUSSIA

ATLANTIC
OCEAN

NETHERLANDS

BELGIUM
LUXEMBOURG

GERMANY

POLAND

BELARUS

CZECH
REPUBLIC

UKRAINE

FRANCE

LIECHTENSTEIN

SWITZERLAND

AUSTRIA

SLOVAKIA

HUNGARY

MONACO

SLOVENIA

CROATIA

ROMANIA

MOLDOVA

PORTUGAL

SPAIN

ANDORRA

SAN
MARINO

BOSNIA AND
HERZEGOVINA

SERBIA

KOSOVO

MONTENEGRO

BULGARIA

Black Sea

CORSICA
(Fr.)

BALEARIC IS.
(Sp.)

SARDINIA
(It.)

ITALY

MACEDONIA

ALBANIA

TURKEY

GIBRALTAR (U.K.)

Mediterranean
Sea

SICILY
(It.)

GREECE

MALTA

CRETE
(Gr.)

CYPRUS

SYRIA

500 mi

500 km

Glossary

A

abolitionist (ab uh LIHSH un ist) A person who worked to get rid of slavery.

activist (AK tih vist) A person who works hard for a cause.

adapt (uh DAPT) To change the way you do something.

adjust (uh JUST) To change or shift.

adobe (uh DOH bee) Sun-dried bricks.

advocate (AD vuh kut) Someone who fights on behalf of a cause.

affect (uh FEKT) To have an influence on.

agricultural region (ag rih KUL chur ul REE jun) A place where there is much flat land and rich soil.

aid (ayd) Help or support.

ancestor (AN ses tur) A relative who lived long ago.

anthem (AN thum) A song of loyalty to a nation.

approve (uh PROOV) To agree to, accept.

area (AIR ee uh) A part of a larger place.

arts (arts) Creations that include paintings, sculptures, songs, poems, stories, and dances.

assembly line (uh SEM blee lyn) When each worker does only one part of a job.

assist (uh SIST) To provide help or support.

aware (uh WAIR) Knowing about something.

B

background (BAK ground) A person's culture, knowledge, and experience.

benefit (BEN uh fit) Useful result.

bill (bil) An idea for a law written down for government to decide on.

C

Cabinet (KAB uh nit) A group of advisors.

canal (kuh NAL) A waterway dug by people.

capital resource (KAP uh tul REE sors) Human-made item used to make other goods.

census (SEN suhs) A count of a population.

charter (CHAR tur) A legal document that describes the powers of local government.

checks and balances (cheks and BAL un sez) Each branch of government can check the power of another.

citizen (SIT uh zun) An official member of a community.

citizenship (SIT uh zun ship) The character and behavior of a citizen.

civic (SIV ik) Refers to the rights and responsibilities of citizens.

civil rights (SIV ul ryts) Rights of all citizens to be treated equally under the law.

civil war (SIV ul wor) A war fought between groups of people who live in the same country.

claim (klaym) To say that something belongs to you.

climate (KLY mut) The weather a place has over a long period.

colonize (KAHL uh nyz) To settle lands for another country.

colony (KAHL uh nee) A place ruled by another country.

communicate (kuh MYOO nuh kayt) When people pass thoughts or information to others.

community (kuh MYOO nuh tee) A place where people live, work, and have fun together.

confederacy (kun FED ur uh see) A formal agreement, or treaty, between groups to work together.

Congress (KONG grihs) The branch of government that makes the laws.

consequence (KAHN sih kwens) The result or effect of an action.

conserve (kun SURV) To save and protect resources.

constitution (kahn stuh TOO shun) A written plan of government that explains the beliefs and laws of a country.

construct (kun STRUKT) To build.

consume (kun SOOM) To eat or drink something.

consumer (kun SOOM ur) User of goods and services.

continent (KAHNT uh nunt) One of seven of the largest land areas on Earth.

continue (kun TIN yoo) To keep on, extend.

convention (kun VEN shun) A large meeting.

converse (kun VURS) To talk back and forth.

convince (kun VINS) To cause someone by the use of evidence to take a course of action or to believe something.

cooperate (koh OP uh rayt) To work together.

cost (kawst) The price needed to get something.

council (KOUN sul) A group that makes laws.

crucial (KROO shul) Very important.

cultural heritage (KUL chur ul HAYR uh tij) The traditions, customs, and artifacts of a cultural group.

cultural region (KUL chur ul REE jun) An area where people who share a similar culture live near each other.

culture (KUL chur) The way of life of a group of people.

custom (KUS tum) A special way of doing something.

cyberbullying (SYE bur bool ee ing) Sending mean messages online.

D

debt (det) Money that is owed to another person.

deed (deed) An action.

defend (dih FEND) To protect or guard from harm.

delegate (DEL uh git) A person chosen to act for others.

design (dih ZYN) Outline, plan, details.

despite (dih SPYT) Without being affected by.

diverse (duh VURS) Different.

document (DAHK yoo munt) A written record or account.

drought (drout) Not enough water.

E

ecosystem (EE koh sis tum) All the living and nonliving things that interact in a certain place.

elevation (el uh VAY shun) The height of land above sea level.

enable (en AY bul) To make possible.

enforce (en FORS) To make sure people obey laws and rules.

equal rights (EE kwul ryts) When people have the same rights as others.

erosion (ee ROH shun) The washing away of soil by rain, wind, and nearby rivers.

essential (uh SEN shul) Absolutely necessary.

ethnic group (ETH nik groop) A group of people who share the same language, culture, and way of life.

exclusion (eks KLOO zhun) Keeping people out of a place.

executive (ig ZEK yuh tiv) The branch of government that carries out laws.

expedition (ek spuh DISH un) A trip made for a special reason.

explorer (ik SPLAWR ur) A person who travels looking for new lands and discoveries.

export (ek SPORT) To send out goods to another country.

F

federal (FED ur ul) National.

financial (fye NAN shul) Relating to matters of money.

fine (fyn) Money paid for violating a law.

fort (fort) A strong building or area that can be defended against enemy attacks.

frontier (frun TEER) A region that forms the edge of a settled area.

fund (fund) To pay for.

G

generation (jen ur AY shun) People born and living about the same time.

gold rush (gold rush) When many people come to an area to search for gold.

goods (goods) Things that workers make or grow.

government (GUV urn munt) A system of ruling people.

governor (GUV ur nur) Head of a state's executive branch.

H

harvest (HAR vist) The crops gathered at the end of the growing season.

hero (HEER oh) Someone who has done special deeds and is a role model for others.

homestead (HOHM sted) An area of land that includes a house and buildings.

human capital (HYOO mun KAP uh tul) A person's skills, knowledge, and experience.

human resource (HYOO mun REE sors) A person's talents and skills.

I

ideal (eye DEEL) An idea we hope will come true.

immigrant (IM uh grunt) A person who moves from one country to settle in a different country.

import (im PORT) To bring in goods from another country.

impose (IM pohz) To bring about by force.

independence (in duh PEN duns) Freedom.

industrial region (in DUS tree ul REE jun) A place where many kinds of factories are located.

influence (IN floo uns) To have an effect upon.

interpreter (in TUR pruh tur) An individual who speaks more than one language who helps a person understand what is being said by someone speaking another language.

introduce (in troh DOOS) To use for the first time.

invention (in VEN shun) Something that is made for the first time.

invest (in VEST) To spend now in the hope of future reward.

irrigate (IR uh gayt) To bring water in through pipes.

issue (ISH yoo) An important public matter.

J

judicial (joo DISH ul) The branch of government that makes certain the laws follow what is in the U.S. Constitution.

L

landform (LAND form) Form or shape of part of Earth's surface.

landmark (LAND mark) An important building or monument.

law (law) An official rule.

layer (LAY ur) A single covering.

legal (LEE gul) Recognized by courts of law.

legend (LEJ und) A story from the past whose facts cannot be checked.

legislative (LEG is lay tiv) Law making.

legislature (LEJ is lay chur) A part of government that makes laws.

local (LOH kul) Things made near where they are sold.

location (loh KAY shun) Where something is.

longhouse (LAHNG hows) An Native American home that was longer than it was wide.

M

material (muh TEER ee ul) An item that something is made of, such as stone, wood, grass, or mud.

mayor (MAY ur) Leader of a community.

method (METH ud) A particular way of doing something.

mine (myn) To dig for materials.

mineral (MIN ur ul) A resource that does not come from an animal or a plant.

mission (MISH un) A settlement that has a church where religion is taught.

modify (MAHD uh fye) To change something.

motive (MOH tiv) A reason.

N

natural resource (NACH ur ul REE sors) Something in nature that is useful to people.

need (need) Something you must have to live.

nonrenewable resource (nahn rih NOO uh bul REE sors) A resource that takes a long time to be replaced or that cannot be replaced after it is used.

O

obey (oh BAY) To follow rules.

observe (ub ZURV) To celebrate in an accepted way.

obtain (ub TAYN) To acquire or get.

occupation (ahk yuh PAY shun) A job.

opportunity cost (ahp ur TOO nih tee kawst) What you have to give up to get something.

option (AHP shun) A choice that can be made.

organize (OR guh nyz) To set up.

original (uh RIJ uh nul) The first.

P

participate (par TIS uh payt) To take part in.

patent (PAT unt) A document giving someone the right to be the only person making or selling an item.

patriot (PAY tree ut) A person who loves and defends the country.

perform (per FAWRM) To present to an audience.

pilgrim (PIL grum) A person who travels for a religious reason.

powwow (POU wou) An American Indian gathering.

prepare (pree PAYR) To get ready.

produce (pruh DOOS) To make or create.

producer (pruh DOOS ur) Maker of goods.

promote (pruh MOHT) To encourage or help.

property (PRAHP ur tee) A piece of land owned by someone.

protect (pruh TEKT) To keep from harm, keep safe.

protest (PROH test) To complain.

provide (pruh VYD) To give, to supply.

public virtue (PUB lik VUR choo) The goodness in all citizens and the willingness to work for the good of a community or nation.

purchase (PUR chus) To buy.

purpose (PUR pus) A goal or reason.

Q

Quaker (KWAY kur) A follower of a religion that believes in peace and equal treatment for all people.

R

recreation (rek ree AY shun) A way of enjoying yourself.

recycle (ree SYE kul) To use an item again.

region (REE jun) A large area with at least one feature that makes it different from other areas.

rely (rih LYE) To depend on; to trust.

renewable resource (rih NOO uh bul REE sors) A resource that can be replaced in a short time.

represent (rep ruh ZENT) To stand for.

representative (rep rih ZEN tuh tiv) A person chosen to speak for others.

require (rih KWYR) To need.

reservation (rez ur VAY shun) Land that the United States government set aside for American Indians.

reside (rih ZYD) To live in or have a permanent home at.

responsibility (rih spahn suh BIL uh tee) A duty.

responsible (rih SPAHN suh bul) Able to be trusted to do what is right.

revolution (rev uh LOO shun) Something that takes place when people want to take over the government that rules them and create a new one.

right (ryt) A basic idea or truth that people value.

risk (risk) A dangerous chance.

role (rohl) A job, duty, or function.

role model (rohl MAHD ul) Someone whose good behavior sets an example for others.

route (root) The course you take to get somewhere.

rural (ROOR ul) Describing a community in the countryside where there is plenty of open space.

S

secure (sih KYOOR) To make something safe and certain.

segregate (SEG ruh gayt) To separate.

services (SUR vis uz) Work that people do.

settlement house (SET ul munt hous) A community center located in a poor area of a city.

significant (sig NIF uh kunt) Important.

slavery (SLAY vur ee) The practice of buying, selling, and owning people.

structure (STRUK chur) Something that is constructed.

suburban (suh BUR bun) Describing a community that is near a large city.

sufficient (suh FISH unt) Enough.

suffrage (SUF rij) The right to vote.

symbol (SIM bul) Something that stands for something else and that has meaning to people.

T

tax (taks) Money paid to a government.

technology (tek NAHL uh jee) The use of science to solve problems and make things work better.

telegraph (TEL uh graf) A machine that sends and receives signals through a thin wire.

territory (TER uh tawr ee) An area of land owned by a country either within or outside the country's borders.

toll (tohl) Money paid for using a road.

trade-off (TRAYD awf) Giving up one thing for another.

tradition (truh DISH un) A special way that a group does something that is passed down over time.

transcontinental (trans kahn tih NEN tul) Across the continent.

typically (TIP ih klee) Usually or in most cases.

U

undertake (un dur TAYK) To begin to do.

urban (UR bun) Describing a large city.

V

vaccine (vak SEEN) A weakened virus given to people to help them fight off a disease.

value (VAL yoo) To think something is important.

vegetation (vej uh TAY shun) Kinds of plant life.

veto (VEE toh) To reject.

violate (VY uh layt) To break or fail to follow a rule or law.

volunteer (vahl un TIHR) To work or give without being paid.

W

wagon train (WAG un TRAYN) A group of covered wagons that traveled together for safety.

want (wahnt) Something you would like to have but do not need to live.

weather (WETH ur) Daily conditions outside.

Glosario

A

abolitionist/abolicionista Alguien que trabajó para eliminar la esclavitud.

activist/activista Alguien que trabaja duro por una causa.

adapt/adaptarse Cambiar la manera de hacer algo.

adjust/modificar Cambiar o alterar.

adobe/adobe Ladrillos secados al sol.

advocate/defensor Alguien que lucha por una causa.

affect/afectar Influir sobre algo.

agricultural region/región agrícola Lugar en el que la tierra es principalmente plana y fértil.

aid/ayuda Asistencia o apoyo.

ancestor/ancestro Familiar que vivió hace mucho tiempo.

anthem/himno Canción de lealtad hacia una nación.

approve/aprobar Estar de acuerdo, aceptar.

area/área Una parte de un lugar más grande.

arts/arte Creaciones que incluyen pinturas, esculturas, canciones, poemas, cuentos y danzas.

assembly line/línea de montaje Cuando cada trabajador hace solo una parte del trabajo.

assist/asistir Brindar ayuda o apoyo.

aware/consciente Que tiene conocimiento de algo.

B

background/formación La cultura, los conocimientos y la experiencia de una persona.

benefit/beneficio Resultado útil.

bill/proyecto de ley Idea que se escribe para que el gobierno decida si va a ser ley.

C

Cabinet/gabinete Grupo de consejeros.

canal/canal Vía de navegación hecha por el hombre.

capital resource/recurso de capital Un artículo hecho por humanos que se usa para producir otros bienes.

census/censo Conteo de la población.

charter/carta Documento legal que describe los poderes del gobierno local.

checks and balances/sistema de controles y equilibrios Cada poder del gobierno tiene maneras de limitar las capacidades de los otros poderes.

citizen/ciudadano Miembro oficial de una comunidad.

citizenship/ciudadanía Carácter y conducta de un ciudadano.

civic/cívico Referido a los derechos y las responsabilidades de los ciudadanos.

civil rights/derechos civiles Derechos que tienen todos los ciudadanos de ser tratados con igualdad ante la ley.

civil war/guerra civil Guerra entre grupos de personas que viven en el mismo país.

claim/reclamar Decir que algo le pertenece a uno.

climate/clima Tiempo de un lugar durante un período extenso.

colonize/colonizar Poblar tierras en nombre de otro país.

colony/colonia Lugar gobernado por otro país.

communicate/comunicarse Transmitir pensamientos o información a otras personas.

community/comunidad Sitio donde las personas viven, trabajan y se divierten.

confederacy/confederación Acuerdo formal, o tratado, que establece la colaboración entre grupos.

Congress/Congreso Poder del gobierno que crea las leyes.

consequence/consecuencia Resultado o efecto de una acción.

conserve/conservar Cuidar y proteger un recurso.

constitution/constitución Plan de gobierno escrito en el que se explican las creencias y las leyes de un país.

construct/construir Fabricar.

consume/consumir Comer o beber algo.

consumer/consumidor Usuario de bienes y servicios.

continent/continente Una de las siete superficies de tierra más extensas del planeta.

continue/continuar Seguir, extender.

convention/convención Reunión de mucha gente.

converse/conversar Hablar con otra persona.

convince/convencer Usar evidencia para hacer que alguien actúe de cierta manera o crea algo.

cooperate/cooperar Trabajar conjuntamente.

cost/costo El precio necesario para obtener una cosa.

council/concejo Grupo de personas que hacen leyes.

crucial/crucial Muy importante.

cultural heritage/herencia cultural Las tradiciones, las costumbres y los artefactos de un grupo cultural.

cultural region/región cultural Área donde las personas que comparten una cultura similar viven cerca una de la otra.

culture/cultura Modo de vida de un grupo de personas.

custom/costumbre Forma especial de hacer algo.

cyberbullying/ciberacoso Acción de enviar mensajes agresivos por Internet.

D

debt/deuda Dinero que se le debe a una persona.

deed/obra Acción.

defend/defender Proteger de daño o peligro.

delegate/delegado Persona escogida para actuar en nombre de otros.

design/diseño Delineación, plan, detalles.

despite/a pesar Sin ser afectado por algo.

diverse/diverso Diferente.

document/documento Registro o informe escrito.

drought/sequía Falta de agua suficiente.

E

ecosystem/ecosistema Todos los seres vivientes y cosas no vivientes que interactúan en un lugar determinado.

elevation/altitud Altura de la tierra sobre el nivel del mar.

enable/permitir Hacer posible.

enforce/hacer cumplir Asegurarse de que las personas obedezcan las leyes y reglas.

equal rights/igualdad de derechos Cuando las personas tienen los mismos derechos que las demás.

erosion/erosión Desgaste del suelo producido por la lluvia, el viento y los ríos cercanos.

essential/esencial Absolutamente necesario.

ethnic group/grupo étnico Grupo de personas que comparten el mismo idioma, la misma cultura y el mismo modo de vida.

exclusion/exclusión Acción de mantener a alguien fuera de un lugar.

executive/ejecutivo El poder del gobierno que hace cumplir las leyes.

expedition/expedición Viaje que tiene un propósito particular.

explorer/explorador Persona que viaja en busca de nuevas tierras y descubrimientos.

export/exportar Enviar bienes a otro país.

F

federal/federal Nacional.

financial/financiero Relativo a asuntos de dinero.

fine/multa Dinero pagado por transgredir una ley.

fort/fuerte Edificio fortificado o un área que sirve como defensa contra los ataques de los enemigos.

frontier/frontera Región que forma el límite de una zona poblada.

fund/financiar Pagar algo.

G

generation/generación Personas que nacieron y viven aproximadamente en la misma época.

gold rush/fiebre del oro Cuando muchas personas van a un área en busca de oro.

goods/bienes Cosas que los trabajadores fabrican o cultivan.

government/gobierno Sistema para dirigir a las personas.

governor/gobernador Jefe del poder ejecutivo de un estado.

H

harvest/cosecha Recolección de cultivos al final de la temporada de cultivo.

hero/héroe Alguien que hizo actos especiales y es un modelo para otros.

homestead/finca Porción de tierra que incluye una casa y otras construcciones.

human capital/capital humano Destrezas, conocimientos y experiencia de las personas.

human resource/recurso humano Talentos y destrezas de una persona.

I

ideal/ideal Idea que esperamos que se vuelva realidad.

immigrant/inmigrante Persona que se va de un país y se instala en otro.

import/importar Hacer entrar bienes desde otro país.

impose/imponer Hacer que algo suceda a la fuerza.

independence/independencia Libertad.

industrial region/región industrial Lugar donde hay muchos tipos de fábricas.

influence/influir Tener un efecto sobre algo.

interpreter/intérprete Persona que habla más de un idioma y ayuda a una persona a entender lo que dice alguien que habla otro idioma.

introduce/introducir Usar por primera vez.

invention/invento Algo que se hace por primera vez.

invest/invertir Gastar dinero en algo ahora con la idea de obtener una ganancia en el futuro.

irrigate/irrigar Llevar agua por medio de tuberías.

issue/asunto Un tema público importante.

J

judicial/judicial El poder del gobierno que se asegura de que las leyes sigan lo que dice en la Constitución de los Estados Unidos.

L

landform/accidente geográfico La forma que tiene una parte de la superficie terrestre.

landmark/sitio de interés Edificio o monumento importante.

law/ley Regla oficial.

layer/capa Una sola cubierta.

legal/legal Reconocido por los tribunales.

legend/leyenda Relato sobre el pasado cuyos datos no se pueden comprobar.

legislative/legislativo Que hace las leyes.

legislature/cuerpo legislativo Parte del gobierno que se encarga de crear las leyes.

local/local Referido a cosas hechas cerca del lugar donde se venden.

location/ubicación Lugar donde está algo.

longhouse/vivienda comunal Casa de los americano nativo que era más larga que ancha.

M

material/material Elemento con lo que algo está hecho, como piedra, madera, pasto o lodo.

mayor/alcalde Líder de una comunidad.

method/método Manera particular de hacer algo.

mine/extraer minerales Sacar materiales de la tierra.

mineral/mineral Recurso que no proviene de un animal o una planta.

mission/misión Asentamiento que tiene una iglesia donde se enseña religión.

modify/modificar Cambiar algo.

motive/motivo Razón.

N

natural resource/recurso natural Algo que existe en la naturaleza y es útil para todos.

need/necesidad Algo que uno debe tener para poder vivir.

nonrenewable resource/recurso no renovable Recurso natural que tarda mucho tiempo en ser reemplazado o que no puede ser reemplazado una vez que se usa.

O

obey/obedecer Cumplir las reglas.

observe/observar Celebrar de un modo aceptado.

obtain/obtener Adquirir o conseguir.

occupation/ocupación Empleo.

opportunity cost/costo de oportunidad Algo a lo que renuncias para tener otra cosa.

option/opción Elección que se puede hacer.

organize/organizar Establecer.

original/original El primero.

P

participate/participar Ser parte de algo.

patent/patente Documento que le da a una persona el derecho de ser la única que puede fabricar o vender un producto.

patriot/patriota Persona que ama y defiende a su país.

perform/actuar Presentarse ante un público.

pilgrim/peregrino Persona que viaja por motivos religiosos.

powwow/pow wow Reunión de indígenas americanos.

prepare/preparar Dejar algo listo.

produce/producir Hacer o crear.

producer/productor Creador de bienes.

promote/promover Alentar o ayudar.

property/propiedad Terreno que le pertenece a alguien.

protect/proteger Cuidar de un peligro, mantener a salvo.

protest/protestar Quejarse.

provide/proporcionar Dar, proveer.

public virtue/virtud pública El bien que hay en todos los ciudadanos y la voluntad de trabajar por el bien de una comunidad o una nación.

purchase/adquirir Comprar.

purpose/propósito Objetivo o razón.

Q

Quaker/cuáquero Alguien que practica una religión que cree en la paz y el trato igualitario para todos.

R

recreation/recreación Manera de divertirse.

recycle/reciclar Usar un objeto más de una vez.

region/región Área extensa con al menos una característica que la hace distinta a otras áreas.

rely/confiar Depender; tener confianza.

renewable resource/recurso renovable Recurso natural que puede reemplazarse en poco tiempo.

represent/representar Significar.

representative/representante Persona escogida para hablar en nombre de otros.

require/requerir Necesitar.

reservation/reserva Tierras que el gobierno de los Estados Unidos apartó para los indígenas americanos.

reside/residir Vivir o tener un hogar permanente en un lugar.

responsibility/responsabilidad Deber.

responsible/responsable Persona en quien se puede confiar que haga lo correcto.

revolution/revolución Algo que ocurre cuando las personas quieren reemplazar al gobierno que tiene el control en ese momento por uno nuevo.

right/derecho Idea o verdad básica que las personas valoran.

risk/riesgo Posibilidad peligrosa.

role/función Rol, ocupación o trabajo.

role model/modelo Alguien que tiene un buen comportamiento y es un ejemplo para los demás.

route/ruta Camino que se toma para llegar a un lugar.

rural/rural Describe una comunidad que está en el campo donde hay mucho espacio abierto.

S

secure/asegurar Hacer que algo sea seguro y no falle.

segregate/segregar Separar.

services/servicios Trabajo que hacen las personas.

settlement house/centro comunitario Espacio para la comunidad ubicado en un área pobre de una ciudad.

significant/significativo Importante.

slavery/esclavitud La práctica de comprar y vender personas como si fueran propiedad.

structure/estructura Algo que se construye.

suburban/suburbano Relacionado con una comunidad ubicada cerca de una gran ciudad.

sufficient/suficiente Bastante cantidad.

suffrage/sufragio Derecho al voto.

symbol/símbolo Algo que representa otra cosa y tiene significado para las personas.

T

tax/impuesto Dinero que se le paga a un gobierno.

technology/tecnología El uso de la ciencia para resolver problemas y hacer que las cosas funcionen mejor.

telegraph/telégrafo Máquina que envía y recibe señales por medio de un cable delgado.

territory/territorio Región gobernada por un país que puede ubicarse dentro o fuera de las fronteras de ese país.

toll/peaje Dinero que se paga por usar un camino.

trade-off/intercambio Renunciar a una cosa para obtener otra.

tradition/tradición Manera especial que tiene un grupo de hacer algo que se transmite a lo largo del tiempo.

transcontinental/transcontinental Que atraviesa el continente.

typically/típicamente Generalmente o en la mayoría de los casos.

U

undertake/emprender Comenzar a hacer.

urban/urbano Relacionado con una gran ciudad.

V

vaccine/vacuna Virus debilitado que se les da a las personas para ayudarlas a combatir una enfermedad.

value/valorar Considerar que algo es importante.

vegetation/vegetación Tipos de plantas que crecen.

veto/vetar Rechazar.

violate/transgredir Romper o no cumplir una regla o una ley.

volunteer/ser voluntario Trabajar o colaborar sin recibir un pago.

W

wagon train/caravana de carretas Grupo de carretas cubiertas que viajaban juntas por seguridad.

want/deseo Algo que a uno le gustaría tener pero no necesita para vivir.

weather/tiempo Condiciones diarias en el exterior.

Index

This index lists the pages on which topics appear in this book. Page numbers followed by *m* refer to maps. Page numbers followed by *p* refer to photographs. Page numbers followed by *c* refer to charts or graphs. Page numbers followed by *t* refer to timelines. Bold page numbers indicate vocabulary definitions. The terms *See* and *See also* direct the reader to alternate entries.

Text Acknowledgments

The Cabrillo National Monument Foundation
An Account of the Voyage of Juan Rodríguez Cabrillo.
Copyright © The Cabrillo National Monument Foundation.

Charles Hard Townes
Quote by Charles Hard Townes after receiving the 1964
Nobel Prize. Copyright © Charles Hard Townes.

David Kupfer
The Final Interview with David R Brower by David Kupfer.
Copyright © David Kupfer

David McCullough
Quote from David McCullough's Speech to Wesleyan
college graduates, 1984. Copyright © David McCullough.

Maya Angelou
Quote from Maya Angelou, Rainbow in the Cloud: The
Wisdom and Spirit of Maya Angelou. Copyright © by The
State of Maya Angelou.

Simon & Schuster
Mine Eyes Have Seen: A First-Person History of the Events
That Shaped America by Richard Goldstein. Copyright ©
Simon & Schuster

Torch Press
Adobe Days: A Book of California Memories by Sarah
Bixby-Smith. Copyright © Torch Press.

Images

Cover
FatCamera/Getty Images

Front Matter
SSH2: Stephen Oliver/Dorling Kindersley ltd.; SSH11: Kirk
Treakle/Alamy Stock Photo; SSH12: Roy H. Anderson/
National Geographic/Getty Images; SSH14: Bst2012/
Fotolia; SSH15: Paul Marcus/Shutterstock; SSH16:
SuperStock/Alamy Stock Photo; SSH17: Jan Hakan
Dahlstrom/Photographer's Choice/Getty Images;

Chapter 01
001: Hero Images/Getty Images; 004: Snehit/Shutterstock;
006L: Csondy/E+/Getty Images; 006R: Texpan/iStock/Getty
Images; 006C: Ron_Thomas/E+/Getty Images; 007L: Texpan/
iStock/Getty Images; 007C: Dennis Macdonald/Photolibrary/
Getty Images; 007R: Zhukova Valentyna/Shutterstock; 008:
America/Alamy Stock Photo; 010: Wollertz/Shutterstock;
012: Tomark/iStock/Getty Images; 014: Nature Collection/
Alamy Stock Photo; 015: Doug Perrine/Alamy Stock Photo;
016: NOAA/Science Source/Getty Images; 018: Naschy/
Shutterstock; 019: Dennis MacDonald/age fotostock/Alamy

Stock Photo; 020: Hero Images/Getty Images; 024: Alistair
Berg/Iconica/Getty Images; 026: Bettmann/Getty Images;
029: Atlantide Phototravel/Corbis Documentary/Getty
Images; 030: Jessica McGowan/Getty Images; 032: Joe
Klamar/AFP/Getty Images; 034: Spring Images/Alamy
Stock Photo; 036: George Ostertag/Alamy Stock Photo;
037: Gordon Chibroski/Portland Press Herald/Getty Images;
038T: USDA Forest Service; 038B: Zack Frank/Shutterstock;
039T: Snehit/Shutterstock; 039B: Joe Klamar/AFP/Getty
Images; 040: Ron_Thomas/E+/Getty Images;

Chapter 02
044-045: Cosmo Condina/Alamy Stock Photo; 047: Mike
Kemp/Blend Images/Getty Images; 049: American Stock/
ClassicStock/Archive Photos/Getty Images; 050: Posnov/
Moment Open/Getty Images; 051: Design Pics Inc/Alamy
Stock Photo; 052: LHB Photo/Alamy Stock Photo; 054:
Transcendental Graphics/Archive Photos/Getty Images; 055:
GraphicsRF/Shutterstock; 056-057: Ian Dagnall/Alamy Stock
Photo; 061: British Dental Association Museum/Science
Source; 062-063: Jon Barlow/Pearson Education, Inc;
064-065: Moxie Productions/Blend Images/Alamy Stock
Photo; 067: Ayse Mardinly/EyeEm/Getty Images; 068L:
Quang Ho/Shutterstock; 068R: GeoStock/Stockbyte/Getty
Images; 070-071: Greg Ryan/Alamy Stock Photo; 072R-073L:
Lisa F. Young/Shutterstock; 072L: Wavebreakmedia/
Shutterstock; 073R: Lurin/Shutterstock; 074: Hurst Photo/
Shutterstock; 075: Asiseeit/E+/Getty Images; 076: Chris
Sattlberger/Cultura Creative (RF)/Alamy Stock Photo; 078T:
Epa European PressphotoAgency b.v./Alamy StockPhoto;
078bkgd: Mclek/Shutterstock; 082: Tcly/Shutterstock;

Chapter 03
084-085: D. Hurst/Alamy Stock Photo; 088: North Wind
Picture Archives/Alamy Stock Photo; 090: Fototeca Gilardi/
Hulton Archive/Getty Images; 092: William S. Kuta/Alamy
Stock Photo; 098: Dorling Kindersley/Getty Images;
094 Burstein Collection/Corbis/VCG/Getty Images; 100:
Grenville Collins Postcard Collection/Chronicle/Alamy Stock
Photo; 102L: Simplebe/Shutterstock; 102R: Stock Montage/
Archive Photos/Getty Images; 103: Stock Montage/Archive
Photos/Getty Images; 104: Jon Bilous/Alamy Stock Photo;
105: Lanmas/Alamy Stock Photo; 106T: Allen Creative/Steve
Allen/Alamy Stock Photo; 106B: Patti McConville/Alamy
Stock Photo; 109: Sean Pavone/Shutterstock; 111: Renault
Philippe/Hemis/Alamy Stock Photo; 112T: GraphicaArtis/
Archive Photos/Getty Images; 112B: PictureNet Corporation/
Alamy Stock Photo; 114: Oleksiy Maksymenko Photography/
Alamy Stock Photo; 115: Photo Researchers/Science
History Images/Alamy Stock Photo; 118: Stock Montage/
Archive Photos/Getty Images; 121: Raymond Boyd/
Michael Ochs Archives/Getty Images; 122: Bettmann/Getty
Images; 124: Anonymous/Getty Images; 126: North Wind
Picture Archives/Alamy Stock Photo; 127: GraphicaArtis/
Archive Photos/Getty Images;128: Christopher Reed/Danita

Delimont/Alamy Stock Photo; 131: Lawcain/iStock/Getty Images; 133T: Klara Viskova/Shutterstock; 133C: Cristophor/Shutterstock; 133B: Nikiteev_konstantin/Shutterstock;

Chapter 04

138-139: Brian Jannsen/Alamy Stock Photo; 142: JT Vintage/Glasshouse Images/Alamy Stock Photo; 144: Chip Somodevilla/Getty Images; 146: Brendan Smialowski/AFP/Getty Images; 147: Jonathan Ernst/Reuters; 148T: Hill Street Studios/Blend Images/Alamy Stock Photo; 148B: Justin Sullivan/Getty Images; 150: Drnadig/iStock/Getty Images; 151: Samuel Corum/Anadolu Agency/Getty Images; 152: Andy Katz/Pacific Press/LightRocket/Getty Images; 153: Good Media/Alamy Stock Photo; 154: Travelwide/Alamy Stock Photo; 160: Louise Wateridge/Pacific Press/LightRocket/Getty Images; 161: Kali9/E+/Getty Images; 162 Dean Hanson/Albuquerque Journal/Albuquerque Journal/ZUMA Press, Inc./Alamy Stock Photo; 163: Jill Schneider/National Geographic/Getty Images; 164: Steve Skjold/Alamy Stock Photo; 168: Michael Ventura/Alamy Stock Photo; 170T: Architect of the Capital; 170B: Matej Hudovernik/Shutterstock; 171: 123rf.com; 172: Xinhua/Alamy Stock Photo; 173: Photowings/Shutterstock; 175: TECH. SGT. ANDY DUNAWAY/KRT/Newscom; 176T: Bettmann/Getty Images; 176B: Orhan Cam/Shutterstock;

Chapter 05

182-183: Pacific Press/Alamy Stock Photo; 186: MonkeyBusinessImages/iStock/Getty Images; 188: Lisa Werner/Alamy Stock Photo; 189: Blend Images/Hill Street Studios/Brand X Pictures/Getty Images; 190: Don Kelsen/Los Angeles Times/Getty Images; 193: Fotokostic/Shutterstock; 195: The Washington Post/Getty Images; 196: John Birdsall/Alamy Stock Photo; 197: Justin Sullivan/Getty Images; 198: AB Forces News Collection/Alamy Stock Photo; 200: Lori Adamski Peek/The Image Bank/Getty Images; 202: Pictorial Press/Alamy Stock Photo; 203: Underwood Archives/Getty Images; 204: Bettmann/Getty Images; 205: Bettmann/Getty Images; 206: Bettmann/Getty Images; 208: Maxfocus/E+/Getty Images; 210: North Wind Picture Archives/Alamy Stock Photo; 211: Anthony Berger/Library of Congress Prints and Photographs Division[LC-DIG-ppmsca-19305]; 212T: National Archives/Stocktrek Images/Getty Images; 212B: National Archives; 213: The Underground Railroad, 1893 (oil on canvas), Webber, Charles T. (1825-1911)/Cincinnati Art Museum, Ohio, USA/Subscription Fund Purchase/Bridgeman Art Library; 214: AFP/Getty Images; 215: David Grossman/Alamy Stock Photo; 216L: Science Source/Getty Images; 216R: Bettmann/Getty Images; 218: Bettmann/Getty Images; 219: IanDagnall Computing/Alamy Stock Photo; 220: Ana Venegas/ZUMA Press/Newscom; 221TC: Blend ImagesKidStock/Blend Images/Getty Images; 221B: Bettmann/Getty Images; 221T: Don Kelsen/Los Angeles Times/Getty Images; 221BC: The Washington Post/Getty Images; 223: Pictorial Press/Alamy Stock Photo;

Chapter 06

226-227: Jim West/Alamy Stock Photo; 234: Photo Researchers/Science History Images/Alamy Stock Photo; 236: Stephanie S. Cordle/AP Images; 239: dibrova/iStock/Getty Images; 241: Bettmann/Getty Images; 247T: Oleksiy Maksymenko/Alamy Stock Photo; 249T: scanrail/iStock/Getty Images; 249C: imaginima/iStock/Getty Images; 247TC: Science & Society Picture Library/Getty Images; 247BC: Tim Caddick/Alamy Stock Photo; 247B: Adrio Communications Ltd/Shutterstock; 249B: kkong/Alamy Stock Photo; 250: Fotosearch/Archive Photos/Getty Images; 253: Prisma Archivo/Alamy Stock Photo; 254: Stefano Bianchetti/Corbis Historical/Getty Images; 255: Al Fenn/The LIFE Picture Collection/Getty Images; 256T: Everett Collection Historical/Alamy Stock Photo; 256B: Martha Holmes/Contributor/Getty Images; 257: Trinity Mirror/Mirrorpix/Alamy Stock Photo; 258: World History Archive/Alamy Stock Photo; 259: drnadig/E+/Getty Images; 260T: Photo 12/Alamy Stock Photo; 260B: State Archives of Florida/Florida Memory/Alamy Stock Photo; 261TL: Bogushenkova Anna/Shutterstock; 261TC: Macrovector/Shutterstock; 261TR: Dacian G/Shutterstock; 261BR: Atlaspix/Shutterstock; 261BL: Aha-Soft/Shutterstock;

Chapter 07

266-267: Monkeybusinessimages/iStock/Getty Images; 270: Ian Dagnall/Alamy Stock Photo; 271: Sergi Reboredo/Alamy Stock Photo; 272: Dszc/iStock/Getty Images; 273: Flame/Alamy Stock Photo; 277: Tony Freeman/PhotoEdit; 277bkgd: Feng Yu/Shutterstock; 278: America/Alamy Stock Photo; 279: Kevin E. Schmidt/Quad-City Times/ZUMA Press Inc/Alamy Stock Photo; 280: JodiJacobson/iStock/Getty Images; 281: Fotog/Getty Images; 282: Jeremy Woodhouse/Blend Images/Getty Images; 284: Andrew Parker/iStock/Getty Images; 286: Delimont Photography/Newscom; 287: ML Harris/Alamy Stock Photo; 288T: Kazuyoshi Nomachi/Corbis Documentary/Getty Images; 288B: MOHAMED EL-SHAHED/Staff/AFP/Getty Images; 290: 615 collection/Alamy Stock Photo; 291: Bettmann/Getty Images; 292: Mark Wilson/The Boston Globe/Getty Images; 293: Frilet Patrick/Hemis/AGE Fotostock; 294T: US Navy Photo/Alamy Stock Photo; 294B: Paul Conklin/PhotoEdit; 296: Gary Conner/PhotoEdit; 297: Ian Dagnall Commercial Collection/Alamy Stock Photo; 298: Andrew Lichtenstein/Corbis/Getty Images; 299: Ricky Fitchett/ZUMA Press, Inc./Alamy Stock Photo; 300: Science Source/Getty Images; 302L: David Grossman/Alamy Stock Photo; 302TR: Alan Wilson/Alamy Stock Photo; 302-303BR: B Christopher/Alamy Stock Photo; 303R: RosalreneBetancourt 5/Alamy Stock Photo; 304: Joel Carillet/iStock Unreleased/Getty Images; 305: Mason Vranish/Alamy Stock Photo; 306: Chuck Place/Alamy Stock Photo; 307: Dennis MacDonald/Alamy Stock Photo; 308: Beau Lark/Corbis/VCG/Getty Images; 312T: Bettmann/Getty Images; 312B: Corbis Historica/Getty Images; 313TL: Jemastock/123RF; 313TR: NotionPic/Shutterstock; 313BL: Cosmic_pony/Shutterstock;